Comics Beyond the Page in Latin America

MODERN AMERICAS

Modern Americas is a series for books discussing the culture, politics and history of the Americas from the nineteenth century to the present day. It aims to foster national, international, transnational and comparative approaches to topics in the region, including those that bridge geographical and/or disciplinary divides, such as between the disparate parts of the hemisphere covered by the series (the US, Latin America, Canada and the Caribbean) or between the humanities and social/natural sciences.

Series Editors

Claire Lindsay is Reader in Latin American Literature and Culture, UCL.

Tony McCulloch is Senior Fellow in North American Studies at the Institute of the Americas, UCL.

Maxine Molyneux is Professor of Sociology at the Institute of the Americas, UCL.

Kate Quinn is Senior Lecturer in Caribbean History at the Institute of the Americas, UCL.

Comics Beyond the Page in Latin America

Edited by James Scorer

First published in 2020 by
UCL Press
University College London
Gower Street
London WC1E 6BT

Available to download free: www.ucl.ac.uk/ucl-press

A CIP catalogue record for this book is available from The British Library.

ISBN: 978-1-78735-756-3 (Hbk.)
ISBN: 978-1-78735-755-6 (Pbk.)
ISBN: 978-1-78735-754-9 (PDF)
ISBN: 978-1-78735-757-0 (epub)
ISBN: 978-1-78735-758-7 (mobi)
DOI: https://doi.org/10.14324/111.9781787357549

Contents

List of figures

List of contributors

Daniel E. Aguilar-Rodríguez is head of the Grupo Recasens de Investigación en Comunicación (GRIC) and a researcher at the Centro de Investigación en Comunicación Política in the Faculty of Social Communication – Journalism, Universidad Externado de Colombia. His research is focused on migration, cultural consumption, graphic narratives and comics, rock music and political participation. He is currently carrying out a research project on comics in Colombia in collaboration with Enrique Uribe-Jongbloed.

Jesús Cossio is the author of *Rupay: Historias gráficas sobre la violencia política 1980–1984* (co-authored with Alfredo Villar and Luis Rossell), *Barbarie: Cómics sobre la violencia política 1985–1990* and *Los años del terror: 50 preguntas sobre el conflicto armado interno*. *Rupay* and *Barbarie* have been published in Spain, France, Austria and Brazil. He is also the author of the comic strip *Las increíbles aventuras del hombre que no se hacía dramas*. He has been invited to comics festivals in Argentina, Chile, Bolivia, Brazil, Colombia, Mexico and the United States. He is currently a drawing instructor for the Concurso de Historietas por la Memoria (Competition of Comics about Memory) organised by Comisión Multisectorial de Alto Nivel para las Reparaciones and a lecturer in photo comics for the Centro de la Imagen in Peru.

Carolina Gonzáles Alvarado is a researcher in graphic narratives at the Tecnológico de Monterrey, in Mexico, where she is completing her doctoral thesis on the work of Craig Thompson. She has undertaken postgraduate study at the Ibero-American University, Mexico, and has held temporary research posts at the University of Glasgow, Scotland,

and the University of Almería, Spain. She also has an education diploma in teaching comics awarded by the École européenne supérieure de l'image (Angoulême, France). Currently, she is contributing to a PAPIME (Programa de Apoyo a Proyectos para Innovar y Mejorar la Educación) project entitled Teaching Audiovisual Languages in the Digital Era, at the School of Political and Social Sciences at the National Autonomous University of Mexico, where she is researching expanded visual experiences of webcomics.

Edward King is a senior lecturer in the School of Modern Languages at the University of Bristol. His research explores contemporary cultures of digital connectivity in Latin America, with a particular focus on the use of multimodal and multimedia texts, from artists' books to comics, to expose and contest the shifting power dynamics of the digital age. He has published two monographs, *Science Fiction and Digital Technologies in Argentine and Brazilian Culture* (Palgrave, 2013) and *Virtual Orientalism in Brazilian Culture* (Palgrave, 2015), and co-authored a book with Joanna Page, *Posthumanism and the Graphic Novel in Latin America* (UCL Press, 2017).

Ivan Lima Gomes is Adjunct Professor of Modern and Contemporary/ Latin American History at the Federal University of Goiás. He holds a PhD in Social History from the Fluminense Federal University, which was supported by funding from CNPq (the Ministry of Science, Technology, Innovation and Communication). His research interests address the historiographical study of cultural practices, with a particular focus on the aesthetic, history and theory of comics, publishing history, visual culture and Latin American history. He is the author of *Os Novos Homens do Amanhã: Projetos e Disputas em Torno dos Quadrinhos na América Latina (Brasil e Chile, anos 1960–1970)* (Prismas, 2018).

Nina Mickwitz works as a lecturer in contextual and critical studies at the London College of Communication, University of the Arts London. She is the author of *Documentary Comics: Graphic Truth-telling in a Skeptical Age* (Palgrave, 2016), and has more recently co-edited two volumes with Ian Hague and Ian Horton, *Contexts of Violence in Comics* and *Representing Acts of Violence in Comics* (Routledge, 2019). Nina is a founding member of the Comics Research Hub at University of the Arts London and her research interests include mobilities and negotiations of social norms and identities in comics, as well as the mobilities of comics.

Cristian Palacios has a PhD in Linguistics (with honours) from the University of Buenos Aires. He is a researcher for CONICET (the National Scientific and Technical Research Council of Argentina) in the fields of discourse analysis, semiotics, linguistics and theatre studies, comics, literature and art, with a specialisation in comic and humoristic discourses. He has received an Honourable Mention from the University of Buenos Aires for his academic work and multiple awards for his artistic work. His last book *Hacia una teoría del teatro para niños* (Lugar Editorial, 2017) has received two awards as the best academic work in the field of theatre by the ATINA association and the ALIJA-IBBY foundation. He is also a writer, actor, playwright and theatre director.

Carla Sagástegui Heredia is a lecturer in literature at the Pontifical Catholic University of Peru. She obtained her doctorate in 2013 from the Pompeu Fabra University in Barcelona with her thesis *Tramas de la ficción externa en la literatura peruana y sus modos ficcionales* (2013). As well as studying orality and writing, her research interests have included comics ever since 2003 when she curated and published the catalogue for the exhibition *Los primeros 80 años de la historieta en el Perú*, held at the Peruvian North American Cultural Institute (ICPNA). As well as contributing book chapters to the collections *Redrawing The Nation: National Identity in Latin/o American Comics* (2009), edited by Héctor Fernández L'Hoeste and Juan Poblete, and *BÚMM! Historieta y humor gráfico en el Perú: 1978–1992* (2016), edited by Alfredo Villar, she is also the author, with Jesús Cossio, of *Ya nadie te sacará de tu tierra* (2019), a comic about agrarian reform in Peru.

James Scorer is a senior lecturer in Latin American cultural studies at the University of Manchester. He is the author of *City in Common: Culture and Community in Buenos Aires* (SUNY, 2016), and the co-editor (with Jorge Catalá Carrasco and Paulo Drinot) of *Comics and Memory in Latin America* (Pittsburgh, 2017), also available as *Cómics y memoria en América Latina* (Cátedra, 2019), and (with Peter Wade and Ignacio Aguiló) of *Cultures of Anti-Racism in Latin America* (ILAS, 2019). As well as Latin American comics, his research interests include Latin American urban imaginaries, especially of Buenos Aires, and Latin American photography.

Jorge Tuset is an architect and a lecturer in architecture at the Faculty of Architecture, Design and Urbanism at the University of the Republic in Uruguay, where he coordinated the course entitled City, Architecture,

Comic between 2014 and 2017. He received his doctorate in architecture from the Higher Technical School of Architecture in Madrid in 2011. His thesis looked at the relationship between architecture and comics in the work of François Schuiten and Benoît Peeters. He has also taught on architecture and comics in the Faculty of Design at the University of Buenos Aires and at the Artigas Teacher Training Institute in Uruguay. He has contributed as a reviewer to the publication *ARQUISUR* and is a member of the investigative collective PACE (Plataforma Académica sobre el Cómic en Español).

Enrique Uribe-Jongbloed is a lecturer and researcher within the Grupo Recasens de Investigación en Comunicación (GRIC) in the School of Social Communication – Journalism, Universidad Externado de Colombia. He researches on issues of media representation and cultural transduction in audiovisual and printed products. He is currently undertaking research on comics in Colombia, and has co-authored a chapter with Fernando Suárez on the Colombian comics industry in *Cultures of Comics Work* (2016), edited by Casey Brienza and Paddy Johnston, and an article with Daniel E. Aguilar-Rodríguez and Sergio Roncallo-Dow on dystopias in Colombian comics.

Laura Vazquez is a CONICET researcher and lecturer in communication at the University of Palermo and the Gino Germani Institute (Buenos Aires). She also lectures at the University of Buenos Aires, where she directs the area of Drawn Narratives, the National University of the Arts and the National University of Moreno. Her research into comics is focused particularly on the publishing industry and on the history of Argentine comics producers, magazines and artistic projects. She is the author of *Fuera de Cuadro: Ideas sobre historieta argentina* (Agua Negra, 2012) and *El oficio de las viñetas: La industria de la historieta argentina* (Paidós, 2010). She has been invited to speak at congresses and seminars in Latin America and Europe and was the director of the International Congress of Comics and Graphic Humour Viñetas Serias (2011–2014).

Acknowledgements

The conversations that underpinned the theme of this book were made possible by The Leverhulme Trust, which funded the three-year international network Comics and the Latin American City: Framing Urban Communities (http://comicsandthelatinamericancity.wordpress.com). I would like to thank everyone who participated in the network and its activities but particularly Alana Jackson, who made everyone's involvement, especially mine, that much more straightforward.

1

Latin American comics beyond the page

James Scorer

Over the past two decades Latin America has seen an expansion in the publication and consumption of comics. This renaissance is benefiting from transnational dialogues and exchanges: in 2017, for example, the publishing house :e(m)r;, based in Rosario, Argentina, produced a groundbreaking compilation of comics by artists from over 10 Latin American countries. With a title suggesting an eruption not dissimilar to the explosion of the *Boom* in Latin American fiction in the 1960s and 1970s, *El Volcán* (The Volcano) (Sainz and Bidegaray 2017) reflects growing regional self-awareness of expansion, exposure and dissemination. In 2017, the book was presented at the Kuš! Komikss festival in Riga and at the Helsinki comics festival, alongside an exhibit of the book's artwork. International attention of this kind has been magnified by efforts to create collaborative links across regions. The Fumetto festival in Switzerland, for example, which hosted the *El Volcán* exhibit in 2018, also included an exhibition of works produced as part of an artistic exchange set up between Brazilian and Swiss comics creators. The festival is looking to establish a similar programme with Colombian comics creators in future iterations.

That *El Volcán* has been consumed both as a book and as an exhibit or discussion topic at festivals demonstrates that enthusiasm for Latin American comics is not confined to the page. From specialist festivals to art exhibitions, from university courses to school workshops, from murals to statues to subway art, and from digital comics to transnational collective blogs, Latin American comics are circulating in all manner of ways beyond traditional paper-based formats. This phenomenon is far from being exclusively Latin American. Something about comics and their use of word and image allows them to be transposed and put into dialogue with different cultural media. These transmedial processes are integral to an epoch drawn to interdisciplinarity, dialogues and exchanges between different media, and the fluid relationships between humans and the material environment.

Drawing on Rosalind Krauss's theory of landscape art, the comics scholar Bart Beaty has referred to the idea of 'comics in the expanded field' (Baetens 2013, 185). That idea, which Beaty uses to frame a planned study of the relationship between form and transmediality provisionally entitled *Comics Off the Page*, can be seen in several chapters in this book. But, unlike Beaty, the authors included here are generally less concerned with determining what constitutes or not a comic. Neither do they follow wholesale the more focused approach of Casey Brienza and Paddy Johnston's fascinating *Cultures of Comics Work* (2016), which addresses the field of comics and 'the primacy of collective creation rather than the formal properties of the comics art object' (7). Even though it only occurs minimally, textual analysis of form and page is not entirely out of place in this book. If some contributors are concerned with comics entirely *off* the page, others include analysis based on expanded notions of a text. For that reason, I prefer the notion of comics *beyond* the page for this book, a phrase that imparts the sense of being on a threshold that is not entirely abstracted from print cultures and the page.

Even if the trends analysed in this book are evident in other regional contexts, Latin America nonetheless offers a unique opportunity to study the role that popular culture plays in a region that remains hugely unequal and politically fractured, and where state funding for public cultural projects, including those related to comics, is precarious. Judith Gociol, for example, has referred to the 'institutionalisation' of comics that took place in Argentina after 2010 (070 Womansplaining 2018). During the presidency (2007–15) of Cristina Fernández de Kirchner, comics were embraced as part of a national-popular political imaginary, not least because they harked back to the 'Golden Age' of comics production during the first period of Peronism in the mid-twentieth century. During Fernández de Kirchner's presidency, the Museo del Humor was opened in Buenos Aires, comics were presented as part of the Frankfurt Book Fair in 2010 at which Argentina was the special guest, and a comics archive was established at the Biblioteca Nacional in 2012. Gociol, who directs that archive, has suggested that this revival was possible only because comics were a 'language in tune' with the Kirchner era. To some degree, then, we might consider whether the recent resurgence in comics runs in tandem with the so-called 'pink tide' that altered the face of Latin American politics during the 2000s. Many populist governments used comics to recall an earlier set of iconographic visual strategies and tropes and earlier forms of cultural expression associated with populist and/or revolutionary governments that were in power in the 1950s, 1960s and 1970s. It is also likely that renewed interest in and enthusiasm for comics has encouraged state entities to try and permeate what has often been seen as a counter-cultural world.

Nevertheless, ventures such as a national comics archive remain rare in Latin America, and the future of such projects is always uncertain when abrupt regime change arrives, as it did in Argentina. Like so many cultural industries in Latin America, comics have a very rich tradition and are at the cutting edge of wider explorations of form, aesthetics and content, but they exist in a milieu of economic, social and political instability. Despite recent changes, Latin America, as we shall see below, lacks what might be called a 'comics industry' and, for all the acceptance of and enthusiasm for comics as a cultural form, there are still very few opportunities within even tertiary education for the widespread study of comics.

But even if the production of comics in the region is generally small scale, precarious and under-funded, grassroots enthusiasm and occasional institutional investment makes for an incredibly diverse, vibrant and often insightful set of cultural products that engage constantly with the region's political and social challenges. One key site of struggle is precisely that, despite having a long-standing autochthonous comics tradition, the region has constantly been faced with transnational exchanges. The importing of US comics books, genres and traditions, for example, a practice that dominated the industry for much of the twentieth century, has meant that local artists and producers have always had to engage with foreign industries and iconographies. At times such relationships have simply been labelled as examples of unequal power relations played out through cultural neocolonialism. Ariel Dorfman and Armand Mattelart's 1971 work *Para leer al Pato Donald* (How to Read Donald Duck (1975)), which read Disney's interventions in Latin America as an attempt to disseminate capitalist ideologies to child consumers, is the best-known example of such criticism. But a long colonial and neocolonial history has meant that Latin Americans are very well aware of the ideologies attached to cultural imports. For that reason, studying how comics function within the Latin American public sphere offers an opportunity to see how cultural forms, genres, characters and tropes from other locales are taken up and refashioned within local traditions.

In the remainder of this introduction, I will demonstrate how the particular nature of Latin America's politics and cultural production, not least as a site on the margins of both US and European comics traditions and industries, has created an environment in which graphic narratives thrive despite their precariousness. Following the cultural neo-imperialism of earlier periods of comics production, I will argue that the diverse manifestations of comics circulating beyond print media demonstrates how they have become a key site for exploring and contesting transnational exchanges, and also for developing dialogues between state-driven narratives of identities, histories and traditions and those fomented by NGOs and comics communities.

I have divided the chapter into three sections that reflect the topics of the contributions that follow. In the first section, 'Comics work, digital comics and (im)material comics communities', I discuss the impact of digital technologies on comics production, the ongoing demand for material interactions with comics, and the way that both of these contribute to the creation of comics communities in Latin America. In the second, 'Comics in public space', I look at the deployment of comics in the cityscape, focusing particularly on different examples from Buenos Aires, including in a subway station and the city's Paseo de la Historieta (Comics Walk). And in the final section, 'Comics for education and protest', I refer to the pedagogical role comics have played in Latin America, whether in popular workshops, secondary schools, or simply as a means to highlight social inequality and injustice in the region.

Comics work, digital comics and (im)material comics communities

Comics production in Latin America is, in many ways, still nascent and not evenly developed across the region. The only period during which certain countries in Latin America had fully fledged comics industries, driven by large publishing houses like Editorial Abril in Argentina (Scarzanella 2016), was the so-called 'Golden Age' of autochthonous Latin American comics production that lasted roughly from the late 1940s until the early 1960s. Such industries were dismantled by the growing globalisation of cultural production and consumption. Nowadays, even in the countries that dominate comics production in the region, principally Argentina, Brazil and Mexico, scholars are reluctant to refer to national comics 'industries'.

Pablo Turnes, for example, suggests that in Argentina 'there is no industry, but there is production and work' (Gandolfo et al. 2017). Similarly, Fernando Suárez and Enrique Uribe-Jongbloed (2016) argue that only over the past decade or so might Colombia be described as having anything approaching a comics industry. And Daniel Jiménez Quiroz, a key figure in Entreviñetas, one of Latin America's most important comics festivals, has described the fact that this event takes place in Colombia as an 'anomaly' precisely because the country lacks a fully fledged industry, specialist publishing houses and an authorial tradition (Jiménez Quiroz 2017). Suárez and Uribe-Jongbloed add that the 'informal business' of comics in Colombia 'makes [the work of comics creators] seldom recognized, economically unstable, and not a proper source of income' (2016, 57). In that sense, it might be more accurate to refer not to a Latin American comics industry but to the world of 'comics work' within Latin America, the term that Casey Brienza and Paddy Johnston use to describe the network of labour practices that underpin the wide range of people involved in producing comics (2016, 3).

Nevertheless, the panorama of comics work within Latin America is changing. A range of comics festivals have taken place across the region in recent decades, including in Argentina (Crack Bang Boom, Fantabaires, Viñetas Serias), Bolivia (Viñetas Con Altura), Brazil (Festival Internacional de Quadrinhos), Chile (Valpocomics), Colombia (CaliComix, Entreviñetas), Peru (Día del Cómic Festival) and Uruguay (Montevideo Cómics). Entreviñetas, for example, not only gathers together artists from Latin America but also puts them into dialogue with peers from the US and Europe. Colombia has also seen some growth in the number of publishing houses that specialise in comics (Rey Naranjo, La Silueta, Cohete Comics, among others), a growth partly due to more accessible – both in terms of cost and availability – forms of producing comics that aid small producers, new university degrees in graphic design, one of the spaces where students are sometimes required to draw comics as part of their studies, and the decision in 2015 to include comics within tax exemptions for print publications (Suárez and Uribe-Jongbloed 2016, 54–7). There are signs that such work is also being recognised abroad, not just in the shape of possible future links to the Fumetto festival, but also with publications such as *Ñ comme viñetas* (Rannou and Salazar Morales 2017), a collection of Colombian comics translated into French as part of the 2017 state-sponsored Année France-Colombie.

The Argentine comics world has also expanded in recent decades. Turnes describes a growing network of activities around comics, an increase in smaller, independent publishers creating what he calls 'a process of postindustrial professionalization', greater diversity in terms of authors, and an increase in international connections between artists and writers and European comics publishing houses (Gandolfo et al. 2017). All of that, he goes on to suggest, has strengthened 'a shared notion of a community of comics creators'. Evidence of some of these advances can be seen in recent exhibits such as 'Pibas' (2019) at the Centro Cultural Recoleta in Buenos Aires, which highlighted a range of recent work by women, or 'Las Dibujantes: Expresiones de lo feminino' (2019) at the Alliance Française, which put three Argentine artists into visual dialogue with three French artists, also with a particular focus on gender.

The growing exposure to and enthusiasm for Latin American comics both regionally and internationally owes much to the expansion in digital technologies.[1] Such technologies have made it easier to produce comics and to disseminate them. It is quicker and cheaper to promote publications and events and to reach much wider audiences more effectively and quickly than ever before. Authors can self-publish on the internet via blogs, Instagram and other forms of social media. In turn, those forms of communication facilitate the growth of networks of producers and consumers. Those networks are often digital manifestations of concrete material worlds that exist in specific locations. But they have also helped develop transnational relationships and connections – artists and enthusiasts across the region now have a much better grasp of work being undertaken in countries other than their own.

Latin America is perhaps extremely apt as a place for reflecting on recent debates about digital comics and online communities because it is a region where the pre-modern and the modern are so often not polar opposites but different faces of the same coin. Edward King (2017) highlights a good example of this multitemporal awareness in his analysis of the Brazilian graphic novel *Morro da favela* (2011) (*Picture a Favela* (2012)) by André Diniz. He demonstrates how Diniz used digital technology to reproduce the style of *xilogravura*, the practice of woodblock printing linked to pre-modern Brazilian culture, a process that demonstrates the 'long history of negotiations between local traditions and the technologies of modernity' (King 2017, 233).

Moreover, Latin American comics have always engaged with a diverse set of narrative and artistic practices that come from imported and sometimes translated comics from the US and Europe, with their accompanying sense of a comics canon, as with domestic artistic, thematic and genre traditions (see, for example, Gandolfo and Turnes (2019) and Laura Vazquez's chapter in this volume).

Digital comics are not the only way that technology has impacted on the world of comics. The internet has also helped establish virtual communities around comics creation, production and consumption. Though we should be conscious of the social inequalities that affect access to technology and digital literacy, not least in a region with stark income disparity and unequal infrastructures, Latin American artists have more opportunities to disseminate their work faster and more widely than ever before. Many use crowdfunding to initiate projects. In Brazil, for example, sites such as Catarse have been 'perceived by social actors as a new way to deal with specific struggles for capital' (Pereira de Carvalho 2016, 253). In his chapter in this volume, King highlights how social media has become a key platform for comics creation. And Turnes has noted that the resurgence in Argentine comics has partly been driven by the internet, suggesting that the blog *Historietas reales*, which was started in 2005, was a trailblazer for online comics in Argentina (and perhaps the region more broadly). These digital interfaces allow consumers and fans to openly and immediately express their preferences and views, sometimes engaging in dialogues with creators. Ángel Mosquito's *La calambre* (2013), for example, first appeared online on the author's blog but mid-way through publication Mosquito announced its cessation due to 'editorial commitments', a reference to the forthcoming print edition with the Barcelona-based publishing house La Cúpula. The subsequent comments posted online reveal the immediacy of the relationship between author and consumer. One reader commented: 'ehee!! vamo a tener que pagar?! BURGUES!!', to which Mosquito replied, 'si, capo, pagáaaaaaaa!!!! leiste 5 años gratis!!! paga la reconcha de tu madre! [heyy!! we're going to have to pay?! BOURGEOIS!! / yes, man, payyyyyyyyy!!!! you've read 5 years for free!!! pay up you piece of shit!]' (Mosquito 2011).

The internet has also helped some underrepresented groups gain greater exposure. Latin American comics remains a predominantly male sphere, both in terms of production and a prevailing set of views about gender and sexuality, what Héctor Fernández L'Hoeste and Juan Poblete called 'a masculinist imagination' (2009, 10). But the past decade has seen wider recognition for women comics creators – some 40 per cent of the contributors to the *El Volcán* collection mentioned above, for example, are women. Daniel Jiménez Quiroz suggests that prior to 2012 only Powerpaola was recognisable as a woman working within Colombian comics (070 Womansplaining 2018) but that her influence has helped other women become more visible. The transgender artist Sindy Elefante, for example, has spoken of what she describes as the 'hermandad' (sisterhood) currently being formed between women working within the comics world (070 Womansplaining 2018). A recent publication by Gabriela Borges, Katherine Supnem, Maira Mayola and Mariela Acevedo (2018) demonstrates how important the digital sphere has been to this growing visibility, whether in terms of virtual spaces (e.g. CarnesTolendas, 365 Mujeres Ilustradas, Tetas Tristes, Minas Nerds, Lady's Comics), or the many authors who have published their work online before – and sometimes instead of – in print.

The collective Chicks on Comics is a good example of how groups can utilise diverse forms of online presence. The membership of Chicks on Comics has fluctuated over time, but members have included Delius (Argentina), Clara Lagos (Argentina), Sole Otero (Argentina), Powerpaola (Ecuador/Colombia), Maartje Schalkx (Netherlands), Bas (Netherlands), Weng Pixin (Singapore) and Zane Zlemeša (Latvia). This transnational group uses three principal online tools. On Twitter (@chicksoncomics) they have over 2,000 followers and describe themselves as 'the feminist fuelled vehicle for an on-going dialogue between 8 female and trans cartoonists across the globe'. Here their work is placed into a wider network of comics dialogue and production with a range of other contributors and interlocutors, including other Latin American artists such as the Colombians La Watson and the aforementioned Sindy Elefante. On Tumblr (chicksoncomics.tumblr.com) they engage in visual dialogues and narratives with each other, riffing from one frame to the next by picking up on particular tropes, ideas or images. And on their website (chicksoncomics.com), they refer explicitly to how social media helps make visible the diverse nature of comics production by women.

Even though the internet has provided alternative means for producing and disseminating comics and comics communities, many artists and consumers still value print media, a point evident in the chapters by Carla Sagástegui Heredia and Carolina González Alvarado in this book. Indeed, I would argue that, concurrent with the expansion in digital comics and digital platforms, Latin American comics artists were simultaneously involved in a number of influential print publications, including *Carboncito* (Peru, 20 issues, 2001–16); *Clítoris: Revista de historietas y exploraciones varias* (Argentina, 4 issues, 2011–12); *Fierro: La historieta argentina* (Argentina, 125 issues, 2006–17); *Revista Larva* (Colombia, 17 issues, 2006–15); and *Suda Mery K!* (Argentina, 5 issues, 2005–7). The comics industry also thrives on highly tactile, material experiences. Many still enjoy the almost fetishistic process of buying physical copies from specialist outlets where the consumer can browse and engage in conversation with specialist staff. Amadeo Gandolfo (Gandolfo et al. 2017) has spoken of how, since the 1990s, the comic-book store in Argentina has become an important 'cog in the local "industry"' by placing imported comics alongside comics published in Argentina.

The comics industry builds on such practices and encounters via the comics festival or comic con, larger-scale, immersive venues for those with a shared interest in comics. Festivalgoers interact via acts of consumption, discussions, book signings, presentations and also via mutual visual and aesthetic practices and ways of seeing. Some festivalgoers dress up, playing out fictional worlds in which their particular costume or make-up not only distinguishes them from others but also draws them and their different genres, global traditions and media together into a shared, fan-based comic world. In cosplay, for example, a practice that developed in Asia in the 1970s, fans dress up as figures from popular culture worlds, including those of *manga*, and the industry can use such embodied experiences to drive forward the comics market (Rahman et al. 2012). Something similar can be seen in the popular zombie marches, which are often linked directly to zombie comics or to the wider phenomenon of zombie popular culture. In recent years, zombie marches have been held in Mexico City (with some 10,000 participants), in San Antonio de los Baños in Cuba, and in Santiago de Chile (with over 20,000 participants) (Ferrer-Medina 2015, 29).

These festivals and marches are, in a context of social frag-mentation brought about by neoliberal market reforms and national identities fractured by right-wing dictatorships or armed civil conflict, a means of grounding a set of identities and social relations through comics. Such shifts are not only citizen led; the fact that national and regional governments are interested in and willing to sponsor such events demonstrates awareness of how culture can 'achieve development, strengthen collective identities, assure governance, and serve as an argument for cultural recognition and self-determination', as Gisela Cánepa puts it in her discussion of religious festivals in Lima (2010, 142).

Entreviñetas, for example, which is funded by both state and private entities, has created an urban comics network in a country that has suffered decades of civil conflict and widespread displacement. In Bogotá, Entreviñetas forms part of wider programmes of urban reform. If progressive mayors were using the material environment of Bogotá to encourage citizen participation and the establishment of wider community links (Berney 2017, 21), then events such as Entreviñetas support such aims. The festival also fits with efforts to promote reading in Colombia, as it lists this as one of its goals. As Marcy Schwartz (2018) has demonstrated, several major Latin American cities have housed public reading programmes that have tried to foment urban belonging. Although her focus is more on reading in public spaces, Schwartz describes how Entreviñetas echoes attempts to promote reading and rejuvenate public spaces through libraries, festivals, book giveaways and writing competitions (2018, 48–9). Schwartz argues that in Bogotá such programmes are designed to help inhabitants overcome hostile urban environments, failing infrastructures, poverty or a sense of alienation produced by displacement (2018, 86).

That Schwartz contextualises such reading programmes by referring to Ángel Rama's famous concept of the lettered city suggests that the kind of reading programmes she analyses fit with the direction of Rama's hints at a democratised set of lettered practices within contemporary urban life. By introducing comics, perhaps one of the most *popular* forms of reading, into that vision of public reading practices, Entreviñetas adds a further dimension to the dismantling of elitist forms of reading and cultural consumption. In the following section, I address how some of these approaches play out in the use of comics in public spaces.

Comics in public spaces

Comics are a spatial form, occupying the territory of the page. For that reason it is no surprise that comics were born with and developed alongside the modern city. Their fragmented nature lends itself to capturing the multiple elements that shape the modern city. And the multimodal nature of most comics, built out of text and image, captures the multifaceted nature of the street. For that reason there are affinities between comics and Walter Benjamin's reading of Parisian arcades: both are built around the patchwork, the threshold, the framed collection of entities, and the lure of word and image.[2]

When comics are placed in the public sphere, they undergo not just a transmediation but also a translocation, from the page to the street or square. In that shift they intervene in a wide range of urban imaginaries, a reminder that comics are a process, a mode of doing, a practice. We might, in that sense, understand comics as a verb, not just a noun: to comic. If space, as Doreen Massey describes it, is formed of multiple trajectories, constantly being formed and reformed in what she calls 'a simultaneity of stories-so-far' (2005, 130), then comics in public spaces form part of the negotiations that shape space. There is, Massey points out, political potential in the negotiations that come about from the 'throwntogetherness' of places (2005, 141–2). Like 'stories-so-far', comics too are constantly being reformed as part of a process of negotiation within a field of 'throwntogetherness'. That fits, moreover, with Jan-Noël Thon and Lukas R.A. Wilde's description of the 'materiality' of comics as 'a dynamic process wherein objects, bodies, and subjectivities only emerge as relational effects' (2016, 235).

Comics should not necessarily be romanticised as a mode of resistance. Nor should we celebrate acts of comics graffiti or impromptu murals as inherent attempts to dismantle urban structures of power or as tactical forms of resistance. What they offer, however, is a means of engaging with others, either at the level of bodily interactions in space (whether between humans, or between humans and their material environment), or at the level of the urban imaginary. They provide a rich site of negotiation since they are visually iconic, readily recognisable and themselves refer to parallel narrative worlds, all of which remind us of the temporal nature of space and the contested nature of producing and engaging with socially constructed narratives and imaginaries.

Comics in public spaces can be cited via historical markers, as street names, or in comics museums or stores. Comic forms and characters can also appear in squares, streets and subway stations. In Buenos Aires, for example, you can find a mural to Alberto Breccia in the neighbourhood of Mataderos, a plaque celebrating Quino/Mafalda's house in the neighbourhood of San Telmo, and the Plaza Oesterheld in Puerto Madero, where you can also visit the Museo de Humor. Strips from Mafalda are printed on walls located in the Plaza Mafalda in Colegiales, and in Nuñez there is a weathered mural of Monumental just a stone's throw from the actual stadium, one based on an image from Héctor G. Oesterheld and Francisco Solano López's comic *El Eternauta*, first published in 1957 (see Figure 1.1).[3]

Figure 1.1 Mural of Monumental stadium in Nuñez based on an image from Héctor G. Oesterheld and Francisco Solano López's *El Eternauta*. Photograph by the author

Comics are also embedded in the cityscape at the level of iconography, examples being those that do not include an obvious sense of graphic narrative but which rely on recognisable figures or forms. Such uses can take quite varied forms, even just as comic fonts, speech bubbles or superhero symbols to promote certain businesses or products. A notable example in this vein is the use of figures inspired by *El Eternauta*, the subject of Cristian Palacios' chapter in this volume. In 2010, a figure was created to promote a political rally in Buenos Aires: ostensibly it depicted *El Eternauta*'s famous time-traveller dressed in his makeshift protective suit and diving mask. Behind the mask, however, was not the face of the Eternaut, Juan Salvo, but that of Néstor Kirchner, president of Argentina between 2003 and 2007. Stencil artists subsequently used the so-called Nestornauta to graffiti buildings. The authors, in this case the Peronist militant group La Cámpora, were creating clear national-populist links between figures perceived to be (Peronist) saviours of a nation threatened by neocolonial external powers. As various authors (Francescutti 2015; Gago 2016) have pointed out, these interventions were not without their controversies: objections were raised by, among others, the then mayor of Buenos Aires, Mauricio Macri, and the editor of the publishing house Editorial Record, on the grounds that Oesterheld's legacy was being inappropriately politicised. Other critics responded with their own figure, the Chorronauta ('chorro' is slang for 'crook' or 'thief'), a reference to accusations of financial corruption under the Kirchners. Whatever the politics of these struggles, the Nestornauta project demonstrates, as Pablo Francescutti argues, the growing value of comics within cultural production (2015, 40). And more than that, it highlights how comics can be used as cultural and political currency to foment widespread cultural-political exchanges beyond print media.

Examples such as the Nestornauta demonstrate how comics function as what we might call, following Elizabeth Edwards' theory of photographs as physical objects, 'material performances' (2009, 130–1). As 'performances', comics renarrate our place in public spaces or imagined communities. The idea of the material performance is a particularly apt way of describing the growing number of comics presented in art galleries as three-dimensional, multifaceted experiences that provide a further dimension to the spatial nature of the form. Jason Dittmer and Alan Latham have described how the British artist Dave McKean's exhibit/comic 'The Rut' enables audiences to create 'an architecture of becoming' through embodied reading (2015, 428). The interactive, performative nature of such works is evident, for example, in works produced by design students at the Universidad de Buenos Aires. Drawing on notions of transmediality, students are required to create what are called 'historietas expandidas' (expanded comics). In one example, 'El camino del campeón', the reader has to don boxing gloves and hit their 'opponent', a comic-book character whose speech bubble says 'Dale gil. No servís para nada [Come on, idiot. You're worthless]'. Striking the opponent simultaneously revolves both the opponent's glove, which the reader must duck to avoid being hit in the head, and a drum that contains a narrative about domestic violence that progresses with the 'fight'. The work requires physical exertion and material interaction to advance the narrative.

The embodied nature of reading can also be seen in the Buenos Aires subway. Several subway stations include works by comics artists, including Horacio Altuna, Quino, Héctor G. Oesterheld, Alberto Breccia, Crist, Roberto Fontanarrosa, Nik, Dante Quinterno and Landrú (a list that reminds us of the gender bias of the Argentine comics canon). But the most significant comics intervention is at Pasteur-AMIA, a station renamed in 2015 to commemorate the bombing of the headquarters of the Asociación Mutual Israelita Argentina (AMIA), the country's pre-eminent Jewish organisation.

The walls of the subterranean entrance hall, the escalators and the platforms are covered with works by comics artists, caricaturists or sketch artists, all of which reflect on the nature of memory and the lack of justice for the victims. Maitena's work shows a frightened woman looking at dark shadowy figures to the words 'asesinos sueltos' (murderers on the loose). Fontanarrosa's famous character Inodoro Pereyra cracks a joke about his grandmother's memory while drinking mate and Liniers' character Enriqueta comments on the ties between justice and memory. In this way, the station has been transformed into an immersive memory experience that creates a cognitive link between travellers' journeys and the artworks. The network experience of the city, with the narrative of the journey being inscribed by collective memory, is intensified by the reading experience of being in spaces of transit turned into civic spaces for urban belonging based around shared practices of reading comics (see Figure 1.2 and Figure 1.3). As the space not only demands justice but also foments an embodied process of remembering, it helps urban dwellers work towards what I have elsewhere called 'memoryscapes that are fashioned in common' (Scorer 2016, 53).

Figure 1.2 Board explaining the rationale for the installations at Pasteur-AMIA metro station with thumbnails of some of the comic murals. Photograph by the author

Figure 1.3 Comics at Pasteur-AMIA metro station. Photograph by the author

Evidently, comics form part of a national cultural heritage, and placing them in public spaces means they function like other state-sponsored monuments and murals that use culture to promote or interpellate a national or regional identity. The Parque del Cómic in Santiago de Chile, for example, with numerous tile figures and four large statues, territorialises a national cultural tradition (Figure 1.4). That national tradition comes in part because the figures are located next to the Casa de la Cultura, housed in a building where Pedro Subercaseaux, creator of the first Chilean comic-book character, Von Pilsener, once lived. The statues provide a ready opportunity for photographs, and walking along the path lined with the tiled figures and statues creates an embodied link with a national visual tradition. As Jorge Montealegre, historian and member of the original committee that proposed the park, puts it, the park attempted to 'concentrate' or 'characterise the municipality', part of a process of the 'positioning' of San Miguel as a comics neighbourhood (interview with the author 2017).

Figure 1.4   Tiles in the Parque del Cómic, Santiago de Chile. Photograph by the author

The Paseo de la Historieta (Comics Walk) in Buenos Aires, inaugurated in 2012 as part of the Unidad de Proyectos Especiales Construcción Ciudadana y Cambio Cultural, a body that pertains to the Ministry of Culture of the City of Buenos Aires, has a rather different audience. Whereas the poorly preserved and poorly publicised Parque del Cómic in Santiago targets a national, even neighbourhood audience, with no explanatory information provided about the characters either in situ or online, the Paseo in Buenos Aires is more obviously a tourist attraction. Though it too celebrates a national cultural tradition, covering a range of characters dating from the 1930s onwards, it is also accompanied by explanatory material both on plaques beneath the figures and online, with maps and historical information available in Spanish and English. Echoing the Comic Book Route in Brussels, the Paseo is an example of the city using comics for urban self-promotion, showcasing itself as a twenty-first-century global metropolis, not least because half the walk takes place in Puerto Madero, a neighbourhood that echoes waterfront regeneration projects in other major world cities. In this case, by placing comics figures between the edges of San Telmo and the Museo del Humor in Puerto Madero, the walk promotes a particularly transnational and predominantly wealthy part of the city, part of the city's rebranding exercise described by Rubens Bayardo as a combination of global cosmopolitanism and unique local cultural production. As he suggests, Buenos Aires's attempt to internationalise itself has relied on understanding culture as a resource for promoting real estate development rather than for encouraging social diversity and citizenship (Bayardo 2013, 115–6).

Bayardo's point is exemplified by the official description of the Paseo, which refers to wanting to 'strengthen a common Argentine identity, using the representation of certain values, and the humoristic critique of our idiosyncrasies and national customs' at the same time as promoting the fact that 'many of our characters and their creators are famous worldwide, especially because Argentine comics is emblematic, and for decades was at the forefront, of Hispanic America'. But the gender politics of the Paseo de la Historieta is sufficient to demonstrate how problematic that vision of a shared, globally famous national comics tradition is. Of the 18 sculptures that currently make up the walk, none were created by women and only three include women: Tía Vicenta (an opinionated but ignorant spinster), Chicas Divito (two impossibly proportioned figures of fashion) and Malfalda/Susanita together (the latter desperate to have children and become a housewife). Moreover, none of the three sculptures located on Marta Lynch Street in the Parque de Mujeres Argentinas (Argentine Women's Park) in Puerto Madero are women. The three sculptors listed on the website are all men, the murals that adorn the walk are all by men and/or about the work of men, and the Consejo Asesor del Museo del Humor, the group responsible for drawing up the list of characters, was made up of six men (Gobierno de la Ciudad de Buenos Aires).

Specific state entities are not the only groups to stake a claim to national traditions, however. The aforementioned mural of Monumental, for example, was created by the Kirchnerist militant group La Cámpora. The description of the mural on the organisation's website refers to Néstor Kirchner as the reincarnation of the collective hero represented by El Eternauta (La Cámpora 2011). Here the use of a national tradition is more specific: the militant group refers to El Eternauta as a symbol of Peronist, national-popular resistance. The choice of Monumental as the subject of an image located just a few streets away from the stadium is its own expression of urban resistance: not only was the home of River Plate football club the site where those resisting the alien invasion came together in Oesterheld and Solano López's comic, but it also symbolises the 1976–83 military dictatorship, which refashioned the stadium for the 1978 World Cup. The mural mobilises comics to reclaim the stadium as a site of popular resistance rather than state repression.

Figure 1.5   Paseo de la Historieta: statue of Nik's character Gaturro adorned with graffiti. Photograph by the author

Similarly, a comic-strip mural in the city of Córdoba, Argentina, was created by Hernán Cappelletti for the Abuelas de Plaza de Mayo Córdoba (Grandmothers of the Plaza de Mayo Córdoba), a work that was subsequently threatened by state intervention. In January 2015, the wall on Humberto Primo Street, which depicts the search for a child who does not know her background until she is reunited with her grandmother, was painted over by the city government. As the scholar Ludmila da Silva Catela wrote on her Facebook page about the presence of an 'urban hygiene' truck at the erasure, 'la memoria no se borra, mucho menos se higieniza [memory shouldn't be erased, and it certainly shouldn't be sterilised]'. The city government claimed that the mural had been mistakenly covered up by a private company hired to carry out works under the #EnsuciaTuCasaNoLaDeTodos initiative (La Voz 2015). In fact, the mural of the Madres had already been subject to unwarranted interventions, including, according to César Carrizo (2015), being daubed with Nazi symbols and having the contact information for the Abuelas that appeared on the strip erased. Such interventions, as is to be expected in public spaces, are not uncommon. When I followed the Paseo de la Historieta in 2017, for example, the Gaturro statue was daubed with the phrases 'Nik facho' and '#MacriGato' (Figure 1.5).[4] Interventions by individual citizens highlight the contested nature of cultural icons and comics in public space. They symbolise the processes of negotiation that circulate around and through these sites, whether in the form of graffiti, political slogans, stolen tiles, traces of pollution, or dirt.

Comics for education and protest

In this final section I will look at the pedagogic and denunciatory quality of comics. Carol L. Tilley and Robert G. Weiner have highlighted that teachers in the US were using comics in the classroom even by the end of the 1920s to foment experiential learning processes and to offer an insight into humour, cultural habits and practices, and linguistic fluency (2017, 358–60). Comics continue to gain ground as objects of study on university programmes around the world. But they are also being used as an alternative pedagogical tool, encouraging students to think about using different ways of expressing critical thinking and analysis. A recent issue of *Tebeosfera* (2019) looks precisely at how comics are being used in different pedagogical contexts in Spain. In Latin America, comics are used on programmes such as the aforementioned course at the Faculty of Design in the Universidad de Buenos Aires or within the Faculty of Arts at the Universidad Nacional de Colombia, as well as in architectural schools in Uruguay, as Jorge Tuset's chapter in this volume demonstrates. In such cases, comics are often created within group dynamics and as part of collective learning approaches that encourage social interaction and deep thinking. Such activities are not dissimilar to the 'comics work' discussed above: it is as much the processes and interactions that precede the page, or which occur simultaneous to the creation of the page, that facilitate new conceptualisations of experience and identity formation.

That comics have an instructive function is well established in Latin America. Dorfman and Mattelart (1971) highlighted precisely the pernicious impact of Disney's cartoons on Latin American children by critiquing their ideological content. Juan Acevedo, who later became famous for his comic strip *El cuy*, created groundbreaking comics workshops in Peru in the mid-1970s. Though influenced by Dorfman and Mattelart, the concept behind these workshops, which took place in impoverished neighbourhoods such as Villa El Salvador, was based on the idea that a full understanding of the critique of imported comics was dependent on understanding the language of the form, something best taught through creating comics (Sagástegui 2009, 141). In a recent interview, Juan Acevedo referred to the project's aims as being 'the democratisation of the comic, freeing it so it could serve the people' (Villar 2016, 191).

These activities eventually resulted in the book *Para hacer historietas* (Acevedo 1978), a manual for drawing comics that included instructions on how to draw faces, expressions and the component parts of bodies, how to construct comics narratives and how to frame images and create speech, all accompanied by practical tasks for the student and illustrated with an impressive selection of images from primary sources. But even though much of the book is not explicitly political, by describing his aim as 'visual literacy' (199), Acevedo locates the project within wider social discourses of popular education projects within Latin America. Indeed, the book comments on cultural imperialism. When discussing onomatopoeia, for example, Acevedo notes how widespread the use of English sound words is within Spanish comics. He points out that it is not simply a case of rejecting such words outright but rather of not simply 'mechanically repeating them [. . .] and denying your own self' (134). As the book progresses, its ideological thrust becomes clearer, with a comment about how traditional comics resist addressing 'work, politics, social contradictions, etc.' (137). In his brief history of comics, Acevedo sets up a contrast between the industrial development of comics emanating from the US around the turn of the twentieth century and the comics represented by his workshop and the comics creators involved in them, what he calls 'the popular comic', which 'wants to incentivise the reader's conscience and encourage action within the medium in which they exist. Popular comics artists aren't crippled by the challenges posed by lack of access to expensive technologies; they turn to the mimeograph, manual duplication, the hectograph, etc.' (ibid., 144). That is to say, the comics industry is here being challenged by a set of artisanal, communal processes in terms of creating comics rather than simply at the level of ideological content.

In the second edition of *Para hacer historietas*, there are a number of subsequent 'popular comics' workshops listed near the end, including ones that took place in Spain, Cuba, Costa Rica, Mexico, Colombia and West Germany in the 1980s. Acevedo also travelled to Nicaragua to aid similar undertakings there (Butler Flora 1984, 177). Visual culture was an important part of the Sandinista revolution, not least as posters could use iconography to convey political messages effectively to a widely illiterate population. Christiane Berth (2017) has demonstrated how the Sandinistas also incorporated comics into their popular education campaign strategies, satirising Somoza, say, at the same time as promoting vaccination programmes. Berth notes that as Nicaragua did not have a strong comics tradition, the Sandinistas drew on similar approaches in both Chile and Cuba (2017, 113–14) and employed other Latin American artists, including Rius and Miguel Marfán as part of their campaigns (125).

Comics were also a fundamental part of activities organised by a group of Colombian intellectuals between 1972 and 1974 on the Caribbean coast to protest land ownership and rural working conditions. The artist Ulianov Chalarka created several short comics, later collated in a single publication (1985), in which he focused on historical injustices and violence, landscape and territory, and grassroots political campaigns, the political intensity of which is increased by the inclusion of photographs of campaigners. But as Joanna Rappaport (2018) has demonstrated, as well as the content of the comics themselves it was the participatory and collaborative nature of the way Chalarka created these comics that made them so politically powerful. Drawing the comics based on conversations with locals in the area of Córdoba, Chalarka then shared his drafts with rural workers and revised his images in the light of their comments. As Rappaport states, the comics 'functioned as a space where both rural workers and external researchers could deploy and combine their imaginative skills' (2018, 140). Something similar can be seen in more recent workshops being run in Ibagué, Colombia. Researchers at the University of Ibagué, together with Fundación Social, are using comics as a way of fomenting a sense of belonging and community in low-income neighbourhoods in the region.[5]

Indeed, comics continue to be used extensively within Latin America to address political violence, social trauma and memory (Catalá Carrasco et al. 2017).[6] Rappaport herself makes the connection between Chalarka's work and the recent Colombian collaborative comic *Caminos condenados* (Ojeda et al. 2016), which explores conflict over land ownership and irrigation in Montes de María, Colombia. One of the most well-known exponents of such documentary comics is the Peruvian Jesús Cossio, who explicitly sees his work as being in the vein of Joe Sacco. Cossio has worked on two extremely important works in Latin American comics, *Rupay: Historias gráficas sobre la violencia política 1980–1984* (Rossell et al. 2008) and *Barbarie: Cómics sobre la violencia política 1985–1990* (Cossio 2010), both of which address the violence that took place in Peru during the apogee of the neo-Maoist group Sendero Luminoso. More recently Cossio has also been involved in an online comic entitled 'La guerra por el agua' that denounces conflicts over water between mining companies and local residents near Arequipa in southern Peru (Ojo Público 2016). The work includes some animation and some sound (wind, birds, recorded sounds of protest and repression, etc.), but the comic aesthetic and the progression of the narrative and speech indicate that the work should be understood as a comic. The layering of frames creates links between images.[7] And the layering of information revealed piecemeal through the images, alongside the multisensory reading experience, intensifies the denunciatory qualities of the work. The pedagogical, instructive qualities of this comic are clear: local peasants explain what crops they grow and how they have been affected by drought; interactive maps highlight the reaches of the multinational mining company Southern Copper Corporation; and interviews with local activists demonstrate the disagreements between local residents dependent on agricultural livelihoods and the government, which prefers to promote large-scale mining enterprises.

Cossio has also been working extensively within educational institutions in Peru, using comics to help schoolchildren process the traumatic legacy of armed conflict. His work is linked to the Programa de Reparaciones Simbólicas de CMAN (Comisión Multisectorial de Alto Nivel para las Reparaciones a afectados del Conflicto Armado Interno), which is a subsection of the Ministerio de Justicia y Derechos Humanos de Perú. Cossio visits schools in areas that were particularly affected by the armed conflict and works with groups of around 30 schoolchildren aged between 14 and 18, all of whom will have been born after 2000, the 'official' end of the period of conflict. He is responsible for instructing the children in how to draw and compose comics. The children then create comics that relate to the violence that took place in their region, and its aftermath, with the school submitting work as part of a wider competition. Cossio estimates that over the course of the project, which has been running for some five years, they now have over 200 comics. In examples taken from the 2015 edition of the competition in the area of Ayacucho, the heartland of Sendero Luminoso, the content is striking for the subjects addressed: hangings, decapitations, burnings of properties with people inside, domestic violence, dogs eating corpses, rape, all to the backdrop of political figures, flags and slogans. One winning entry is notable for its dark poetry: 'and if you didn't speak then obviously you were hung in dramatic fashion, swinging from the cypress'. Cossio's work as both artist and facilitator, therefore, exemplifies the activist potential of comics production, one that comes firmly out of the tradition of the work of artists like Sacco and Acevedo. It is fitting, therefore, that the concluding contribution to this book should be Cossio's graphic reflection on his experiences working with CMAN. His comic indicates how such projects can open up not just comics consumption but also their creation to wider, more diverse audiences. That, we might suggest, is the most pressing challenge for contemporary Latin American comics work.

Comics Beyond the Page in Latin America: Overview

In the chapter that opens the first of the three sections into which this book is loosely divided, Nina Mickwitz analyses the aforementioned publication *El Volcán* (2017) as a node around which Latin American comics creators have formed a network of cultural production. She argues that the anthology format has created a space and set of activities that has encouraged the development of transnational alliances that can promote work usually only circulated more locally by small presses. Such transnational networks are not only characteristic of contemporary Latin American comics production. As Laura Vazquez demonstrates in her chapter on the world of Argentine comics, during the mid-century 'Golden Age' the comics industry in Argentina was highly transnational, complicating the nostalgic national gaze of some historians. And she also highlights how, in the long decline of that era, artists and producers have constantly had to renegotiate their profession as a result of the tensions between nation and globalisation, and between industry and craft. Vazquez's chapter also presents a recurring theme in this book: that we cannot really talk of Latin American comics industries. Enrique Uribe-Jongbloed and Daniel E. Aguilar-Rodríguez make a similar point in their study of the changing nature of comics consumption in Colombia. Though they welcome the recent growth in comics production in bookstores and festivals, they also highlight that, whereas comics used to be rented and exchanged at kiosks and other consumption spaces in working-class districts of Colombian cities, comics are now the domain of more middle-class consumers who can afford imported and locally published comics. Uribe-Jongbloed and Aguilar-Rodríguez are, nonetheless, tentatively positive about the future of Colombian comics. Carla Sagástegui Heredia also highlights some of the positive developments of changes in the publishing of comics in Peru. She argues that the growth in the publication of comic books and fanzines has produced a kind of revalorisation of the figure of the author. Looking at the way that three authors published by Contracultura have constructed their own authorial selves, not least in an increasingly transnational environment, Sagástegui Heredia argues that, though these artists are still not able to live off comics, they have helped comics become more widely accepted as forms of political and social expression.

The following two chapters expand on the digital dimensions of contemporary comics production. In her chapter on digital comics in Mexico, Carolina González Alvarado demonstrates how authors and producers utilise their web presence to interact with readers and develop a fan base that sometimes results in the publication of hard copies, making the latter a kind of repository. Referring in particular to the work of Alejandra Gámez, González Alvarado demonstrates how contemporary comics readers have to draw on new forms of 'multimodal competence' to construct meaning. Such multimodality is also evident in Edward King's study of the links between social media and digital comics in Brazil. King looks at how certain digital comics put autobiographical selves into visual and textual exchanges with wider technological networks, a process that highlights the ongoing negotiations that are taking place between transnational digital citizenships and grounded identities.

The following two chapters pick up on the presence of comics in material space but focus more on the relationship between comics and urban landscapes. Ivan Lima Gomes looks at how Alberto 'Tito' Serrano's comic graffiti in Rio de Janeiro created a comic narrative via the cityscape itself. The comic places the character of Zé Nobody, an impoverished immigrant displaced in this hostile environment, firmly within the city. As such, Lima Gomes argues, the comic draws together the practice of reading comics with that of reading the city. Cristian Palacios also looks at a comic-book character in the urban landscape: Héctor G. Oesterheld and Francisco Solano López's El Eternauta. Analysing the debates that circulated around the way that a Peronist political group amalgamated the character with former president Néstor Kirchner, Palacios highlights how comic-book characters, when they take on a social existence beyond the space in which they were originally conceived, can become highly contested sites of political expression.

The book's final two contributions focus more directly on the pedagogical and denunciatory function of comics. Jorge Tuset argues that, despite resistance from some academics, comics have proven to be an extremely valuable means of opening up different perspectives for students of architecture at the Universidad de la República in Uruguay. Drawing on the links between comics and architectural practitioners, Tuset demonstrates how students' sophisticated use of the comic form has enabled them to engage with building practices in Uruguay and beyond in new ways. Finally, Jesús Cossio reminds us of the power of comics to engage with pressing social and political issues not just as objects of scrutiny but also as a practice.

Even though Latin America lacks a comics industry, this brief overview of the chapters included in this book highlights the social and political impact of comics beyond the page. Latin American comics work is vibrant, diverse, influential and reveals a great deal about the changing nature of cultural consumption in a digital world, about shifts in the fan base of popular cultural forms, and about the way that Latin American cultural creators must constantly negotiate the tensions and possibilities of the national and transnational flows and identities that criss-cross the region. This book does not set out to romanticise either the national or the global, or to celebrate either the digital or the material. Instead, it demonstrates how diverse groups, from state institutions to NGOs to comics artists and others, mediate between them, variously contesting and embracing them. At the book's heart lies the belief that comics have the potential to cut across diverse reading and consumption groups, to build alliances and foment encounters – material and digital – between people of different nationalities and from diverse social groups. Looking at comics beyond the page highlights the mesh of experiences and negotiations that underpin that belief.

Notes

1 For more on digital comics in a non-Latin American context, see McCloud (2009), Groensteen (2013), Goodbrey (2013) or Wilde (2015).
2 A number of scholars have highlighted this affinity between comics, the city and architectural forms (Ahrens and Meteling 2010; Van der Hoorn 2012; Labio 2015; Bordes 2017).
3 They can also, though I do not have any Latin American examples of such an approach, appear in more complex fusions between comics and architectural space, as in the way one building in Hong Kong has become a canvas for a comic narrative. Mélanie van der Hoorn writes that, in this work 'the comic strip has revealed itself as a multifunctional art form' (2012, 205), highlighting how 'to many architects the comic strip is much more than a means of communication; it literally contributes to the production of architecture' (17).
4 'Nik facho' is a critique of political views expressed by cartoonist Nik (Cristian Dzwonik), creator of the character Gaturro. The hashtag #MacriGato refers contemptuously to the former Argentine president Mauricio Macri. As an insult, 'gato' has various meanings, including, in prison slang, an inmate who works on behalf of someone higher up in the internal hierarchy.
5 My thanks to Edward Muñoz for providing me with this information.
6 And such trends are evident in transnational projects such as Positive Negatives, which uses comics to address human rights issues from various countries around the globe. Positive Negatives includes one story from Latin America, 'Enrique's Shadow', which relates the story of a boy's kidnapping and disappearance in Colombia (http://positivenegatives.org/comics-animations/enriques-shadow/comic/).
7 'Cossio had to split up the images in layers: backgrounds, environment, characters, fragments of drawings that needed to interact. "It took me some time to think of the drawings not as complete detailed compositions but as parts of a whole that, together with the text, had to give a sense of interaction with the reader and make the most of the potential of the digital format", he explained' (Amancio 2016).

References

070 Womansplaining. 2018. 'Casi como un hombre, pero con cuerpo femenino'. Last accessed 12 September 2018. https://cerosetenta.uniandes.edu.co/podcast-casi-como-un-hombre-pero-con-cuerpo-femenino.

Acevedo, Juan. 1978. *Para hacer historietas*. Madrid: Editorial Popular.

Ahrens, Jörn and Arno Meteling, eds. 2010. *Comics and the City: Urban Space in Print, Picture and Sequence*. New York and London: Continuum.

Amancio, Nelly Luna. 2016. 'Entender el conflicto: Experimentarlo todo'. *La guerra por el agua*. Last accessed 12 September 2018. https://laguerraporelagua.ojo-publico.com/es/#como-se-hizo.

Baetens, Jan. 2013. 'Learning From Comics (and Bart Beaty): On the Institutionalization of Comics: An Interview with Bart Beaty by Jan Baetens', *Interférences littéraires – Literaire interferenties* 11: 179–88.

Bayardo, Rubens. 2013. 'Políticas culturales y economía simbólica de las ciudades: "Buenos Aires, en todo estás vos"', *Latin American Research Review* 48: 100–28.

Berney, Rachel. 2017. *Learning from Bogotá: Pedagogical Urbanism and the Reshaping of Public Space*. Austin: University of Texas Press.

Berth, Christiane. 2017. 'Comics in a Revolutionary Context: Educational Campaigns and Collective Memory in Sandinista Nicaragua'. In *Comics and Memory in Latin America*, edited by Jorge Catalá Carrasco, Paulo Drinot and James Scorer, 108–37. Pittsburgh: University of Pittsburgh Press.

Bordes, Enrique. 2017. *Cómic, arquitectura narrativa*. Madrid: Cátedra.

Borges, Gabriela, Katherine Supnem, Maira Mayola and Mariela Acevedo. 2018. 'Historieta feminista en América Latina: Autoras de Argentina, Chile, Brasil y México', *Revista Tebeosfera*, 6. Last accessed 5 June 2019. https://www.tebeosfera.com/documentos/historieta_feminista_en_america_latina_autoras_de_argentina_chile_brasil_y_mexico.html.

Brienza, Casey and Paddy Johnston. 2016. 'Introduction: Understanding Comics Work'. In *Cultures of Comics Work*, edited by Casey Brienza and Paddy Johnston, 1–17. New York: Palgrave Macmillan.

Butler Flora, Cornelia. 1984. 'Roasting Donald Duck: Alternative Comics and Photonovels in Latin America', *Journal of Popular Culture* 18, no. 1: 163–83.

Cánepa, Gisela. 2010. 'Performing Citizenship: Migration, Andean Festivals, and Public Spaces in Lima'. In *Cultures of the City: Mediating Identities in Urban Latin/o America*, edited by Richard Young and Amanda Holmes, 135–50. Pittsburgh: University of Pittsburgh Press.

Carrizo, César. 2015. 'Historieta mural Abuelas de Plaza de Mayo Córdoba'. Last accessed 10 September 2018. http://lahistorietaenlaescuela.blogspot.cl/2015/03/historieta-mural-abuelas-de-plaza-de.html.

Catalá Carrasco, Jorge, Paulo Drinot and James Scorer, eds. 2017. *Comics and Memory in Latin America*. Pittsburgh: University of Pittsburgh Press.

Chalarka, Ulianov. 1985. *Historia gráfica de la lucha por la tierra en la Costa Atlántica*. Bogotá: Fundación del Sinú.

Cossio, Jesús. 2010. *Barbarie: Cómics sobre la violencia política 1985–1990*. Lima: Contracultura.

Diniz, André. 2011. *Morro da favela [Picture a Favela]*. São Paulo: Barba Negra/ Leya Editora.

Dittmer, Jason and Alan Latham. 2015. 'The Rut and the Gutter: Space and Time in Graphic Narrative', *Cultural Geographies* 22, no. 3: 427–44.

Dorfman, Ariel and Armand Mattelart. 1971. *Para leer al Pato Donald* [How to Read Donald Duck]. Valparaíso: Ediciones Universitarias de Valparaíso.

Edwards, Elizabeth. 2009. 'Photography and the Material Performance of the Past', *History and Theory* 48, no. 4: 130–50.

Fernández L'Hoeste, Héctor and Juan Poblete. 2009. 'Introduction'. In *Redrawing the Nation: National Identity in Latin/o American Comics*, edited by Héctor Fernández L'Hoeste and Juan Poblete, 1–16. New York: Palgrave Macmillan.

Ferrer-Medina, Patricia. 2015. 'El zombi caníbal entre la colonialidad y la diferencia ecológica: Una breve arqueología de ideas'. In *Terra zombi: El fenómenon transnacional de los muertos vivientes*, edited by Rosana Díaz-Zambrana, 29–45. San Juan: Editorial Isla Negra.

Francescutti, Pablo. 2015. 'Del Eternauta al "Nestornauta": La transformación de un icono cultural en un símbolo político', *Cuadernos de Información y Comunicación* 20: 27–43.

Gago, Sebastián. 2016. 'El lugar de la utopía en la recuperación del pasado: El caso del "Nestornauta" en la Argentina', *Sociedad y Discurso* 29: 134–60.

Gandolfo, Amadeo and Pablo Turnes. 2019. '"Fresh off the Boat and off to the Presses": The Origins of Argentine Comics Between the US and Europe', *European Comic Art* 12, no. 2 (forthcoming).

Gandolfo, Amadeo, Pablo Turnes and Gerardo Vilches. 2017. 'Historia de dos industrias: Un debate en torno a la historieta argentina y española', *Cuadernos de cómic* 8: 103–30.

Gobierno de la Ciudad de Buenos Aires. n.d. 'Paseo de la Historieta'. Last accessed 10 September 2018. https://turismo.buenosaires.gob.ar/sites/turismo/files/paseo_de_la_historieta_print.pdf.

Goodbrey, Daniel. 2013. 'From Comic to Hypercomic'. In *Cultural Excavation and Formal Expression in the Graphic Novel*, edited by J.C. Evans and T. Giddens, 291–302. Oxford: Inter-Disciplinary Press.

Groensteen, Thierry. 2013. *Comics and Narration*. Jackson: University Press of Mississippi.

Jiménez Quiroz, Daniel. 2017. 'Extracts from a Discussion about Comics Festivals with Andrés Accorsi, Diego Agrimbau and Daniel Jiménez Quiroz'. Last accessed 12 September 2018. https://comicsandthelatinamericancity.wordpress.com/podcast-estudio-tourmalon.

King, Edward. 2017. 'Prosthetic Memory and Networked Temporalities in *Morro da Favela* by André Diniz'. In *Comics and Memory in Latin America*, edited by Jorge Catalá Carrasco, Paulo Drinot and James Scorer, 224–44. Pittsburgh: University of Pittsburgh Press.

La Cámpora. 2011. 'Mural homenaje a Solano López en Núñez'. Last accessed 10 September 2018. http://www.lacampora.org/2011/12/18/mural-homenaje-a-solano-lopez-en-nunez/.

La Voz. 2015. 'La Municipalidad tapó un mural de Abuelas de Plaza de Mayo Córdoba'. Last accessed 10 September 2018. http://www.lavoz.com.ar/politica/la-municipalidad-tapo-un-mural-de-abuelas-de-plaza-de-mayo-cordoba.

Labio, Catherine. 2015. 'The Architecture of Comics', *Critical Inquiry* 41, no. 2: 312–43.

Massey, Doreen. 2005. *For Space*. London: Sage.

McCloud, Scott. 2009. 'The "Infinite Canvas"'. Last accessed 12 September 2018. http://scottmccloud.com/4-inventions/canvas.

Mosquito, Ángel. 2011. 'La calambre', 17 January. Last accessed 10 September 2018. http://granjerodejesu.blogspot.com/2011/01/la-calambre.html.

Mosquito, Ángel. 2013. *La calambre*. Barcelona: La Cúpula.

Ojeda, Diana, Pablo Guerra, Camilo Aguirre and Henry Díaz. 2016. *Caminos condenados*. Bogotá: Cohete Cómics.

Ojo Público. 2016. *La guerra por el agua*. Last accessed 10 September 2018. https://laguerraporelagua.ojo-publico.com/es/.

Pereira de Carvalho, André. 2016. 'Reconfiguring the Power Structure of the Comic Book Field: Crowdfunding and the Use of Social Networks'. In *Cultures of Comics Work*, edited by Casey Brienza and Paddy Johnston, 251–63. New York: Palgrave Macmillan.

Rahman, Osmud, Liu Wing-sun and Hei-man Cheung. 2012. '"Cosplay": Imaginative Self and Performing Identity', *Fashion Theory* 16, no. 3: 317–41.

Rannou, Maël and Roberto Salazar Morales, eds. 2017. *Ñ comme viñetas: Anthologie de Bande Dessinée Colombienne*. Laval: L'Égouttoir.

Rappaport, Joanne. 2018. 'Visualidad y escritura como acción: Investigación Acción Participativa en la Costa Caribe colombiana', *Revista Colombiana de Sociología* 41, no. 1: 133–56.

Rossell, Luis, Alfredo Villar and Jesús Cossio. 2008. *Rupay: Historias gráficas sobre la violencia política 1980–1984*. Madrid: La Oveja Roja.

Sagástegui, Carla. 2009. 'Acevedo and His Predecessors'. In *Redrawing the Nation: National Identity in Latin/o American Comics*, edited by Héctor Fernández L'Hoeste and Juan Poblete, 131–50. New York: Palgrave Macmillan.

Sainz, José and Alejandro Bidegaray. 2017. *El Volcán: Un presente de la historieta latinoamericana*. Rosario: :e(m)r; and Musaraña Editora.

Scarzanella, Eugenia. 2016. *Abril: Un editor italiano en Buenos Aires, de Perón a Videla*. Buenos Aires: Fondo de Cultura Económica.

Schwartz, Marcy. 2018. *Public Pages: Reading Along the Latin American Streetscape*. Austin: University of Texas Press.

Scorer, James. 2016. *City in Common: Culture and Community in Buenos Aires*. Albany: State University of New York Press.

Suárez, Fernando and Enrique Uribe-Jongbloed. 2016. 'Making Comics as Artisans: Comic Book Production in Colombia'. In *Cultures of Comics Work*, edited by Casey Brienza and Paddy Johnston, 51–64. New York: Palgrave Macmillan.

Thon, Jan-Noël and Lukas R.A. Wilde. 2016. 'Mediality and Materiality of Contemporary Comics', *Journal of Graphic Novels and Comics* 7, no. 3: 233–41.

Tilley, Carol L. and Robert G. Weiner. 2017. 'Teaching and Learning with Comics'. In *The Routledge Companion to Comics*, edited by Frank Bramlett, Roy Cook and Aaron Meskin, 358–66. New York: Routledge.

Van der Hoorn, Mélanie. 2012. *Bricks & Balloons: Architecture in Comic-Strip Form*. Rotterdam: 010 Publishers.

Villar, Alfredo, ed. 2016. *BÚMM!: Historieta y humor gráfico en el Perú: 1978–1992*. Lima: Reservoir Books.

Wilde, Lukas. 2015. 'Distinguishing Mediality: The Problem of Identifying Forms and Features of Digital Comics', *Networking Knowledge* 8, no. 4: 1–14.

2

El Volcán: Forging global comics cultures through alliances, networks and self-branding

Nina Mickwitz

Introduction

This research grew from a chance encounter at the Helsinki Comics Festival 2017, the main themes of which included Latin American comics. As the website states: 'Helsinki Comics Festival, organised by Finnish Comics Society, is the largest annual comics festival in Northern Europe. The festival features an exciting gathering of comics artists and publishers from all around the world, and attracts ca. 11,000–20,000 visitors each year' (Helsinki Comics Festival 2019). In 2017, the invited guests included different generations of Argentine comics creators (José Muñoz and Berliac), and the editors and contributing artists of the newly published anthology *El Volcán: Un presente de la historieta latino-americana* (2017). This encounter with an anthology of Latin American comics at an event in the far north-eastern reaches of Europe brought into focus the fact that comics studies still has work to do when it comes to the global circulation of comics.

Comics studies has grown exponentially over the past 10 to 15 years. Since the *International Journal of Comic Art* (1999–present), other journals have emerged: *European Comic Art* (Berghahn, 2008–present); *The Journal of Graphic Novels and Comics* (Routledge, 2010–present); *Studies in Comics* (Intellect, 2010–present); *Mechademia* (2006–present); *Inks: The Comics Studies Society Journal* (University of Ohio Press, 2017–present); *Revista Latinoamericana de Estudios sobre la Historieta* (2001–10); *Nona Arte: Revista Brasileira de Pesquisas em Histórias em Quadrinhos* (2012–present); *Comicalités: Études de culture graphique* (2013–present); and *Deutsche Comicforschung* (2005–present). Online journals dedicated to comics include *ImageText: Interdisciplinary Comics Studies, Comics Grid, Closure, SANE Journal: Sequential Art Narrative in Education* and *Scandinavian Journal of Comic Art*. Alongside the longstanding publisher of comics scholarship, the University Press of Mississippi, with its Great Comics Artists Series, Rutgers University Press run a series entitled Comics Cultures, McFarland & Co has published numerous monographs and edited collections on the topic, as have Routledge's Advances in Comics Studies and Palgrave's series Studies in Comics and Graphic Novels. Regularly occurring conferences are too numerous to list here.[1] The maturing of the field can be observed in the emergence of scholarly readers that attempt to set out key concerns and debates. *The Language of Comics: Word and Image* (2001) edited by Christina Varnum and Gibbons, *A Comics Studies Reader* (2009) edited by Kent Worcester and Jeet Heer, and Matthew J. Smith and Randy Duncan's *Critical Approaches to Comics: Theories and Methods* (2012) have been followed by volumes such as *The Routledge Companion to Comics Studies* (2017) edited by Frank Bramlett, T. R. Cook and Aaron Meskin, *The Cambridge Companion to Graphic Novels* (2017) edited by Stephen A. Tabachnik, and *Comics Studies: A Guidebook* (forthcoming) edited by Bart Beaty and Charles Hatfield. The Anglo-American weighting of the listed outputs is undeniable. That does not mean that contributing scholars are limited to these particular geographies, nor that the subjects of study are necessarily located within these parameters. In fact, a cursory glance across the contents pages of most journals and collections of essays demonstrates substantial cultural and geographical diversity when it comes to examples examined and histories explored. It is nevertheless fair to say that production cultures with long established international circulation, namely North American comics, Franco-Belgian *bandes dessinée* and Japanese manga, have tended to dominate scholarship across borders.

Coming across *El Volcán* in Helsinki brought to the fore a number of related questions concerning global networks, encounters and identities, and cultural and linguistic translation in relation to comics. In some ways, this encounter represents a connection between two cultural contexts – Latin America and Finland – that can both be framed as peripheral. This has certainly been the case in relation to international comics circulation, as each has provided markets for the import of comics to a degree significantly exceeding their capacity to access foreign markets for their own production. In a broader sense, neither belongs to a dominant cultural paradigm. Within Europe, Finland can be described as a small nation at some remove from the continent, both geographically and in terms of political and economic muscle.[2] The economic and political dominance of the United States has historically also positioned Latin America as marginal. But this dynamic is complicated by the fact that Finland belongs to the privileged global north, while Latin America is a constituent of the global south. In this sense, a centre–margin relation remains part of the overall equation.

Thirty years ago, Arjun Appadurai argued that the contemporary global cultural economy is now 'a complex, overlapping, disjunctive order that cannot any longer be understood in terms of existing centre-periphery models (even those that might account for multiple centres and peripheries)' (1990, 588), while Ulf Hannerz (1990) suggested that a centre-periphery dynamic still effectively holds sway, not least in the way dominant 'world' languages uphold advantages for certain sections of global populations. Since then, the tectonic plates of geo-political alliances and economic power (and their fault lines) have shifted considerably and technological developments have shaped, further deterritorialised and reconfigured global cultural landscapes. But the unevenness of flows that constitute the global cultural economy has, if anything, intensified. Asymmetrical relations of mobility and exchange are often entrenched and reproduced by further disparities in terms of visibility and attention. At the same time, the global marketplace requires and encourages differentiation, and cultural identity can be utilised for such purposes.

El Volcán: Un presente de la historieta latinoamericana identifies its offering ('presente' can be translated as 'gift', which makes the subtitle suggestive of a benevolent act of sharing) through cultural and regional identity. At the Helsinki festival, *El Volcán*'s celebration of the idiosyncratic and often hand-crafted clearly connected with the sensibilities of Finnish small press and independent creators on show. These local counterparts were selling comics and other merchandise on tables in one of the smaller halls on the festival site. As invited international guests, the *El Volcán* editors and contributors were a focal point of the festival programme, including an exhibition of artwork and interviews and panel appearances on stage. The intention of this chapter is to examine how regional and cultural identity (as constructed by *El Volcán*) works as performative identification and as a category through which products are engaged with and understood.

The study of comics, like that of many other cultural forms, often applies a national frame. Approaches to Latin American comics (L'Hoeste and Poblete 2009; Manthei 2011; Vergueiro 2009; Ostuni et al. n.d.; Gociol and Rosemberg 2000; Suárez and Uribe-Jongbloed 2016; Gomes 2016) are no exception. Ana Merino (2017, 70) has rightly argued that histories of comics production in different Latin American countries have been shaped by distinct socio-economic and political contexts and demand specificity of address and attention. Yet national labels tend to obscure mobilities and exchanges that continually take place across borders, and which have multiplied with the growth of the internet. On the whole, geo-political and cultural categorisations are often more complex than national frameworks can adequately account for. 'It is so taken for granted that each country embodies its own distinctive culture and society that the terms "society" and "culture" are routinely simply appended to the names of nation-states' (Gupta and Ferguson 1992, 6–7). A regional frame is no less at risk of flattening internal differences, but can help account for cultural resonances, commonalities and collaborations not beholden to national borders.

Using *El Volcán* as a case study, and with the generous assistance of José Sainz, Alejandro Bidegaray, Muriel Bellini, Joni B., Jesús Cossio, Powerpaola[3] and Júlia Barata, I have been able to develop these thoughts further. Rather than focusing on the visual or narrative comics work included in the book, this chapter approaches *El Volcán* in its capacity as a networking tool, examining how this publication enables the construction of comics communities both within Latin America and beyond.

Following a brief summary of genesis and contents, the chapter considers the anthology format and its functions. It then goes on to explore how various levels of belonging – local, national and regional – are articulated within *El Volcán*. How does this publication embody specific and local comics cultures? How do creators themselves place their practice, especially in relation to wider comics cultures, and what is at stake in mobilising the regional? Having considered these questions, attention turns to the networks of transactional relationships that connect publications, exhibitions and international festivals. The chapter thus argues that a publication such as this requires consideration as both text and project, and, in terms of global comics cultures, as a networking node in its own right.

An outpouring of talent

El Volcán: Un presente de la historieta latinoamericana is a 25 by 20 centimetre tome, and by comparison with UK and US paperback formats its production values are striking. The book opens with a contents page and editor's foreword, and ends with three pages of short biographical notes. These introduce the 42 comics creators. These paratextual elements bookend 272 glossy pages of short form comics, some in monochrome but many rendered in uncompromising full colour. They convey a busy and energetic impression in clear correspondence with the title, and eponymous bursting forth of flames from the volcanic crater on Javier Velasco's front cover (see Figure 2.1).

Figure 2.1 *El Volcán: Un presente de la historieta latinoamericana* (2017), with cover artwork by Javier Velasco. Photograph by Alejandro Bidegaray

Edited by José Sainz and Alejandro Bidegaray, *El Volcán* was published by Editorial Municipal Rosario[4] and Musaraña Editora in 2017. The project first took shape as the brainchild of Bidegaray, who originally ventured into publishing to provide financial support for this bookshop. Musaraña Editora has since grown into an autonomous proposition. Its inaugural and most high-profile title to date is *Vapor* by fêted Spanish creator Max[5] in 2013, originally published in Spain by La Cúpula (2012), and later brought to Anglophone readers by Fantagraphics (2014). Between then and early 2018, the imprint has published a string of graphic artists' work and currently counts 18 titles in several formats: pocket books; larger albums; fanzines; and risograph fanzines (Alejandro Bidegaray, email to author, 23 April 2018). Bidegaray asked fellow comics aficionado and promoter José Sainz to join the *El Volcán* project early on. Sainz, based in the city of Rosario in Santa Fé province, had in 2015 published *Informe: Historieta argentina del siglo XXI* with the collaboration of local authority-run publisher Editorial Municipal Rosario (EMR). EMR's involvement with comics began with the 2014 publication of the Spanish translation of *Johnny Jungle – Première Partie* (Deveney et al. 2013) with the support of the Victoria Ocampo Publishing Assistance Program of L'Institut français d'Argentine. Sainz describes EMR as 'a public publishing house but with the mindset of an independent, alternative publisher', giving specific mention to director Oscar Taborda, editor Daniel García Helder and designers Lis Mondaini and Juan Manuel Alonso (José Sainz, email to author, 23 April 2018). Previously instrumental in reinvigorating discussions around contemporary poetry, EMR's initial comics publications came out of national cartoon competitions (Concurso Nacional de Historieta Roberto Fontanarrosa 2008 and 2010). Since *Informe* (2015), EMR has published several individual works as well as *El Volcán* (2017) and the anthology *Historieta LGTBI* (Various authors 2017).[6]

El Volcán's 42 contributors are distributed across roughly 13 countries, a map occasionally complicated by multiple affiliations. The largest clusters represent Argentine, Brazilian, Peruvian and Colombian comics cultures, and most contributors are born in the 1970s and 1980s, with some exceptions at either end. Max Cachimba, who worked on the magazine *Fierro* in the mid-1980s,[7] can probably be identified as something of a lodestar, while other Argentine creators include Muriel Bellini, Juan Vegetal, Mónica Naranjo Uribe, Diego Parés, Jorge Quien, Jazmín Varela and Javier Velasco. Chilean contributors are Amanda Baeza (resident in Portugal), Catalina Bu and

Maliki, while the Brazilian contingent includes Mariana Paraizo, Pedro Frantz, Laura Lannes, Jaca, Fabio Zimbres and Diego Gerlach. Puiupo and Júlia Barata are both Portuguese, although Barata is now based in Argentina. Bolivia is represented by Marco Tóxico and Cuban-born Frank Arbelo, Costa Rica by Edward Brends, Uruguay by Maco, Paraguay by Regina Rivas, Venezuela by Carlos Sánchez Becerra and Ecuador by Powerpaola. Powerpaola is now an active member of the Colombian comics scene, alongside Mariana Gil Ríos, Truchafrita, Jim Pluk, Stefhany Yepes Lozano, La Watson and Joni B. Mexican creators include Inés Estrada, Abraham Díaz and Pachiclón, while Peru's contribution numbers Jesús Cossio, Rodrigo La Hoz, David Galliquio, Eduardo Yaguas, Jorge Pérez-Ruibal, Amadeo Gonzales and Martin López Lam (who lives in Spain). The challenges of determining precise boundaries and criteria for the project indicated in this summary overview flag up issues of identity and regionality central to this chapter. But before tackling these questions, the format of the publication deserves some attention.

The anthology as themed selection and statement

Chris Couch (2000) has claimed that 'the first comic books were anthologies of newspaper strips', although these were collections of previously published material. Capitalising on popular products that, having circulated among readers, had most likely been thrown away rather than kept, these publications were motivated by maximising sales. 'Usually the publishers of such books were the newspapers in which they had first appeared' (Sabin 1996, 25). Before simply adopting the term 'anthology' for such early historical examples, it is helpful to consider its defining features and provenance. What, for example, is the distinction between a collection and an anthology? Anne Ferry (2001) defines the anthology by multiple authorship, and thus something distinct from a collection of works by the same creator (which in the case of comics might be taken to mean the same creator, or group of creators). An anthology is most commonly associated with a themed selection of writing in book form. Magazines, for instance, might be identified by a specific theme and usually also consist of entries by multiple contributors, but are not considered to be anthologies. Not solely a consequence of publication format, the anthology is a genre designation weighted with ideas of cultural worthiness and esteem. Despite the value attached to these publications in retrospective and revisionist accounts, the word 'anthology' thus seems incongruous with the very early comic books that redistributed newspaper strips. However, by the 1990s, comics anthologies – clearly positioning themselves as such – played a vital role in shaping the publishing landscape.

Bart Beaty has traced the contemporary international comics anthology of 'avantgardist traditions and independent tendencies' (2007, 28) to L'Associacion, the French publishing co-operative that announced itself with the collection *Logique de Guerre Comix* in 1990. The characterisation of L'Association, in terms of 'an ideology of independence, autonomous production, and selection that privileges an idea of creation as founded exclusively in the arena of personal expression and individual style' (Beaty 2007, 43), transfers to the approach taken by Bidegaray and Sainz with remarkable ease, as does the observation that, during the 1990s European comics renaissance, the earlier emphasis on authorship in comics shifted towards visual creatorship.

The importance of anthologies appears particularly pronounced for small press, independent and self-publishing creators, as a means of visibility and reach. Where the national context is too limited to sustain a comics culture, anthologies offer a useful means of widening exposure, either by placing local creators alongside peers from other national contexts, or by collecting locally produced work that addresses wider readerships and professional networks. Among Beaty's examples, the Spanish magazine *Nosotros somos los muertos* (1995–2007) and the Portuguese anthology *Para Além dos Olivais* (Cotrim and Saraiva 2000) appear to share the outlook and ambitions of Bidegaray and Sainz. Closer to home, and 10 years prior to *El Volcán*, Jorge Siles (2007) wrote in celebratory tones about 'The Boom in Bolivian Comics' by mentioning titles such as the anthology magazine *Crash* (published by Eureka and initially headed up by Frank Arbelo) and *Suda Mery K!* The latter is especially interesting in terms of transnational efforts. Published from 2005 to 2008, in five bi-annual editions, this title was a joint project between three independent comics publishers – the French-Argentine Ex Abrupto, Bolivian Eureka and Chilean Ergo Comix – under the label ABC (Siles 2007). Since the early 2000s, comics events in the region have ranged from relatively small scale to the massive FIQ (Festival Internacional de Quadrinhos) in Belo Horizonte, Brazil. This belies the idea of a sudden eruption, instead suggesting that the contemporary comics scene represented in *El Volcán* has evolved gradually through multiple efforts and networking initiatives.

Following Beaty's (2007, 28) observations of 'high art' values in comics, the anthology format is a logical development on two accounts. The contemporary comics anthology, as Beaty (2007, 63) points out, takes on an increasing correspondence with traditions of artists' books. And formed by processes of selection and constitutive of framed bodies of work, anthologies can have a gate-keeping function and contribute to canon formation. The process through which *El Volcán* contributors were identified and selected indicates Bidegaray and Sainz's editorial sensitivity to the gate-keeping function and implicit weight of their choices. A decision not to duplicate any of the creators already included in the earlier *Informe* (2015) is described as deliberately guarding against overweighting towards the Argentine cohort, the local scene most familiar to the editors. Moreover, had some names been included in both anthologies they would have tacitly been positioned as particularly 'deserving' (José Sainz, email to author, 20 March 2018).

The selection criteria for *El Volcán* were plural and intersectional; some names included were 'obvious choices, and I mean obvious in a good way' (José Sainz, email to author, 20 March 2018). For example, publishing Powerpaola's work is perceived to cement the standing of Musaraña Editora (Alejandro Bidegaray, email to author, 23 April 2018) which underscores her position. Max Cachimba is an internationally fêted creator with an impressive back catalogue of work and, like David Galliquio, a recurring presence on competition juries. Amadeo Gonzales, Fabio Zimbres, Frank Arbelo, Marco Tóxico, Joni B, Maliki, Diego Parés and Jesús Cossio command similar esteem. These artists built careers in the precarious first decade of the twenty-first century, long after the collapse of the comics industry but before a newer notion of a Latin American comics scene had begun to coalesce. More recent arrivals currently in the process of making their names are identified by Sainz and Bidegaray as the following 'wave'. The anthology thus brings together creators already commanding recognition with others who are less established to set out and expand its field.

Association with respected peers works as a validation mechanism. Bellini expresses her admiration for many of the other contributors, describing being included in *El Volcán* as 'an honour' (Muriel Bellini, email to author, 20 February 2018). Júlia Barata mentions the opportunity for her work 'to travel' and gain access to different geographical locations and contexts beyond her own direct reach, and the importance of her work being positioned 'between a lot of artists that I admire' (Júlia Vilhena, email to author, 6 February 2018).

Jesús Cossio (email to author, 21 February 2018), if from a patently different perspective, offers a similar understanding:

> It is a good opportunity to disseminate my work in other circuits, outside Peru. And to support an initiative that will surely help introduce the work of several colleagues in places where they were previously unknown. The project also offers an overview of the range and plurality of what is being done in South America.

That inclusion works as a form of validation and recognition for creators clearly points to the role of anthologies in canon formation (Ferry 2001, 6) and the vital and formative role of editors. However, Jeffery Di Leo has suggested that '[a] more progressive and optimistic view of anthologies locates their value in the topologies of the literary world that they create' (2004, 3). He continues: 'A topical anthology literally creates a place or region – a topos – that can be easily visited or identified.' In an anthology based on regional identification such as *El Volcán*, the cultural topology constructed has two dimensions, one related to Latin American comics production and the other temporal (the early decades of the twenty-first century). Similarly picking up on both time and place, Bidegaray (email to author, 23 April 2018) outlines the intention to illustrate what has 'been going on in comics here in the last 15 years, [. . .] since we started thinking about ourselves as part of something bigger than our national borders'. The aims of the project were always two-fold: to consolidate connections within the region and to promote the creative momentum of regional comics cultures further by reaching out to wider, in particular European, audiences (José Sainz, email to author, 12 August 2018). This calls for some further unpacking of relations between the local and transnational, and of how the regional frame figures in the context of international exchange.

Labels and identifications: Thinking through the local, regional and transnational

In work presented in *El Volcán*, the local appears inscribed and asserted in narrative terms, in the use of language and through specific historical, visual and cultural references, and by its representation of clusters of creators in various localities and national contexts. Creators might be geographically dispersed and still conceive of themselves as part of a wider community. Yet the principle of agglomeration, as it 'arises from spatial proximity' (Rosenthal and Strange 2010, 278), also supports the emergence of distinct nodes of activity in urban centres. The term 'scene' better captures the fluidity and temporal indeterminacy involved here. The benefits and 'enabling circumstances' (Mommaas 2009, 46) of such scenes include validation through shared interests and social aspects but also professional knowledge exchange and organisation, generation of readerships and reputation building. Thus, Júlia Barata tells of regularly meeting with other women creators in Buenos Aires to sketch and make artwork together (Júlia Vilhena, email to author, 6 February 2018). The importance of these meetings and networks to her practice supports this picture of a localised community and social interaction between creators. Powerpaola has similarly described partaking in weekly creator meet-ups and collective drawing sessions in La Paz (Paola Silguero, email to author, 12 March 2018). If *El Volcán* has facilitated and strengthened regional networks between such local nodes of cultural activity, its very existence also depended on them.

The local now works in tandem with digital networks, platforms and interactions offering deterritorialised spaces and means of interaction. This is likely to be of particular importance for independent artisanal comics producers outside large-scale industry and publishing structures, such as newspaper and weekly magazines. Certainly, websites and blogs play a significant role in presenting work, linking with professional networks, constructing and maintaining a visible profile. Such extended capacities of visibility, access and connectivity do not, however, diminish the vital role played by local support networks. These clearly provide the creative and professional conditions that make possible a groundswell of productivity and the collectivity implied in the term 'comics cultures'. Nor has the transnational reach of digital cultures rendered the national frame obsolete.

National identifications and beyond

Despite globalising forces and flows – of people, capital, information, technology and ideas – that exceed the boundaries of nation states (Appadurai 1990), the nation is far from an exhausted framework where the analysis of culture is concerned. It remains relevant for understanding histories and developments intrinsically bound to specific economic, political and cultural institutions and policies. Even when fundamentally outward looking, such structures tend to be founded on the state as a sovereign administrative unit. National identity functions as a useful device not only for analytical endeavour but also as a curatorial concept. Both funding opportunities and promotional strategies often remain tied to and reproduce association with national identity.

In other words, the conditions that form specific historical comics cultures are contingent on national contexts. The nation's importance for the way comics are produced and circulate consequently informs approaches to their study. Héctor Fernández L'Hoeste and Juan Poblete's *Redrawing the Nation* (2009) uses national identity as its organising principle and the contributors offer informative accounts of specific comics histories. 'Latin American countries have historical backgrounds linked with their cultural differences that represent long traditions' (Merino 2017, 70). Merino nevertheless recognises that contemporary Latin American comics creators are increasingly engaging in transnational dialogue and collaboration, both through online spaces and in the form of events and festivals. Fernando Suárez and Enrique Uribe-Jongbloed (2016) have elaborated on this contemporary context, one that might be described as post-industry comics production. Here the discussion is framed and articulated specifically through national histories and conditions, as in writing about independent comics publishing (Reati 2009, 100; Vergueiro 2009, 165) that also forms part of *El Volcán*'s genealogy.

However, as a whole the anthology resolutely transcends national parameters. It describes belonging beyond citizenship, formed instead through affiliations, cultural practices and consumption rarely restricted by national boundaries. Such transnationality has more often given cause for discussion in fandom and audience studies (Morimoto 2018), but is no less pertinent when considering creators. The intent here is not to offer a detailed examination of the stylistic or aesthetic qualities of *El Volcán*'s individual contributors. Indeed, such interpretation is inevitably subject to situated cultural knowledge and reference points. For instance, finding the scratchy lines and expressionist linework in Pachiclón's story 'Grosería' (Sainz and Bidegaray 2017, 61–8) of two nihilist punks reminiscent of the German expressionist Georg Grosz might reveal more about my arts education than the artist's influences (see Figure 2.2).

Figure 2.2 Excerpt from the short story 'Grosería' by Pachiclón in *El Volcán*. © Pachiclón

If the aim is to establish an art-historical genealogy, relying on creators' own accounts would be equally problematic; such accounts are likely to be impacted by potentially short-lived enthusiasms and displays of cultural capital. However, creators' responses offer some indication of how they position themselves in relation to others in the field, and indeed how they conceive their practice. For instance, that Cossio cites Joe Sacco and Edilberto Jiménez as influences comes as no surprise (see Figure 2.3).

Figure 2.3 Excerpt from Jesús Cossio's contribution to *El Volcán*. © Jesús Cossio

Cossio's retrospective renditions of the political violence that has ravaged Peru are based on research by the Peruvian Truth and Reconciliation Commission and witness testimonies. It thus offers clear correspondences with Sacco's work, in particular *Footnotes in Gaza* (2010). Jiménez is likewise known for drawings and paintings informed by witness testimony that deal with the internal armed conflict in Peru's recent past.[8] Cossio's interest in experiential narration, memory and factual modes in comics, and international reference points, are reflected in the mentions of Chester Brown, Phoebe Gloeckner and Sarah Glidden, Paco Roca and Emmanuel Guibert (Jesús Cossio, email to author, 21 February 2018).

Powerpaola's cited influences include Julie Doucet's *My New York Diary* (1999) and the anthology publications *Twisted Sisters* (1976–1994) edited by Aline Kominsky and Diane Noomin (Paola Silguero, email to author, 12 March 2018). Her other mentions, beyond the Peruvian David Galliquio,[9] also suggest a broadly international positioning. Colombian creator Joni B.'s responses (email to author, 21 February 2018) highlight how comics histories of transnational circulation predate contemporary attention to authors and creators. He notes that his earliest comics influences – *Cementeria* (*Cimiteria*), *La Gata* and *El Libro Vaquero* – did not identify authors. Having believed these were Mexican comics, he only later learned that they were in fact Italian imports. Joni B. goes on to mention the US underground and a later influx of names from the 1980s and 1990s, mainly North American and Spanish.

On the whole, the cited influences are temporally and geographically diverse while positioning the respondents squarely in creator-centred and 'arts'-affiliated comics cultures. This tendency towards eclecticism and arts is even more explicit in the responses from Muriel Bellini and Júlia Barata. Bellini cites Nell Brinkley, the self-taught and prominent early US illustrator and comics creator, but also British twentieth-century poets and contemporary artists, US painters and film-makers among her influences. Her Latin American reference points were the Spanish-born illustrator based in Argentina Alejandro Sirio (1890–1953) and *El Volcán* co-contributor Rodrigo La Hoz (Muriel Bellini, email to author, 20 February 2018). Júlia Barata's range is similarly broad-reaching, and includes canonical European film directors and US singer-songwriters. Her mention of Mauricio de Sousa's *Turma de Mónica* thus stands apart as a singular representation of popular and specifically Latin American comics traditions (Júlia Vilhena, email to author, 6 February 2018).

The editors' foreword states their desire to represent a particular strain of Latin American comics production, one succeeding prior comics cultures devastated by the economic crisis of the 1990s, and one they claim is now growing ever more buoyant and vigorous: 'Latin American comic languages of the first decades of the twenty-first century, which cover a wide stylistic spectrum, expand and diverge through a magma of experimentation that includes all the levels of content and expression' (Sainz and Bidegaray 2017). While this description aptly summarises the diversity of the contributions, it also indicates the editorial emphasis on expression and experimentation, which is echoed in the creators' responses. Beyond an evident 'art world' (Beaty 2012) positioning and a number of current names receiving attention, certain comics periods repeatedly emerge as reference points: the US underground of the 1960s and 1970s; the authorial 1990s in both North America and Europe. The impact of women creators and autobiographical approaches is also considerable for many of the creators consulted here. The responses suggest that, while factors that determine influence include proximity, they are as likely to indicate wider and often transnational consumption practices.

El Volcán's aesthetics appear to be shaped through distinctly trans-national influences, stylistic affiliations and taste cultures. How, then, do these aspects relate to the regional identification in the anthology's very title?

Regionalism

Notions of the regional have undergone various and important historical shifts, and have included discussions directly addressing Latin America. However, these debates often deal with economic, fiscal and political concerns (Riggirozzi and Tussie 2012) that go beyond the scope of this chapter. When it comes to writing specifically about Latin American comics, approaches adopting a regional frame include Flora (1984), Page and King (2017) and Catalá Carrasco et al. (2017). The notion of regional networks, as symbolically construed and presented by El Volcán, seem particularly meaningful in the context of precarious conditions, and financially fragile and often short-lived publication initiatives (Suárez and Jongbloed 2016). I will limit my discussion to two contributions, neither of which speak directly to a Latin American context but both of which are useful for the purposes at hand. The first is Leo Ching's (2001) thesis that globalisation and regionalism are tied in a mutually constitutive dynamic, and importantly, that rather than conceived exclusively through an economic lens, these concepts are also always cultural and therefore simultaneously exist in a symbolic realm. He rejects the notion that either one of these, economic or cultural, is determined by the other, but instead conjures an image of a mutually formative dynamic.

> If globalization is to be taken as a process in space, and localization is to be understood as a specificity in place, the regional appears to be a terrain 'in between,' a geographic reality and a constructed discursivity that is both spatialized in its transnational deterritorialization and yet reterritorialized in a specific configuration bounded by historically invented geography.
>
> (Ching 2001, 284)

Rikke Platz Cortsen and Ralf Kauranen's article on Nordic comics anthologies argues that regional identity can function as a 'brand effect' and that 'the relatively small countries of the North have a better chance of getting noticed if they pool their efforts together and make their promotional strategies abroad under the heading "Nordic"' (2016 n.p.). Territories and populations of the Nordic region are tiny compared with Latin America, but in both regions artisanal and small press comics cultures depend on niche markets. Expanding the reach of their output by accessing globally scattered readerships supports sustainability, and a consolidated effort identified by a regional label is a useful strategic move.

Ching (2001) and Platz Cortsen and Kauranen (2016) concur that regionalism is a discursive construct. It has no autonomous or given meaning, but 'is always directed against another territorial discourse (the world system, nationalism, or other regionalisms)' (Ching 2001, 285). According to Platz Cortsen and Kauranen the regional label 'is not used as an epithet for a stylistic or thematic commonality, but instead a platform for [regional] collaboration in the comics field' (2016, n.p.). This analysis fits the pan-regional approach of *El Volcán*, yet the notion of 'difference' carries distinct weight in relation to the region's cultural and historical colonial legacies. The very term 'Latin American' has been rejected by many for its homogenising effect, its erasure of many ethnic and social groups. Its qualification appears to underline the US's claim to American-ness while obscuring the extent to which it is, in fact, itself a Spanish-speaking nation. The term moreover lends itself to an external 'interpretive network of aesthetic values, judgements and myths which continue to invent the discourse of "Latin American" art as elsewhere and "Other"' (Genocchio 1998, 4–5). Sainz and Bidegaray's discussion of the regional banner as it relates to their selection criteria conjures a more nuanced and reflective interpretation:

> When we asked ourselves, what it means to be Latin American, comics-related and in the context of globalization, we answered that nationality or territory are of course important but not defining terms. So, we started to consider those who aren't obvious at all because you may not think of them as Latin American, maybe because they don't live here or don't publish here or maybe because they weren't born here, and we thought it was important to have them in the book since mixture, fusion, miscegenation or whatever you may call it is one important part of Latin American identity.
>
> (José Sainz, email to author, 20 March 2018)

The regional identification of *El Volcán* acts as an assertion of collective purpose and internal dialogue between participating comics cultures. The editors' responses suggest that the anthology's intention is to support and further embolden comics production in locations where it remains fragmentary. But it simultaneously provides a label that has purchase in markets beyond the region. According to Ching, current mobilisations of regional identity are not merely signifiers of colonial pasts, but serve different and more strategic purposes. In the contemporary global cultural economy 'difference itself exists only as a commodity, a spectacle to be consumed in a globalized capitalist system precisely at the moment when exteriority is no longer imaginable' (Ching 2001, 285).

The *El Volcán* project includes a small, simply printed and stapled leaflet of translations to accompany the anthology, as and when required. Its eight pages include the editors' foreword and the textual elements and dialogue from each comic translated into English by Micaela Ortelli. This freestanding publication is in itself an interesting response to the thorny issue of translating comics, a form where textual elements are uniquely integral to the visual composition of a panel and page. Extricating them in order to carry out linguistic translating thus often presents an impossible task. Moreover, this leaflet indicates the wider address of this anthology and ambition to circulate this collected showcase not only within but also beyond the region itself.

Expanding transactional networks

'We live now in an era of the enterprising self. Emphasis is increasingly placed on the entrepreneurial aspects of creative talent with the artist and cultural producer encouraged to find a niche, fill a gap, know their audience, innovate, promote, package, brand and sell him/herself and their work' (McCall and Houlihan 2017, 154). As constitutive aspects of contemporary comics cultures as professional and entrepreneurial networks, the mutual relations between publication and events are fairly self-evident. Publications beget promotional events, and events bring people together to stimulate further undertakings, creative and/or enterprising. Such dynamic affordances are corroborated by Bidegaray, explaining how his bookshop has not only given rise to a publishing venture but also related events: 'From Musaraña we also produce exhibitions and festivals, Festival Fanzín (fanzines) and Festival Sudestada (drawing and illustration). I work as a creative director in both, and as a curator in several exhibitions outside our own space' (Alejandro Bidegaray, email to author, 23 April 2018). The festival event, characterised by its particular and spatial qualities and temporal specificity (Peaslee 2013, 815), is a crucial network node in its capacity to bring together people and offer fertile grounds for further collaborative endeavour. In this capacity, festivals align particularly well with a changing conception of culture into 'something much more open and horizontal, but also more commercial' (Mommaas 2009, 45). They work as platforms for performing 'notions of artistic professionalism, the cultural resourcing of artistic creativity, the composition of critical audiences, artistic role models, and the reputation of creative careers' (ibid.).

Sainz (email to author, 23 April 2018) recounts being introduced to Kalle Hakkola, the executive director of the Helsinki Comics Festival, who was attending a comics festival in Buenos Aires as an invited guest, and a subsequent chance meeting at Fumetto (the annual International Comics Art Festival in Lucerne, Switzerland) in 2016. The connection initiated in Buenos Aires and Lucerne was instrumental in bringing *El Volcán* to the Helsinki Comics Festival in 2017. The transactional nature of this exchange is evident in the financial arrangements: helped by grant funding at either end, the festival organisers took care of exhibition production and accommodation costs for the guests, while the delegates covered their own travel costs. 'It was expensive, of course, but sales were really good in Helsinki and the book ended up paying for it' (José Sainz, email to author, 23 April 2018). This is a relationship of mutual benefits as well as contributions. The festival offers important promotional and sales value for the book, while in return the anthology presents thematic coherence, plurality of content and cultural interest in line with a cosmopolitan outlook and taste cultures. An introduction to the artistic director of Fumetto, Jana Jakoubek, in 2016 also set in motion events resulting in *El Volcán*'s inclusion in the 2018 Fumetto festival programme. At this event, *El Volcán* benefited from being placed next to the Swiss-Brazilian project Magma, which was one of the festival's main exhibitions (José Sainz, email to author, 23 April 2018). Touring with the anthology and exhibition has not just been a promotional endeavour but has also enabled first-hand encounters with other comics cultures: 'We thought of *El Volcán* as a bridge in both directions and it seems to be working' (José Sainz, email to author, 23 April 2018).

It is worth noting that, like conventions,[10] the festivals mentioned here involve panel discussions, signings and prizes, but also often emphasise their production of spaces set apart from events involving large-scale franchises and syndication. Fumetto, for instance, characterises itself as a 'non-commercial' event, focused on 'alternative, independent comics story-telling' and located at the intersection of 'comics, visual arts and performance' (Jakoubek 2017). A focus on creators, often with exhibitions of artwork as a prominent feature, further cements the cultural standing of these events, and they are highly compatible with the values represented by the *El Volcán* anthology. Officially endorsed and sponsored by municipal arts funding and state sponsorship (Beaty 2007, 121), such festivals play an important role in local and municipal strategies for cultural investment (O'Brien 2014). These comics festivals often adopt a model of international cultural exchange, in alignment with notions of cosmopolitan tastes and competencies (Hannerz 1990, 239). This creates a context in which the regional identification and markers of cultural specificity/difference of *El Volcán* accrue particular value.

Conclusion

El Volcán functions as a consolidation and reification of contemporary Latin American comics culture. It combines selection, representation and a strategic assertion of regional identity. The anthology moreover offers an interesting case study of post-industry growth of comics production within which creators (rather than characters or story-worlds) assume a central position. Idiosyncratic aesthetic markers, strongly evocative of processes of making, further underline the creative agency of creators. These creators often position themselves within communities of practice and traditions that span local and regional, but also globally dispersed, contexts. The project's regional identity potentially works to strengthen networks beyond national borders within the continent and has also proven a successful platform for promoting and extending outward-facing networks.

By mobilising and collating small press and artisanal comics work on a regional basis, *El Volcán* is aligned well with certain international comics networks and festivals, and the anthology's Latin American-ness is an identifier that effectively supports global circulation. This commodity-concept provides a theme and umbrella that works in productive alignment with transnational agendas, both its own and that of others. In the context of international festivals, the regional identification offers a focal point and fits with the organisers' aims. The anthology form is equally conducive, as its comprehensive range of content and individual approaches offers plurality. *El Volcán* thus functions as a collective calling card and transactional networking tool as it participates in and contributes to transnational networks of creative and entrepreneurial comics cultures.

Notes

1 For more information see www.comicsresearch.org; some of the content is dated but this is still a decent resource and useful starting point.
2 Finland is a country with a population of just over 5.5 million, which in relation to its area makes it sparsely populated. In terms of global economics Finland is well off, if statistically some way behind its Nordic neighbours. Historically a young country, before achieving independence in 1917 it was a province either of the Swedish kingdom or the Russian empire. From 1947 to the early 1990s Finland was tied in to bilateral trade and cultural exchange programmes with the Soviet Union, but since 1995 has been a part of the EU (Hjerppe, n.d.). Culturally, Finland has a distinct heritage, and the Finnish language sits apart from the Germanic roots shared by Scandinavian languages. Having a very small population, a relatively small economy in relation to direct neighbours, and an isolated language, Finland found it necessary to adopt the use of a *lingua franca*, which since the mid-twentieth century has been English. The country's limited cultural heterogeneity in part derives from the absence of a colonial past, and for economic reasons emigration has been a stronger historical feature than immigration. All these factors contribute to Finland's position as simultaneously privileged and peripheral.
3 While referred to as Powerpaola in text, material derived from email communications will be referenced by the creator's given name, Paola Silguero. Similarly, email communications from Júlia Barata will be referenced using Júlia Vilhena.
4 Rosario is the largest city in the centre-east Argentine province of Santa Fé and host to the annual *Crack, Bang, Boom* convention initiated in 2010 by Eduardo Risso, whose collaborations with Brian Azzarello have cemented his international reputation as a comics

artist. The Puro Comic bookshop and associated publishing venture Puro Comic Ediciones also contribute to Rosario's status as a significant comics hub.

5 For more on Max (also known as Francesc Capdevila) as an exemplar of the transnational small-press comics creator, see Beaty (2007, 116–8).

6 Two contributors in *El Volcán*, Júlia Barata and La Watson, also appear in *Historietas LGBTI* (2017*)*, and Jazmín Varela's *Crisis Capilar* (2016) was published by EMR.

7 'The pages of *Fierro* mixed articles on art movies, detective and noir literature, science fiction, and the history of comics' (De Santis 2009, 197). Pablo De Santis describes *Fierro* as a product of the cultural revitalisation that followed the reinstatement of democratic rule.

8 His book *Chungui: Violencia y trazos de memoria* (*Chungui: Violence and Traces of Memory*) was published in 2009; a revised second edition followed a year later.

9 In an interview on the comics blog Comic Noveno Arte (2009), David Galliquio himself cites US underground figureheads Robert Crumb, Gilbert Sheldon and Harvey Pekar.

10 Conventions have drawn scholarly attention in particular as platforms for transnational franchises and fandoms (Jenkins 2012; Geraghty 2015).

References

Appadurai, Arjun. 1990. 'Disjuncture and Difference in the Global Cultural Economy', *Theory, Culture & Society* 7, no. 2–3: 295–310.

Beaty, Bart. 2007. *Unpopular Culture: Transforming the European Comic Book in the 1990s*. Toronto: University of Toronto Press.

Beaty, Bart and Charles Hatfield, eds. 2020. *Comics Studies: A Guidebook*. New Brunswick: Rutgers University Press.

Bramlett, Frank, T.R. Cook and Aaron Meskin, eds. 2017. *The Routledge Companion to Comics Studies*. New York: Routledge.

Catalá Carrasco, Jorge, Paulo Drinot and James Scorer, eds. 2017. *Comics and Memory in Latin America*. Pittsburgh: University of Pittsburgh Press.

Ching, Leo. 2001. 'Globalizing the Regional, Regionalizing the Global: Mass Culture and Asianism in the Age of Late Capital'. In *Globalization*, edited by Arjun Appadurai, 279–306. Durham, NC: Duke University Press.

Comic Noveno Arte. 2009. 'Entrevista a David Galliquio (Parte 1) Como Hacer Comic en el Perú', 16 November. Last accessed 1 June 2019. http://comicnovenoarte.blogspot. co.uk/2009/11/entrevista-david-galliquio-parte-1-como.html.

Cotrim, João Paulo and Nuno Saraiva, eds. 2000. *Para além dos Olivais*. Lisbon: Bedeteca de Lisboa.

Couch, Chris. 2000. 'The Publication and Formats of Comics, Graphic Novels, and Tankobon', *Image & Narrative* 1: n.p. Last accessed 3 June 2019. http://www.imageandnarrative.be/ inarchive/narratology/chriscouch.htm.

De Santis, Pablo. 2009. 'The Fierro Years: An Exercise in Melancholy'. In *Redrawing the Nation: National Identity in Latin/o American Comics*, edited by Héctor L'Hoeste and Juan Poblete, 191–203. New York: Palgrave Macmillan.

Deveney, Jean-Christophe, Jerôme Jouvray and Anne-Claire Jouvray. 2013. *Johnny Jungle: Première Partie*. Grenoble: Glénat.

Deveney, Jean-Christophe, Jerôme Jouvray and Anne-Claire Jouvray. 2014. *Johnny Jungle: Primera Parte*. Rosario: EMR.

Di Leo, Jeffrey R. 2004. 'Analyzing Anthologies'. In *On Anthologies: Politics and Pedagogy*, edited by Jeffrey R. Di Leo, 1–27. Lincoln and London: University of Nebraska Press.

Ferry, Anne. 2001. *Tradition and the Individual Poem: An Inquiry into Anthologies*. Stanford: Stanford University Press.

Flora, Cornelia B. 1984. 'Roasting Donald Duck: Alternative Comics and Photonovels in Latin America', *The Journal of Popular Culture* 18, no. 1: 163–83.

Genocchio, Ben. 1998. 'The Discourse of Difference: Writing "Latin American" art', *Third Text*, 12, no. 43: 3–12.

Geraghty, Lincoln. 2015. 'Heroes of Hall H: Global Media Franchises and the San Diego Comic Con as Space for the Transnational Superhero'. In *Superheroes on World Screens*, edited by Rayna Denison and Rachel Mizsei-Ward, 75–93. Jackson: University Press of Mississippi.

Gociol, Judith and Diego Rosemberg. 2000. *La historieta argentina: Una historia*. Buenos Aires: De la Flor.

Gomes, Ivan Lima. 2016. 'Recognizing Comics as Brazilian National Popular Culture: CETPA and the Debates over Comics Professional Identities (1961–1964)'. In *Cultures of Comics Work*, edited by Casey Brienza and Paddy Johnston, 81–95. New York: Palgrave Macmillan.

Gupta, Akhil and James Ferguson. 1992. 'Beyond "Culture": Space, Identity and Politics of Difference', *Cultural Anthropology* 7, no. 1: 6–23.

Hannerz, Ulf. 1990. 'Cosmopolitans and Locals in World Culture', *Theory, Culture & Society* 7(2–3): 237–51.

Helsinki Comics Festival. 2019. Last accessed 3 June 2019. https://sarjakuvafestivaalit.fi/in-english.

Hjerppe, Riitta. n.d. 'An Economic History of Finland'. *Economic History Association*. Last accessed 3 June 2019. https://eh.net/encyclopedia/an-economic-history-of-finland/.

Jakoubek, Jana. 2017. 'Fumetto Festival (Lucerne) – A Comic Festival Built on Bridges', Delhi Comic Arts Festival (DECAF). Last accessed 3 June 2019. https://www.youtube.com/watch?v=Sz-u9TsstkY.

Jenkins, Henry. 2012. 'Superpowered Fans: The Many Worlds of San Diego's Comic-Con', *Boom: A Journal of California* 2, no. 2: 22–36.

Jimenez, Edilberto. 2018. *Chungui: Violencia y trazos de memoria*. Lima: Instituto de Estudios Peruanos.

L'Hoeste, Héctor and Juan Poblete. 2009. 'Introduction'. In *Redrawing the Nation: National Identity in Latin/o American Comics*, edited by Héctor L'Hoeste and Juan Poblete, 1–16. New York: Palgrave Macmillan.

Manthei, Jennifer. 2011. 'How to Read Chico Bento: Brazilian Comics and National Identity', *Studies in Latin American Popular Culture* 29: 142–63.

Max. 2012. *Vapor*. Barcelona: La Cúpula.

Max. 2013. *Vapor*. Buenos Aires: Musaraña Editora.

Max. 2014. *Vapor*. Seattle: Fantagraphics.

McCall, Kerry and Maeve Houlihan. 2017. 'The Artist as Cultural Entrepeneur'. In *Arts and Business: Building a Common Ground for Understanding Society*, edited by Elena Raviola and Peter Zackariasson, 148–62. New York and Abingdon: Routledge.

Merino, Ana. 2017. 'Comics in Latin America'. In *Routledge Companion to Comics*, edited by Frank Bramlett, Roy T. Cook and Aaron Meskin, 70–8. New York and London: Routledge.

Mommaas, Hans. 2009. 'Spaces of Culture and Economy: Mapping the Cultural-Creative Cluster Landscape'. In *Creative Economies, Creative Cities* 98, edited by Lily Kong and Justin O'Connor, 45–59. Dordrecht: Springer.

Morimoto, Lori. 2018. 'Transnational Media Fan Studies'. In *Routledge Companion to Media Fandom*, edited by Melissa A. Click and Suzanne Scott, 280–8. New York and Abingdon: Routledge.

O'Brien, Dave. 2014. 'Comic Con Goes Country Life: On British Economy, Society and Culture', *The Comics Grid: Journal of Comics Scholarship* 4, no. 1, Art.10. DOI: http://doi.org/10.5334/cg.au.

Ostuni, Hernán, Fernando García, Norberto Rodríguez Van Rousselt and Javier Mora Bordel. n.d. 'Politics, Activism, Repression and Comics in Argentina During the 1970s', translated by L. Eisner and L. Bolton.

Page, Joanna and Edward King. 2017. *Posthumanism and the Graphic Novel in Latin America*. London: UCL Press.

Peaslee, Robert M. 2013. 'Media Conduction: Festivals, Networks, and Boundaried Spaces', *International Journal of Communication* 7: 811–30.

Platz Cortsen, Rikke and Ralf Kauranen. 2016. 'New Nordic Comics – A Question of Promotion?', *Journal of Aesthetics & Culture* 8, no. 1: 30253. DOI: http://dx.doi.org/10.3402/jac.v8.30253.

Reati, Fernando. 2009. 'Argentina's Monteneros: Comics, Cartoon, and Images as Political Propaganda in the Underground Guerrilla Press of the 1970s'. In *Redrawing the Nation: National Identity in Latin/o American Comics*, edited by Héctor L'Hoeste and Juan Poblete, 97–110. New York: Palgrave Macmillan.

Riggirozzi, Pia and Diana Tussie, eds. 2012. *The Rise of Post-Hegemonic Regionalism: The Case of Latin America*. Dordrecht: Springer.

Rosenthal, Stuart S. and William C. Strange. 2010. 'Small Establishments/Big Effects: Agglomeration, Industrial Organization and Entrepreneurship'. In *Agglomeration Economics*, edited by Edward L. Glaeser, 277–302. Chicago: University of Chicago Press.

Sabin, Roger. 1996. *Comics, Comix & Graphic Novels: A History of Comic Art*. London: Phaidon Press.

Sacco, Joe. 2009. *Footnotes in Gaza*. London: Jonathan Cape.

Sainz, José and Alejandro Bidegaray, eds. 2017. *El Volcán: Un presente de la historieta latinoamericana*. Rosario: Editoria Municipal de Rosario and Musaraña Editora.

Sainz, José, ed. 2015. *Informe: Historieta argentina del siglo XXI*. Rosario: Editoria Municipal de Rosario.

Siles, Jorge. 2007. 'El Boom De La Historieta Boliviana', *Latin American Review of Studies on The Historieta*, 28, 15 December. Last accessed 3 June 2019. https://www.tebeosfera.com/documentos/el_boom_de_la_historieta_boliviana.html.

Smith, Matthew J. and Randy Duncan. 2012. *Critical Approaches to Comics: Theories and Methods*. New York: Routledge.

Suárez, Fernando and Enrique Uribe-Jongbloed. 2016. 'Making Comics as Artisans: Comic Book Production in Colombia'. In *Cultures of Comics Work*, edited by Casey Brienza and Paddy Johnston, 51–64. New York: Palgrave Macmillan.

Tabachnik, Stephen A., ed. 2017. *The Cambridge Companion to Graphic Novels*. Cambridge, UK: Cambridge University Press.

Various authors. 2017. *Historieta LGTBI*. Rosario: EMR.

Varnum, Robin and Christina T. Gibbons, eds. 2001. *The Language of Comics: Word and Image*. Jackson: University of Mississippi Press.

Vergueiro, Waldomiro. 2009. 'Brazilian Comics: Origin, Development, and Future Trends'. In *Redrawing the Nation: National Identity in Latin/o American Comics*, edited by Héctor L'Hoeste and Juan Poblete, 151–70. New York: Palgrave Macmillan.

Worcester, Kent and Jeet Heer, eds. 2009. *A Comics Studies Reader*. Jackson: University of Mississippi Press.

3

From the Golden Age to independent publishing: Mass culture, popular culture and national imaginaries in the history of Argentine comics

Laura Vazquez
Translated by Alana Jackson

Introduction: Legendary tales of a (perhaps) successful past

In this chapter I focus on a crucial moment in the history of the Argentine comics publishing industry with the aim of setting out the fluctuations of a market predominantly subject to tensions established by processes of transnationalisation, displacement and the circulation of capital in the global economy. In a world characterised by a growing transnational culture (which often produces a degree of centralisation and homogenisation), it is important to determine how questions of national identity and cultural autonomy were viewed in other historical periods. Here I focus on the second half of the twentieth century.

From the 1960s on and until around the end of the last century, an important scene emerged around what I refer to here as 'the national and popular comics industry'. In Argentina, analyses of comics have focused on two particular issues following the decline of the so-called Golden Age of comics in the 1940s and 1950s, namely the legitimisation of comics and the marginality of the form.[1]

For decades, importing and exporting comics, as variables of a highly transnationalised market, was linked to the defence of national manufacturing. Making and producing comics on the periphery was often regarded as a relatively autonomous practice characterised by artisanal practices in comparison with other mass media. During a period dominated by theories of cultural dependency, especially during the 1960s and 1970s, the prevailing discourse within different intellectual and professional sectors was that comics could also be an instrument of economic politics and that they could counteract the effects of capitalism in the region.

In that sense, it is worth highlighting that, though the Latin American comics market is irregular in terms of the quantity of its output, the publishing industry does have traits in common with the shifts and temporalities of the region as a whole. For that reason it is possible to determine trends in the modes of production, circulation and market strategies that span different countries.[2]

However, if popular culture must be analysed in relation to dominant culture (Bourdieu 1988) the possibilities for autonomy in the struggle for cultural capital in the market of symbolic goods are practically zero. Linking the comics market to national industry meant reading it as a sort of 'welfare state' whose developmentalist and industrialist project entered into decline during the 1950s.

The experience of Peronism in Argentina during the first presidencies of Juan Domingo Perón (1946–55) fomented the social mobility of large sectors of the middle and working classes. The democratisation of the welfare state began prior to the 1930s during the government of Hipólito Yrigoyen (1916–30). Improvements in quality of life in various areas, something agreed on by historians (Schteingart 2014), also laid the groundwork for the foundation of a populist rhetoric that penetrated social subjectivity. Following the overthrow of Perón in 1955 by the de facto government of General Aramburu (1955–58), a set of shared meanings was established around a period known as the Golden Age of Argentine comics.[3]

Following Beatriz Sarlo (1998), populist mythologies require epic, edifying stories to establish a firmly ideological rhetoric with a strong sense of identity. The Golden Age of the Argentine comic worked in this way as an effective mythical narrative that could help to construct (in tune with other narratives, such as the figure of the gaucho, tango or football) a unifying sense of Nation and People:

> Argentines identified with a series of propositions that were to a
> large extent based on mythology but which also had a unifying
> effectiveness: compared to post-war Europe, Argentina was an

abundant country, where you could eat better than anywhere else in the world; compared to the rest of Latin America, Argentina was the country of the industrial working class, the educated middle classes, with the highest consumption of newspapers and books, with complete literacy and full employment.

(Sarlo 1998, 3)

In this context and from both 'miserabilist' and 'legitimist' positions (Grignon and Passeron 1991), editors, intellectuals and professionals constantly located themselves in a field in which the routines of serialised production were interwoven with discourses of the avant-garde, art and the media.[4] Considered a 'lesser form' to other kinds of narratives, comics were immersed in the newspaper industry. In some cases, the permanent tension between art, business and the market was 'resolved' via the validation of an apparent 'marginality' that was seen as representative of what was national and popular. Since the 1970s a question has persisted in cultural sociology: 'does popular culture exist beyond the act which suppresses it?' (De Certeau 1999, 69). Here, the essentialist adjective 'popular' (making it folkloric and objectifying it as something pure and autochthonous) implies denying the structural relationships of domination (Alabarces 2002).

Behind these arguments lie the unsettling shadows of 'Argentine culture' and 'the popular'. Nevertheless, what local imaginaries and subjectivities mobilised these histories? Where should we look for what is 'Argentine' in comic strips and series? In the nationality of the authors? In the subject matter of the stories? In their audiences? And, in any case, what are we talking about when we refer to 'national comics'?[5] If the comics industry was transnational ever since its inception, the defence of a local tradition with its own characteristics (and the references to a supposed 'Argentine School' of illustrators pays testament to such a view) must be analysed against the backdrop of a series of rhetorical gestures that inevitably have their own interests at heart.

My aim here is not to offer an exhaustive historical overview but rather to rethink these issues starting with the transnational networks of markets that are in constant convergence and contiguity. In that sense, the so-called Golden Age that took place in the 1940s and 1950s generated readings by intellectual critics as well as the authors who formed part of that professional 'boom era' which were contradictory, and in a certain sense deterministic.

In effect, as well as producing comics for the internal market, Argentine scriptwriters and artists have historically also worked for transnational markets. The fact that their works circulate worldwide does not necessarily imply that the Argentine comic has lost its identity. This concern gathered momentum in the 1970s and from then on has more or less been a constant preoccupation of the field. But the idea that the past era of comics was a better one is more closely tied to the absence of local publishing practices than to a supposed 'foreignisation' of strips and magazines.

The highpoint of the industry in the Golden Age would never be repeated and, ever since, with some upturns, there has been a downward arc in the production and consumption of comics in Argentina. Nevertheless, the sense that something had been lost that could never be recovered has more complicated facets. Even though the volume of magazines and comics produced and consumed in the 1960s differs substantially from the Golden Age, the transformation of the internal market, the expansion of a comics readership and the inventiveness of publishers in developing different survival strategies demonstrated decisive shifts.

In this chapter, therefore, I foreground the dimensions of a problem plagued by paradigmatic tensions that circulate around a complex cultural field in which relationships between art and the market, experimentation and the profession, mass culture and politics all coexist. My hypothesis is that the production sector of comics in Argentina is strongly conditioned by the dominant centres of international comics production.[6] Thus, though in certain periods of the history of Argentine comics we might refer to a 'national comics industry', the growth of internal consumption was strong not only due to the economic and cultural measures that produced its development, but also as a result of a context that favoured sustaining both market demand and service provision.

The drawing of a sequential narrative is based on a unique config-uration of language. As a product of the cultural industry, comics participate in the establishment of subjectivities as well as in the wider construction of hegemony (Vazquez 2010). In that sense, we are dealing with a form of communication that enables as much as any other field the development of diverse social experiences that cover both high and low culture (Bourdieu 1995). Putting to one side the theoretical discussion over the phenomenon of the graphic novel, I share the views set out by Pablo Turnes about the 'unease' of thinking of the comic as an object of study and the need to analyse it as a language and means of communication, beyond marketing strategies, publishing houses and the circumstances indicated by the market and production standards: 'The possibilities of breaking with the boundaries comprised of the spheres of legitimation described by Bourdieu are unique when it comes to comics: it struggles internally not to be something more accepted but something better' (2009, 4).

In other words, it is a medium with particular characteristics in the market of standardised and mass products, which means that the relationship between high culture, mass culture and popular culture becomes especially complex within this context. Neither purely mass entertainment nor a product refined for minority consumption, comics can no longer be understood purely in terms of its owners of consumption and production. It is necessary here to consider its historical progression within the framework of capitalist and neoliberal societies but also its transformative potential in terms of aesthetics and narrative. We should take up, perhaps, Oscar Masotta's premise that comics should be placed at the heart of wider political and ethical concerns, taking into account their expansive potential at both structural and signic levels.[7] Indeed, analysis of the social codes and languages (cultural products of modern and contemporary mass societies) allows for the recovery of the 'signic density' of the media. In Lucas Berone's words:

> The (perhaps contradictory) theoretical and critical discourse of Masotta has the virtue of indicating, teaching and demonstrating a problematic knot in terms of mixed languages or codes: the interaction between the semiotic properties of word and image. And that knot is only meaningful (from a pedagogical point of view) because it is related to the *moral condition* of comics, since comics always constitutes a moral/moralising discourse about the society in which it is produced, and because that contradiction between image and word opens up the possibility of a political intervention that resolutely alters the symbolic practices of modern capitalist consumer societies.
>
> (Berone 2008, 2)

Indeed, from the 1960s on, the incorporation of comics as an object of study foregrounded the tension between mass culture and the market, as well as bringing up to date debates about the aesthetic dimension of the arts and their modes of legitimation. The different contributions of the pioneers did not progress uniformly, however, but threw up contradictions, agreements and discrepancies. Nevertheless, we can still trace certain trends not only in relation to approaches to comics, but also, more notably, in the theoretical (and political) position from which comics are analysed.[8]

These approaches sustained a particular way of thinking about the publishing and national comics industries, tying the latter to the mythification of a previous, more celebrated era. In other words, there is a circular way of thinking about what is popular and what is mass culture, and of understanding the national industry in and from the cultural margins connected to the Peronist discourse of the time. In broad terms, the essays of Oscar Steimberg, Oscar Masotta, Carlos Trillo, Eduardo Romano, Guillermo Saccomanno, Jorge Rivera and Juan Sasturain set out a historical account that promotes the banner of 'the inaugural', as in each moment of a decline in production a number of more or less explicit 'rescue' programmes and manifestos emerge to 'salvage' the industry.

Peronism and mass culture

Classic studies of comics fuelled the mythical construction of a national Golden Age, which demonstrated the benefits of a cultural industry that included and helped the advancement of the popular classes. The way in which Argentine cultural industries were consolidated during the 1940s and 1950s is intrinsically related to government policies that enacted protectionist and social distributive economic measures in the internal market, boosting the development of small and medium-sized companies, generating employment, and incentivising the consumption of cultural goods and services.

During this period, comics not only became a major product in the culture industry, but they also started to shape their own public, to consolidate their professional system and to define their own graphic aesthetic. The publishing houses Abril, Códex, Columba, Dante Quinterno, Frontera and Manuel Láinez collectively produced a broad market of weekly editions.

Production and consumption data of the comics industry demonstrate a peak in expansion that was incomparable to previous periods. During the 1940s, the magazine *Patoruzito* reached a print run of 300,000 weekly copies and *Intervalo* 280,000. Both of them, together with the humour publications *Rico Tipo* and *Patoruzú*, would make up around 50 per cent of the total circulation of Argentine magazines.[9] This period marks a historic moment when the state and the market take the same approach to cultural media and goods.

Towards the mid-1950s, around 60 comics magazines were being edited in the country, not including those from abroad, which were usually from Mexico. By comparison, in the US around the same time, there were around 300 publications which existed in a system of syndicates, with monthly sales running to 60 million copies. No less than 49 per cent of the North American population identified as habitual consumers of comics (Rivera 1992, 5).

Albums with complete comics gradually replaced series of continual instalments, and by the end of the Golden Age, the serial graphic novel had become an anachronism in permanent decline. The transformation of magazines into monthly albums is an indicator of a shrinking industry. It was an era in which editors had to appeal to sectors with higher purchasing power and capture the attention of new readerships. As they became more expensive and had higher print quality, the aim was to legitimise albums as 'graphic literature' with complete stories in vertical format.

Even in the early years of the 1960s, the signs of gradual erosion were clear. The impact of imported products, the lack of official and private policies, and greater dynamism in external markets, produced a shrinkage that would produce a clear crisis in the years to follow. In 1961, for example, *Patoruzito* sold 78,719 copies per week, while in 1967 its print run was 30,726. *D'Artagnan*, during the same time period, published 48,527 and 40,811 copies respectively. *Intervalo* went from a print run of 53,585 to 41,706 and *Patoruzú* from 99,407 to 59,058 (Rivera 1992, 5).

At the start of the 1960s, it was not only magazines owned by Frontera that failed economically (*Hora Cero Mensual* ceased publication in 1963 and *Hora Cero Semanal* had disappeared by 1959), but also successful magazines like *Misterix, Patoruzito* and *Rico Tipo*. The only publishing house that survived these ups and downs was Columba, which saved its publications by lowering publishing quality. One of its strategies was to modernise its products by introducing colour and adapting films and novels.

At the start of the 1960s, *Patoruzito* suffered significant changes: its size was reduced, its numbering restarted as a monthly magazine, and it introduced complete and imported comics, thereby abandoning its formula of monthly instalments of national titles. This switch from weekly to monthly was fundamental not only to magazines by Quinterno, but also to strategies adopted by the rest of the companies. Among other reasons, this was partly due to the arrival of Mexican publications distributed by the Novaro publishing house. According to Jorge Rivera, even though they were inferior in content, 'they were notable for more modern graphics, colours, size and relatively cheaper price' (Rivera 1992, 52).

Other details that demonstrate the scale of the decline include: a decrease in the number of readers due to falling salaries suffered by the middle and working classes;[10] stiff competition from the import and dissemination of foreign titles; the opportunities for comics artists to take salaried work overseas; and the expansion of television. None of these were individually fatal but put together they caused the market to take a downward spiral beginning in the late 1950s.

Parallel to the circuit of 'serious' or 'adventure' comics, there were also developments in other publications. At the same time as the depreciation of the adventure comic market, children's magazines were growing. In the mid-1960s *Anteojito* (1964) and *Lúpin* (1966) were founded, and at the end of the decade, magazines published by Cielosur (1969) had a significant impact. On the other hand, although the García Ferré publications never repeated the print runs that they had achieved during the Golden Age, they nevertheless kept the periodicals industry alive.

Although production rates had fallen by the end of the 1950s, and even before, it was not until the end of the following decade during a publishing crisis that the need for bringing about a moment of glory was considered. The reasons for this ambiguity and misalignment can perhaps be found in the way that media operations during the Peronist era were understood. During this period, modernisation allowed for the invention of a cultural renewal in which this division seemed to have left no trace (Varela 2006).

Towards the end of the 1960s, the idea of a Golden Age was characterised by expressions of nostalgia, the worshipping of the past, and the respectful citation of the 'maestros', all of which were referred to in relation to the term 'national industry'. The invention of a Golden Age undoubtedly forms part of a wider chapter in the history of the media, and accounts of comics are not unique in terms of how the cultural industry of that period was understood. On the one hand, at the end of the 1950s, authors, critics and editors were extolling the virtues of comics as an indicator of values and 'national idiosyncrasy'; on the other, production depended increasingly on patterns imposed by international industries. Thus the comics artist and editor Ramón Columba ('founder and president of the Asociación Argentina de Editores de Revistas') emphatically claimed: 'Our comics magazines publish 150,000,000 copies per year! No other country in the world surpasses us in this area. [. . .] We produce meat, grains . . . and comics!' (Columba 1954).

The issue of 'what was acquired' as opposed to 'what was received' resulted in a dispute which broke out in the market: at stake was the import and export of comics series. Once again, it was an attempt to 'Argentinise' a market increasingly flooded with globalised cultural assets.

> We need Quixotes, both among students and professionals, but also among editors! Because we have tremendous historical responsibility. Comics can raise the morals of a nation, as well as the cultural value of 'people who don't have time', or who do not care about increasing their cultural knowledge. In the US, for example, scholars and university students learn more about history or other subjects from comics than from dry, antiquated texts. The illustrator owes something to progress, they should give themselves to Humanity.
>
> (Lipszyc 1957)

The enthronement of the US comic ran parallel to an 'internationalist' vision that aimed to incorporate the Argentine comic into an international field and which extolled it as a tributary of a certain 'native idiosyncrasy'. The characteristics of the so-called 'Argentine School of Comics' support this hypothesis. The controversy centred on the opposition between the vernacular and the foreign, between being contemporary and lagging behind. The emphasis placed on singular features valued local work over competing markets.

Arguments to support such views included references to the unfavourable conditions of Argentine professionals or the lack of recognition their creative labour received. The discourses expressed a view of the foreign in which the celebration of 'the local' is wrapped up in a chauvinist and nationalist perspective. The historical cycle that had given comics a privileged place in the industry entered a steep decline in the 1960s: levels of production were never the same despite the development of certain business ventures.

Boom, decline and transnational markets

The coup d'état in March 1976[11] brought to an end an era where ideas emerged from a complex interweaving of culture, politics and the market. During the most critical period of dictatorial repression (1976–9), various factors would interrupt the small resurgence in comics that had taken place in the first half of the 1970s. The exile of some professionals and the disappearance of others, censorship and self-censorship, and, more generally, the economic crisis in the publishing industry, all meant that during this period few notable works were produced.

But with the advent of the transition period (1980–2), even though the actions of the military could not be mentioned directly, the range of topics tackled by comics expanded and some publications included critical views, with the aim of increasing the possibility of public intervention and targeting a new readership. Finally, with the elections of 1983, when comics production started operating once again under democracy, the political debate resurfaced in the shape of a discussion over the relationship between nation and popular culture.

The displacement of an internationalised national industry by a globalised national industry implies being involved wholesale from the start of the process (Sigal 1991; Terán 1993). The transition from a strongly nationalised to a 'globalised' industry disrupted an economic history that was inseparable from the period's cultural and political debates. Following the military coup of 1955, debates about the condition of the petit bourgeoisie and the question of 'what to do with the Peronist masses' (Altamirano 2001; 2007) ushered in a period in which intellectuals questioned the notion of a modernising nationalism and its cultural industries. The internationalisation of tastes and the deterritorialisation of production implied a rethinking of relationships in the midst of a process of globalisation that emerged in a contradictory manner, depending on the perspective from which it is considered. For some professionals, the new situation of comics meant the possibility of joining the international market and producing comics within a context of better working conditions; for others the closure of a national industry implied the development of a sphere from which they were disastrously excluded.

In other words, the national/foreign dichotomy was not a debate centred on market competition among comics-producing countries, nor was it limited to a debate around whether foreign comics should be given a space in the market or if the best comics were those produced by national authors. The conflict included a problem linked to a long-standing tension in Argentine politics in which the construction of a system of opposites is arranged around political tensions.

The history of Argentine comics was, in fact, characterised from its very beginnings by the importing of models from the US and Europe. This dependency was permanently undermined by a national publishing industry and by the selection of magazines produced entirely within the country. But from the second half of the 1970s and even more so in the following decade, the consolidation of a global market and delocalisation of the workforce was striking.

This contradiction becomes apparent whenever the expression of the status of the field (in terms of rupture, advancement or renovation) demands a return to the point of origin. An often romantic and idealistic reading of that past is inscribed in an ideological and strategic operation in which the question of legitimacy becomes the key focal point. The tension between an idealised past and concern over an uncertain future was reworked in the publications that date from the period of democratic transition during the 1980s. It became an amalgamation of meanings in which the residual and the emerging could apparently coexist harmoniously, the 'old school' alongside the avant-garde of comics. From then on, through events and publications, those linked to comics took on glorifying enterprises, the motto of which appeared to be the evocation of a lost past.

Paradigmatically, the process, ushered in at the end of the 1960s with the First International Comics Biennial of the Instituto Di Tella, began with a series of events and festivals which took place in the province of Córdoba between 1972 and 1986, when there were six National and International Biennials of Graphic Humour and Comics.[12] At these kinds of events, reverence for the past and deference and homages to classic comics authors and national graphic humour took centre stage.

This tendency can be linked to the expansion of the culture of memory that is characteristic of recent history. In fact, in more global terms, this period has been defined as 'an era of collectors'.[13] The majority of perspectives on comics are not excluded from this homage to the past (in which the idea of the retro played a key role).

The reconstruction of these positions emerged from a key fact: intellectuals interested in comics in the 1970s and 1980s used a previous era as a point of reference, marked by the expansion of the industry. Researchers produced a history founded on the quantitative growth of the publishing market and the idea of a thriving national industry. Thus, the history of comics is also a history of its debates, businesses and projects. At the end of this illustrious era, marked by the promise of an auspicious future, a large number of tributes and homages to the 'masters' of the medium marked not just the end of a historic moment, but also the limits of a publishing and cultural industry caught up in the circumstances of the era.

The legendary reconstruction of a 'national golden age' largely ignored a central fact: the permanent connection and interdependence of the local industry on international markets. To analyse the labour market in which comics artists and professionals[14] have been immersed it is necessary to explain the manner in which transnational networks of cultural production work (Mato 2004). Argentine comics authors have always been immersed in scenarios of meaning production on a global scale. But, to date, there has still been no exhaustive study of the different methods and systems of work that artists and scriptwriters from Argentina have established over time in relation to the 'publishing centres' (mainly the US, Spain, Italy and France). I do not have the space to explore this issue in more detail in this chapter, but I note here the potential importance of further research into interactions which are global-local in nature and also into the restrictions that the practices of social actors in the aforementioned centres impose on production methods domestically.

Of course, it is not simply a case of studying how artists and scriptwriters work for syndicates and publishing industries, but also of analysing how these actors participate actively in social networks of negotiation and conflict. We must study the manner in which they are linked and how, along with their practices and discourses, they contribute to this mode of strengthening contemporary processes of globalisation. A theoretical problem emerges from this context which is also in some way a political question.

Independent editions, festivals and revivals

The displacement in the production and consumption of comics generated a new cultural phenomenon. With the arrival of the transition to democracy (the 1980s) came tendencies such as comic collecting (exchange or barter clubs for out-of-print editions and the buying and selling of 'rare' materials) and the organising of exhibitions and events dedicated to comics. This (ongoing) period takes up a familiar debate: at every convention, exhibition and festival, there is some reference to the crisis in national comics production and to the need to reinvigorate the form.

Alongside explanations as to why booming, large-scale publishing houses did not manage to recover from their cyclical periods of decline came distinctions, homages and praise for the protagonists of those 'rich and memorable' times. Two general movements within 'independent comics' are evident during the 1980s and 1990s: the first is linked to the cultural and political framework of the democratic transition and is in tune with other artistic expressions of the period. The second is seen in the initiatives of artists in the second half of the 1980s, which heralded the boom in fanzines that would occur in the 1990s.

Edited in different cities around Argentina, the first fanzines were presented as alternatives to dominant modes of production. Without a doubt, *El Subtemento Óxido*, which began as an insert in the magazine *Fierro* in February 1984, was key in consolidating the aesthetic expressions of the 'new generation'. In the 1990s, various magazines that were circulating ceased publication and the most important comics businesses discontinued their activities: *Fierro* (Ediciones De La Urraca) stopped in 1992; the publication of *Puertitas* and *Puertitas Super Sexy* (El Globo Editor) concluded in 1994; 1996 saw the last issue of *Skorpio* (Editorial Récord); and even though Editorial Columba remained in the market until mid-2000 it had long been surviving on the reissuing of materials that were already tried and tested in the market.

The fall in the purchasing power of the middle and working classes, the parity of the peso-dollar that enabled the import and sale of foreign magazines, the transnationalisation of consumption and people's changing entertainment habits are some of the factors that changed the course of a market that, at several moments, was characterised by diversity.

The publishing crisis brought about revamped practices in the production circuit that, though they did not manage to relaunch the industry, did guide production towards other cultural areas. The emergence of small ventures (not only in the comics sector but in the publishing industry in general) that were precarious and only partly competitive was indicative of the situation. In the field of comics, publishing houses, independent magazines and cooperative publishers were aware of a new trend: for the first time, comics artists gathered around administrative collectives presented themselves as cultural producers rather than as business people.

In the final years of the 1990s, hundreds of publications with different programmes, ambitions and publishing policies 'invaded' stands at festivals, magazine kiosks and comic stores. Taking the format of fanzines, these independent magazines and comic books coexisted in a heterogeneous and broad market.[15]

The creation of the Association of Independent Comic Artists (AHI in its Spanish acronym) in mid-1998, a collective that spanned hundreds of magazines across the country, indicated the extent of the expansion in the market. In Buenos Aires, the movement's meetings took place in a space belonging to the Argentine Workers' Union (CTA in its Spanish acronym). It was here that the first incarnation of the event Historieta Bajo Tierra took place in August 1998. Some years later, as a result of discrepancies in objectives and publishing policies, the group responsible for the general organisation split up and started its own publishing house: La Productora.[16] In time, nearly all the subsidiaries broke up, with the exception of the one in Rosario, which subsequently organised the Leyendas festival. More recently international festivals, such as Viñetas Sueltas (2008, 2009, 2010, 2012), Crack Bang Boom (2010–16) and Comicópolis (2013–17), indicate a new strategy of cultural legitimation.

Given that the new generation of artists and scriptwriters no longer enjoyed a professional environment in which they could publish their comics, self-publishing became a common strategy, even though many such publications did not get as far as being distributed in kiosks. Their print runs were meagre and most did not get past a first or second issue. Young (and not so young) comics artists formed part of a movement that, despite their differences, was united around a common discourse: they 'came to occupy' a vacant space. Magazines like *Cazador* (1990–2001) and *Comiqueando* (1994–2002) or publishing houses such as Domus, Doeyo Editores, Thalos, Llanto de Mudo and Loco Rabia gradually consolidated an alternative space that not only responded to generational change but also, fundamentally, to the emerging conditions of editorial production. As a result, their magazines supported both personal and collective aspirations. In general, their objective was not to earn money from these productions but, with a little luck, to recoup expenses.

Fanzines, which varied in terms of graphic quality and were sold hand to hand, were not a profitable venture. Photocopied drawings assembled with staples, folded in the middle, and in most cases covered with a piece of card or thick paper, fanzines always had low print runs and were printed with 'personal touches'. These irregularities invoked the idea of being 'homemade and by hand' and harked back to the 'do-it-yourself' traits of the industry.

These comics artists had to become publishers 'by chance' or circumstance: there was no lineage or tradition. In effect, unlike their 'maestros' who had to follow strict rules imposed by publishing houses, these young artists created their own rules, administered their own resources, defined their own habits, schooled their own preferences and produced their own symbolic merchandise.

A sense of community has been a strong part of such production, not least because of a dramatic difference between the Golden Age and the 1990s with regards to the relationship between the market, art and trade. It is well known, for example, that there was a cut-off between production and the assembly line. Those who had grown up reading comics magazines did not have a space where they could promote and publish their creations. Unlike their 'maestros' who had 'learnt on the job' in comics magazines, these self-taught artists had their own magazines as test sites but had to pay for them.

In this way comics, which had ceased to be an industry, instead became a cultural practice. Public space was crucial in this context. Imitating street vendors, the 'fanzine' generation constructed their own identity and acquired social visibility. The act of producing or buying a magazine and attending festivals indicates that the industry had become an 'atmosphere'. During this period, that notion was linked to a playful understanding of comics activity. In the events and at stands, social gatherings and camaraderie formed part of the act of publishing itself. Those who were showing, producing and distributing their magazines also participated in social activities. The festivals had their own rules of organisation and classification: as in any club, 'everyone knew everyone', and to enter the club newcomers had to partake in initiation rituals. During this period the figure of the 'fan' became increasingly prevalent.

Fantabaires, which first took place in November 1996, was undoubtedly the event that brought together the new generation of comics artists into a space where 'artists sold their work to other artists'. The slogan 'Comic, Science Fiction, Terror and Fantasy' gives us a glimpse into the heterogeneity of their objectives: the comic was one among several products for sale. With all its limitations, this space worked as a meeting place for both aspirational young people (who had read comics during their childhood) and renowned national and international professionals who had been invited to the event. Further editions of this festival would continue for a number of years, though eventually organisational problems would bring it to an end.

Following an insightful reading by Iván Lomsacov (2010), other significant events demonstrated the conditions of a market that was becoming more and more cross-disciplinary with regards to production, circulation and consumption. Lomsacov cites a number of comics festivals: Leyendas (Rosario), Tinta Nakuy (San Miguel de Tucumán), Aquelarre (San Nicolás, Province of Buenos Aires), Frontera (Morón, Province of Buenos Aires) and Viñetas Sueltas (Buenos Aires). Worth noting, too, was the Congreso Bienal Internacional de Historietas y Humor Gráfico, Viñetas Serias (2010, 2012, 2014), which created a space for encounters and exchange between critics, academics and professionals.

At these events comics artists often produced their drawings in front of potential future readers or followers. Unlike professional artists in other eras who experienced specific demands to produce a great deal in short periods of time, these authors were not faced with time pressures, even if they could often be seen sketching speedily and diligently as if faced with a deadline. This practice was not by chance. Praise of manual work does not hide a desire for professionalisation and prominence. The young people who were producing fanzines created a 'we' that refused any sense that they were 'childlike'. They wanted to be like their 'maestros' and belong to an industry. In that sense, they were competing over a legacy without heirs in which, ultimately, the market is the legitimising force.

With the economic crisis of 2001 and the effects of the Convertibility Plan implemented in the 1990s under the neoliberal policies of the government of Carlos Menem, independent publishers were virtually wiped out and stopped circulating in their traditional spaces. Since then, fragmented into different publishing ventures with erratic circulation and limited length, comics production has been subject to ups and downs. The return of *Fierro* to kiosks in November 2006 (this time as a supplement to the newspaper *Página 12*) was perhaps the clearest example. Sixteen years after its first appearance, its aim was no longer so much related to the continuity of values or to recover the national industry but rather to stabilise a symbolic space of production and consumption at a time when anthologies in book format and newspapers at events and festivals have come to occupy the small opening that the field of comics occupies in the market of cultural goods.[17]

Conclusion

Maybe the belief in a possible return to the Golden Age has finally reached its conclusion. Or perhaps it is just that nothing is as it was before in the world of Argentine comics. The current crisis in the comics market is increasingly widespread and the promise of cultural development and the joyous future of modernisation have reached their economic limits. The romanticised views of professionals and artists are often the result of a social position in which nostalgia forms the basis of oral narratives of an idealised historic past. Such constructions are dependent on a selective memory which obfuscates the contradictions and cracks of a defunct cultural and political model. As Raymond Williams states, every golden age is 'the recurrent myth of a happier and more natural past' (1973, 40).

In recent years, digital publishing has constituted a new strategy for expressing viewpoints, criticism and communication between authors and readers. The increase in professional sites and comics blogs requires further study but the phenomenon extends to authors with very different trajectories and spans diverse publics. An amateur with no previous experience can set up a blog in much the same way as an internationally renowned and recognised author.[18]

The ultimate objective, in all cases, is contact with readers and product dissemination. It is of no little consequence that, while the first edition of *Fierro* contained the subheading 'comics for survivors', in its second iteration this motto was replaced with the statement 'The Argentine Comic', as if the ambitious programme of continuity with the Golden Age were being minimised, in the end, to a handful of familiar names, a 'football team', as Juan Sasturain liked to describe it in his editorials.

As 'trials of public opinion' and spaces of exchange, these digital productions are often preludes to professional projects. Nonetheless, with the collapse of the industry and faced with a paralysing sensation of loss, comics artists created a dynamic which involved not just a different form of production but also alternative circulation and consumption practices of cultural merchandise. But before we talk of the disappearance of an industry, it is worth considering the new cultural and economic conditions of a field in continual synergy and transformation. For example, although 'wholesale comics publishers' no longer exist as they did in the mid-twentieth century, professional authors can be involved in anthologies or individual editions of their serialised creations (via the longer format of the graphic novel). In other decades, it would have been unthinkable for an artist from Columba, Quinterno or Récord to be able to disseminate their work to a reduced circuit of readers, let alone with the possibility of widespread recognition and creative autonomy. As Roberto Von Sprecher states in his reading of the features of the new comic that emerged in the 1990s out of the circuit of independent publishing:

> When the new appears relatively consolidated, within a field that has modified its central norms, the agents, criteria and mechanisms of recognition only refer to sales as being of secondary importance and they include agents, considerations and discussions that circulate in the comments on comics blogs, blogs which specialise in criticism, comic magazines such as Comiqueando, events, internet forums, Facebook, and spaces of university research,

among other channels of communication in which creators, consumers, researchers, editors etc. communicate with each other with reasonable ease, a situation unheard of in previous eras. These spaces of exchange are an indicator of the consciousness and self-reflection of members of the field and are a consequence of the existence of spaces of autonomy that favour creative renovation.

(Von Sprecher 2010)

Thus, bearing in mind that the comic as a site of production of symbolic goods is regulated not only by national and regional contexts of industrial production and purchase and consumption markets, but also, as we have seen, by global characteristics of international markets, the relative autonomy achieved through independent publishing creates advantageous channels for exercising both aesthetic and narrative experimentation.

Although the new forms of self-publishing do not generate profits and in some cases only manage to recover costs (current examples of this type of venture are the publishing houses Hotel de las Ideas, Editorial Común and Maten al Mensajero), they not only enable works by professional artists to be disseminated, but they also foreground the heterogeneity of their catalogues. While during the Golden Age the genres and styles of 'to be continued' comics responded to patterns more or less standardised and governed by central comics academies and industries, following the crisis of the 1990s and with increasing appeal, the Argentine comic is finding its own way of creating a voice in conditions which are both adverse and, at the same time, liberating.

The artists and scriptwriters who incorporate different registers into their graphic production have found new channels for their work via new media and technology. Graphic design, communication design and editorial illustration are new niches in the market. Such activity has seen a growth in the blurring of boundaries to such an extent that the questioning of the margins (and from 'the margins') is no longer where the comics industry is going, but rather where the limits and boundaries of the language of comics lie.

Notes

1 A number of works address this issue. While it is not my objective here to examine the critical and intellectual discourses about Argentine comics, helpful studies that deal with these interventions in the field are Lucas Berone (2011), Berone and Reggiani (2012), Von Sprecher and Reggiani (2010) and Vazquez (2010).

2   See also, in this volume, Enrique Uribe-Jongbloed and Daniel E. Aguilar-Rodríguez's chapter on Colombia and Carla Sagástegui Heredia's chapter on Peru.

3   As Daniel Schteingart states: 'Perón's absence generated a historical memory – which has lasted, in large degree, to this day – in which the working classes constituted an ideal that they wanted to return to. Worker demands post-1955 wanted the return of that Edenic and lost past of the 1945–1955 period, in which they achieved a political-civic status they had never previously had (or would ever have again) in Argentine history' (Schteingart 2014, 77).

4   I address some of these issues in my doctoral thesis 'Oficio, Arte y Mercado: Historia de la Historieta argentina entre 1968 y 1984', Universidad de Buenos Aires. A version of the same was also published in my book *El oficio de las viñetas* (2010).

5   As Daniel Mato writes: 'The most analytically advantageous way of approaching the analysis of what [. . .] I've referred to as transnational articulations which are global-local and local-local in nature is not to study only the practices of individual actors, nor institutions and discourses, nor large social processes. Rather, the most beneficial approach is to study the forms in which they link to each other, the forms in which through their practices actors produce and participate in institutions, discourses and processes, and the forms of "translational complexes". These complexes, comprised of actors acting in institutional and social contexts (specific and objects of study) that at the same time they are constantly producing, constitute the forces that produce and outline the aforementioned translational articulations and, in turn, contemporary processes of globalisation' (2003, 331).

6   Referring to the transnational character of the production of series for the European market, Oscar Steinberg claimed that 'the eventual return of exported material, edited years later on the back of its success in the metropolitan centres, will later be both mobiliser and symptom within a context always partly fearful of and partly dependent on external cultural dynamism' (1977, 13).

7   'If Pop artists have been able to take the comic as an "example" or as a theme, that is because there was something more in comics than just being a product of industrial society. That extra dimension is surely to be found in the aesthetic dimensions that exist in the new visual reality shaped by comics' (Masotta 1968, 211).

8   Saccomanno and Trillo contend that, despite the instability of the institutional order and the adverse conditions of the market, the intrinsically marginal nature of the work carried out by Argentine comics artists meant that they subsisted off the structural changes of the system (1980). Endorsing this thesis, Juan Sasturain connects the marginal elements of comics and the constitution of national identity to affirm the key role that marginal expressions have in the historical cultural evolution of the nation: 'The field of marginality – that is, production that takes place beyond the usual forms and circuits of consumption – has provided the truest expressions of Argentine national and popular culture [. . .]. All such production was systematically ignored or undervalued at the time, only for it to be accepted later on, with the exception of official culture which usually tries to appropriate it' (1980, 186).

9   For an analysis of this period, see Bróccoli and Trillo (1971); Steimberg (1977); Saccomanno and Trillo (1980); Rivera (1972); Rivera (1992); Romano (1972); and Sasturain (1995).

10 Take-home wages fell by 25.5 per cent in 1959 after a very small rise after 1955. See Llach and Sánchez (1984).

11 24 March 1976 marked the start of a dictatorship that called itself 'Process of National Reorganisation'. It ended on 10 December 1983 with the return to democracy. In the mid-1970s, levels of political and social unrest were very high. See, for example, James (1993).

12 On the characteristics of these Biennials, see Rugnone (2018).

13 On the marketing of nostalgia and the globalisation of memory, see Huyssen (2002).

14 I would like to highlight the contingent relationship between artist-professionals more than any separation that attributes specific features to either. In effect, avoiding the tension which exists in the creation and the marketing of comics is not a convincing way forward. Indiscriminately sustaining the terms 'artist' or 'professional' is, in fact, to explicitly omit the unstable and ambiguous nature of comics work. Artists and professionals are subject to the rules of a particularly contradictory cultural market. It is a profession which supports this double meaning and which turns the circularity between the rules of art (Bourdieu, 1995) and those of the market into its trademark. I have explored this issue in more detail in Vazquez (2010). See also Rivera (2000), Steimberg (1977), Von Sprecher and Reggiani (2011) and Berone and Reggiani (2012).

15 I list here some examples of these ventures of 'independent' publishers. Fanzines: *Acero Comics, Alas, El Aquelarre, Asesinos, Asfalto Caliente, Aspid, La brigada del buen gusto, Buitre, Catzole, Che, loco, Dark Comics, Doppie Charasca, Elvisman, Extraño Camello, Doble V, Falsa Modestia, Kapop!, La Fiera, Kamikaze, Maldita garcha, Megaultra, Morón Suburbio, El muerto, Neurosis de angustia, Océano y charquito, La metáfora, Pluma negra, El niño azul, El Lápiz Japonés* and *El tripero*. 'Independent magazines' (commercially distributed in kiosks): *Arkanov, Cabeza de Gorgona, Cóctel, El Tajo, Quajas, Gritos de ultratumba, Planeta Caníbal, La Parda* and *Óxido de Fierro*. Comic books (distributed in kiosks in a North American format): *Animal urbano, Cazador, El ojo blindado, El laucha, Mitofauno, Caballero Rojo, La negra* and *Pin 8*.

16 During this period various independent publishing houses had already started to emerge, including La Productora and Llanto de Mudo. Around this time, in the middle of 2000, some productions changed to an A5 format and started to be distributed in kiosks: *Asesino 55, Bulgan Bator, Mutant Comic, 4 Segundos, Mikillo, Ultra* and the first titles published by La Productora: *Morón Suburbio, Road Comic, Grájal, Villa Tesei, Perfecto, Ecos y Tinieblas, El otro, Néstor Comics I: decadencia, Néstor Comics II: Puerto Kapruccia, Copérnico* and *El Destino Invisible* (my thanks to Diego Agrimbau and Andrés Accorsi for providing this information).

17 While the expansion of digital comics falls outside the scope of this chapter, it is worth noting the importance of the online blog *Historietas Reales* (2005–18), which was a pioneer of e-zines and was a beacon for a whole range of individual and group web projects. For a reading of webcomics in Argentina see the study 'Digitalización: Los blogs de historietas, El caso de "Historietas Reales"', by Roberto von Sprecher and José Pestano (2015).

18 As Von Sprecher puts it: 'The appearance of blogs as a free publishing space on the internet ushered in, on 30 December 2005, the most important comics event of the years that followed: Historietas Reales, a blog that brought together numerous well-known and unknown authors, from both Buenos Aires and the interior – some of whom would be replaced over the course of the five years it lasted – and which included daily installments on autobiographical themes, with the occasional exception. Historietas Reales forms the basis of the new generation of real cultural creators, scriptwriters and artists' (Von Sprecher 2010).

References

Alabarces, Pablo. 2002. 'Cultura(s) [de las clases] popular(es), una vez más: La leyenda continúa. Nueve proposiciones en torno a lo popular'. *VI Jornadas Nacionales de Investigadores en Comunicación*, 17–19 October, Córdoba. Last accessed 29 June 2019. https://popularyma-siva.files.wordpress.com/2010/03/nueve_proposiciones.pdf.

Altamirano, Carlos. 2001. *Peronismo y cultura de izquierdas*. Buenos Aires: Temas.

Altamirano, Carlos. 2007. *Bajo el signo de las masas (1943–1973)*. Buenos Aires: Emecé.

Berone, Lucas Rafael. 2008. *Oscar Masotta y la 'literatura dibujada': Reflexiones sobre la disolución de un objeto*. Last accessed 29 June 2019. http://www.descartes.org.ar/masotta-berone.htm.

Berone, Lucas Rafael. 2011. *La fundación del discurso sobre la historieta en Argentina*. Córdoda: Universidad Nacional de Córdoba.

Berone, Lucas and Federico Reggiani, eds. 2012. *Creencias bien fundadas: Historieta y política en Argentina, de la transición democrática al kirchnerismo*. Córdoba: Universidad Nacional de Córdoba.

Bourdieu, Pierre. 1988. *La distinción*. Taurus: Madrid.

Bourdieu, Pierre. 1995. *Las reglas del arte: Genésis y estructura del campo literario*. Barcelona: Anagrama.

Bróccoli, Alberto and Carlos Trillo. 1971. *Las historietas*. Colección La Historia Popular, N° 77. Buenos Aires: CEAL.

Columba, Ramón. 1954. 'Paseo triunfante su lápiz por el mundo', *Dibujantes* 4.

De Certeau, Michel. 1999. *La cultura en plural*. Buenos Aires: Nueva Visión.

Grignon, Claude and Jean-Claude Passeron. 1991. *Lo culto y lo popular: Miserabilismo y populismo en sociología y literatura*. Buenos Aires: Nueva Visión.

Huyssen, Andreas. 2002. *En busca del futuro perdido: Cultura y memoria en tiempos de globalización*. Mexico City: Fondo de Cultura Económica.

James, Daniel. 1993. *Resistance and Integration: Peronism and the Argentine Working Class, 1946–1976*. Cambridge: Cambridge University Press.

Kusch, Rodolfo. 2008. *La negación en el pensamiento popular*. Buenos Aires: Las Cuarenta.

Lipszyc, Enrique. 1957. *La historieta mundial,* Buenos Aires: Enrique Lipszyc Editor.

Llach, Juan and Carlos Sánchez. 1984. 'Los determinantes del salario en la Argentina: Un diagnóstico de largo plazo y propuesta de políticas', *Estudios* 29: 3–47.

Lomsacov, Iván. 2010. 'El campo de la producción, edición y distribución de historietas realistas en Argentina entre 2003 y 2009', *Nostromo: Revista Crítica Latinoamericana* 3, 16 July. Last accessed 29 June 2019. https://historietasargentinas.wordpress.com/2010/07/16/37-el-campo-de-la-produccion-edicion-y-distribucion-de-historietas-realistas-en-argentina-entre-2003-y-2009-pablo-ivan-lomsacov.

Masotta, Oscar. 1968. *Conciencia y estructura*. Buenos Aires: Ediciones Jorge Álvarez.

Mato, Daniel. 2003. 'Actores sociales transnacionales, organizaciones indígenas, antropólogos y otros profesionales en la producción de representaciones de "cultura y desarrollo"'. In *Políticas de identidades y diferencias sociales en tiempos de globalización*, edited by Daniel Mato, 331–5. Caracas: FACES–UCV.

Mato, Daniel. 2004. 'Actores globales, redes transnacionales y actores locales en la producción de representaciones de ideas de sociedad civil'. In *Políticas de ciudadanía y sociedad civil en tiempos de globalización*, edited by Daniel Mato, 67–93. Caracas: FACES–UCV.

Rivera, Jorge B. 1972. 'Para una cronología de la historieta'. In *Historia de la literatura universal: Las literaturas marginales*, edited by Jorge B. Rivera, Buenos Aires: CEAL.

Rivera, Jorge B. 1992. *Panorama de la historieta en la Argentina*. Buenos Aires: Coquena Grupo Editor.

Rivera, Jorge B. 2000. *El escritor y la industria cultural*. Buenos Aires: Atuel.

Romano, Eduardo. 1972. 'Examen de la historieta'. In *Historia de la literatura universal: Las literaturas marginales*, edited by Jorge B. Rivera, Buenos Aires: CEAL.

Rugnone, Andrea. 2018. 'La 3ra Bienal del Humor y la Historieta: hacia lo internacional', *Testimonios* 7, no. 7: 20–30. Last accessed 29 June 2019. https://revistas.unc.edu.ar/index.php/testimonios/index.

Saccomanno, Guillermo and Carlos Trillo. 1980. *Historia de la historieta argentina*. Buenos Aires: Editorial Récord.

Sarlo, Beatriz. 1998. 'Una comunidad llamada Nación', *Perfil*, 8 June 1998: 3.

Sasturain, Juan. 1980. 'Epílogo'. In *Historia de la historieta argentina*, edited by Carlos Trillo and Guillermo Saccomanno. Buenos Aires: Editorial Récord.

Sasturain, Juan. 1995. *El domicilio de la aventura*. Buenos Aires: Editorial Colihue.

Schteingart, Daniel. 2014. 'La democratización del bienestar en el peronismo (1945–1955): ¿Ruptura o continuidad con el pasado?', *Realidad Económica*, 74–108.

Sigal, Silvia. 1991. *Intelectuales y poder en la década del sesenta*. Buenos Aires: Puntosur.

Steimberg, Oscar. 1977 [2013]. *Leyendo historietas: Textos sobre relatos visuales y humor gráfico*. Buenos Aires: Eterna Cadencia.

Terán, Oscar. 1993. *Nuestros años sesentas: La formación de la nueva izquierda intelectual argentina*. Buenos Aires: Ediciones El Cielo por Asalto.

Turnes, Pablo. 2009. 'La novela gráfica: Innovación narrativa como forma de intervención sobre lo real', *Diálogos de la Comunicación* 78. Last accessed 29 June 2019. http://www.dialogos-felafacs.net.

Varela, Mirta. 2006. 'Intelectuales y televisión: historia de una relación', *Revista Argentina de Comunicación, Identidad y memoria de los Estudios de Comunicación en la Argentina*, FADECCOS, 1, no. 1.

Vazquez, Laura. 2010. *El oficio de las viñetas: La industria de la historieta argentina*. Buenos Aires: Paidós.

Von Sprecher, Roberto. 2010. 'Estudio de la historieta como campo: Las luchas por la construcción de lo nuevo y de lo viejo, en Argentina, desde los noventa', *VI Jornadas de Sociología de la UNLP*. Last accessed 29 June 2019. http://www.memoria.fahce.unlp.edu.ar/trab_eventos/ev.5712/ev.5712.pdf.

Von Sprecher, Roberto and Federico Reggiani, eds. 2011. *Teorías sobre la historieta*. Córdoba: Universidad Nacional de Córdoba.

Von Sprecher, Roberto and Federico Reggiani, eds. 2010. *Héctor Germán Oesterheld: De El Eternauta a Montoneros*. Córdoba: Universidad Nacional de Córdoba.

Von Sprecher, Roberto and José Manuel Pestano. 2015. 'Digitalización: Los blogs de Asociación Argentina De Especialistas en Estudios del Trabajo 270 historietas. El caso de "Historietas Reales"', *deSignis* 22. Last accessed 29 June 2019. http://www.designisfels.net/publicaciones/revistas/22.pdf.

Williams, Raymond. 1973. *The Country and the City*. Oxford: Oxford University Press.

4
The comics scene in Colombian cities

Enrique Uribe-Jongbloed and Daniel E. Aguilar-Rodríguez

Introduction

Colombia has recently entered what could be considered a new era after the signing of a peace agreement between the government and the oldest guerrilla movement in the world, the FARC. This historical moment has been accompanied with other changes in many other areas of Colombian society, from film production – now with tax exemptions for foreign productions produced in the country – to the inclusion of the country in the OECD and as a partner of NATO. Moving away from an image of crime and despair in relation to the war on drugs, even despite the fictional worlds evident in series such as *Narcos* (2015), Colombia has become a site of renewed hope, whether in the creative industries – as the recently elected president, Iván Duque, has openly admitted – or tourism. The peace dividend is expected to start paying off soon.

Colombia has not been very famous for its comics. Ana Merino (2017), for example, dedicates most of her recent overview of 'Comics in Latin America' to the historically dominant markets of Argentina, Cuba and Mexico. Colombia is only referred to in relation to Colombian/Ecuadorian artist Powerpaola's fame and the cultural importance of the Entreviñetas festival. Nevertheless, despite the general lack of scholarly recognition, the recent nomination of Lorena Alvarez to the Eisner awards in 2018, the release of the animated film version of Powerpaola's *Virus Tropical* (2017), and the gold medal given to Pablo Guerra and Henry Diaz's *Two Aldos* at the 2018 Japan International Manga Award, have started to turn the spotlight on an art form and communication medium seldom discussed, even in Colombia. These achievements echo the sentiment expressed by comics connoisseur Felipe Ossa (2019, 243) who states that 'it can be said that the development of comics in Colombia is only beginning'.

Such achievements have come about owing more to the dedication of the creators of comics, graphic novels and festivals rather than to any concerted national effort to valorise comics. Nevertheless, shifting conditions in the consumption and presence of comics in Colombian cities have also influenced the growth of comics production. Over the past 40 years the main four cities in the country have witnessed renewed interest in comic-book reading. This process has seen the decline of the kiosk as the site of comic display, trade and acquisition and the concurrent rise of specialised bookstores and of comics at festivals and fairs. Universities have also played an important role, promoting courses in graphic design and similar areas and educating professionals in the possibilities of using comics as relevant media for expression and communication. All of these elements constitute the comics scene in Colombia.

The comics scene in Colombia: Stores, clubs, festivals and events

As part of our research into new urban spaces for comics consumption, we interviewed comic-book artist Fernando Suárez, known for his work as a cartoonist for the newspaper *El País* in Cali in the 1980s and 1990s and a famous collector; managers of comics-related events, namely César Ramírez – recently in charge of the academic elements of Comic-Con in Medellín and Bogotá – and Santiago Suescún – head of FICCO, a festival for independent comic-book artists in Bogotá; and managers of clubs and stores, including Boris Ríos and José Barbosa – owners of Valkyrias y Dragones in Barranquilla, a site for comic-book sales and events – and Champe Ramírez – co-founder of El Cómic en Línea and manager of Casa Friki in Medellín. We put their memories and experiences into dialogue with our own to set out a panorama of the events, stores and festivals where comics were to be found. We also draw on information taken from various documentary sources to develop a historic memory of the many places, activities and initiatives that have placed comics at the heart of the cityscape. Although we limit most of our discussion to the four largest cities in the country – Bogotá, Medellín, Cali and Barranquilla – their cases are symptomatic of other Colombian cities. In fact, even small cities such as Armenia have been important in the development of a comics culture, as will be discussed below. Taken together, we hope to present a broad perspective of all the diverse elements that constitute the comics scene in Colombia.

In this chapter we think of comics in relation to the city in terms of a 'scene'. We understand scene here in the sense presented by Woo et al. (2015, 288), who argue that 'such "scene thinking" can map (always incompletely, to be sure) how social and cultural life are lived in space', as well as in relation to other groups, institutions and works. Thinking about the comics scene in Colombia shows how different groups of people or communities become integrated. As Woo et al. go on to argue, 'like networks, scenes enable, mediate and constrain action, emphasize the relationality of their members, and have an emergent, decentralized order' (290). The scene requires spaces of gathering or encounter, which may be physical or virtual, and which enable interaction with the comic book as a product. Those places of gathering include events, stores and festivals. They may extend to other types of places, where comics have a role within a larger array of objects. Within the scene, 'the possession and accumulation of social capital, the network of relationships that the agent builds in different spaces, enable contact between disseminators and instances of mediation, all of which allows social capital to be reproduced as a medium of cultural appropriation' (Fernández and Gago 2012, 88).

The scene is a conceptual category to promote a holistic perspective of the relationship between comics and the city. It is not a closed concept but rather a prism through which we can connect different elements that would not usually be brought together. To that end, we explore the places of the city where comics are relevant and the people who pass through those places, based on the memories of a group of people who have a long-standing engagement with comics. Of course, this approach cannot give us the whole picture, but we believe that this current chapter opens up a set of issues related to the Colombian comics scene that might be used as the starting point for a deeper study of such interactions and oral histories.

Comics disappear from the cityscape: Magazine kiosks and trade-in shops

In the early 1980s, as throughout the 1970s, comics were big sellers in Colombia. At the end of the 1960s most of the market was cornered by Mexican comics, which continued to dominate during the 1970s and early 1980s, alongside comics from the US that were translated into Spanish. Pareja (1982; 1985), in fact, issued a warning about the potential risk for children who were consuming too many imported comics, both because of the extreme commercialisation of these products, and because of the topics covered in them. This moral panic, as would be the case for other media, emerged simultaneously with an expansion of comic-book consumption throughout the late 1960s, 1970s and early 1980s. Probably as the consequence of the moral panic, comics started to be heavily taxed, something criticised by Ossa (1984) in the Sunday supplement 'Tiras Comicas' (Comic Strips) of the national newspaper *El Tiempo* on 6 May 1984: 'Today it's comics, tomorrow it will be other magazines, and then books, films, albums . . . . All for a "handful of dollars". I do not believe that prohibiting the import of illustrated magazines will prevent the squandering of our dollar reserves.' The tax brought expansion to a halt and caused the gradual disappearance of most of the comics scene until the tax was overturned in 2013.

Comics imports were sold at magazine kiosks that proliferated during the period prior to the comics tax. Similar to newspaper stands in the US, these kiosks offered a variety of newspapers and magazines, as well as small candy bars and bubblegum. Two dynamics of consumption were often carried out among kiosk customers: the first consisted of acquiring new comics; the second was to engage in exchanges and trade-ins. The trade-in tended to be more common in working-class neighbourhoods, in which kiosks worked as an exchange hub for avid comics readers. Although none of the Colombian-made comics were very successful, often ending after a first issue, kiosks provided a variety of products that were mostly consumed by young people, including Disney titles and *Archie* alongside the Mexican publications *Kalimán*, *Memín* and *Águila Solitaria*, and the Chilean *Condorito*.

Aside from formal trade at kiosks and magazine stands, an informal trade took place inside private dwellings or neighbourhood shops, where people would also buy, exchange and sell comics (akin to the exchange or barter clubs in Argentina referred to by Laura Vazquez in this volume). The informal neighbourhood comics stores were often found in the garages of houses. Similar to early video rentals, families could rent magazines for on-site reading for a small fee. Kiosks and informal neighbourhood shops became the principal spaces for reading and trading comics. Most customers were children who had little money to spend and would thus limit their acquisitions to a few issues and then engage in trade-ins once they had read the whole magazine.

As far as kiosks were concerned, it was possible for comics enthusiasts to keep their personal collection on track by visiting these sites regularly, and they became a recognisable part of the urban landscape. Such kiosks were present in the four largest cities in Colombia – as well as in some of the smaller ones – turning them into an urban experience common across the country. For Fernando Suárez, who grew up in the small town of Pradera, near Cali, the place to get comics as a child was the kiosk on the main square, and when he moved to Cali to study at the School of Fine Arts he states that he bought comics:

> [...] at the Librería Nacional bookstore and a few kiosks there. There was one [kiosk] near the bus station, on the side of the Estación Avenue, a small kiosk, next to a Clinic that is still there . . . there was this guy that sold comics, and another in the city centre, diagonally across from the Bank of the Republic, on Eighth Street.
>
> (Interview with Fernando Suarez, 2018)

This experience was similar to Enrique Uribe-Jongbloed's in Cali, where he would go with his grandfather to buy newspapers and comics at the kiosk near the city centre, at what is now Jairo Varela Square. Fernando Suárez adds:

> When I was a little kid I remember seeing kiosks everywhere. And also in [neighbourhood] shops, where they sold everything from buttons to plates, as well as comics.
>
> (Interview with Fernando Suarez, 2018)

That kind of 'miscellaneous shop' was key to the informal market mentioned above. It existed in houses or neighbourhood stores where comics readers would exchange or trade in comics with other attendees or the business owner. Trade-ins were carried out by handing over old editions, or volumes, and adding a small amount of money to buy a new comic. Even though kiosks were present in most areas of the cities connected to public transport networks, trade-in shops were located primarily in middle-class and lower-middle-class neighbourhoods. In these places, it was also possible to rent a comic to be read on the sidewalk or the front porch of the house for up to an hour. In warmer cities – Medellín, Cali and, in particular, Barranquilla – sidewalk reading was very common (such reading practices were not as usual in Bogotá because of the colder and rainier weather). César Ramírez remembers:

I was living in Envigado [near Medellín] back then. They sold comics at a place called *El Ocio*, and they did trade-ins, so you would read a comic and the week after you could take your comic book with you and, giving over something extra [money], you could get the next instalment.

(Interview with César Ramírez, 2018)

Similarly, in the city of Barranquilla kiosks based on trade-in dynamics were widely accepted in the popular sectors of the city, where inhabitants could increase and update their personal collections of *'paquitos'*, as comic books and magazines were commonly called in the northernmost regions of Colombia.[1]

By the end of the 1980s kiosks started to disappear as the tax on imported comics took hold. The early 1990s saw comics retreat from open-air kiosks and move into supermarkets that only offered comics from the Disney catalogue, all of them in Spanish, and the Chilean *Condorito* and its catalogue, which meant Mexican comic books were absent. Comics also appeared in select bookstores, some of which became quite specialised, offering primarily North American and European comics, in big, sometimes luxurious, formats. Bookstores tended to concentrate on larger format European comics (e.g. translations of *Tintin* or *Asterix*, for example, or *Mortadelo y Filemón* and the like), compilations in small format (e.g. *Olafo, el amargado* (Hagar, the horrible) or *Garfield*, also translated), small format Argentinian compilations (e.g. *Boogie el aceitoso*, and *Mafalda*), and US comic books that were not translated into Spanish (e.g. Marvel Comics). When kiosks disappeared, trade-in shops in middle- and lower-middle-class neighbourhoods continued to provide a space for comics consumption. Bookstore customers were usually upper- and upper-middle-class children who could afford their merchandise, which highlights that the dynamics of trade-ins had a significant class connotation in Colombia.

Kiosks and neighbourhood shops were spaces where working- and middle-class children could buy and trade in comics, and supermarket stalls and bookstores were the place for middle- to upper-class comics consumption. The decline of kiosks brought about the disappearance of an important space of cultural exchange for comics in working- and lower-middle-class neighbourhoods. Comics became more highbrow, and with the concurrent rise of graphic novels, the comics fan base moved further away from the mass consumption of classic Mexican comics. Slowly but surely, with the move from public spaces to specialised shops, bookstores, festivals and book fairs, the consumption of comics in Colombia became increasingly elitist. Unlike in Argentina, where magazine kiosks still abound in cities like Buenos Aires, they are no longer seen in Colombia. The traditional space of comics was no longer in public spaces but private stores.

Specialist stores and hobby clubs: The 'nerd culture' of urban comics consumption

The changes enacted by the 1991 Constitution had an ambiguous impact on comic book consumption and the presence of comics in urban settings. On the one hand, a cultural fund established by the government promoted projects such as *ACME* magazine. On the other hand, in 1993, the so-called 'book law' classified comics as culturally irrelevant, placing them in the same category as pornographic and crossword puzzle magazines, which meant they were unable to receive the tax exemptions introduced for scientific and culturally relevant printed works (Suárez and Uribe-Jongbloed, 2016). Through this categorisation, the tax on comics from the 1980s continued during the 1990s and 2000s. Unsurprisingly, during the 1990s there was a shortage of comic books and magazines. Editorial CINCO, which was the largest importer and distributor of comics, stopped bringing comics to Colombia altogether. The book law, which made other books tax-free and raised the tax for comics and graphic novels, had a significant impact on the market – and on the disappearance of the kiosks. Comic fans and enthusiasts soon found themselves without many opportunities for accessing graphic stories, other than in the weekend funnies of newspapers.

During this period the specialised comic-book store and the hobby club replaced the kiosk as a space of interaction. The kiosk disappeared from Colombian streets and squares in the early 1990s almost simultaneously with the disappearance of national comics publications. Unlike in the US, where the lack of comics at newsstands led to the development of specialised comics bookstores (Pustz 1999, 6), in Colombia comics that were no longer available at kiosks or newspaper stands were found only in second-hand bookstores or magazine re-sellers, such as El Loco Pensante in Bogotá – a shop that is still open for business. The comics then found in established bookshops were usually expensive European large-format comics (such as *Tintin* and *Asterix*) or translated Marvel and DC comics.

Bookstores also bought into another trend at the beginning of the 1990s: the cultural scene that brought together comic books, sci-fi novels, role-playing games (RPGs) and, more recently, collectable card games and collectable figures. The main bookstore in Bogotá which sold all of these in one space was Librería Francesa. At that time, it was the centre of Colombian 'nerd culture', a term understood to refer to:

> [...] a set of interests and hobbies that includes reading or collecting comic books; playing certain kinds of games (e.g. role-playing games; collectable card games; miniatures games, 'German' board games and to a lesser extent video or digital games); engaging with science, technology and other scholastic pursuits; and participating in fandoms for certain genres and texts (e.g. science-fiction and fantasy; horror and cult media).
>
> (Woo 2012, 261)

Nerd culture was centred around sci-fi, fantasy and RPGs, which became popular in the early 1990s, mainly among children who brought TSR products (such as Dungeons & Dragons books) from the US. The growth in Librería Francesa's sales correlates with two important developments. On the one hand, Gilles Fauveau, the manager of the bookstore, was a dedicated RPG fan and comic book aficionado. He was also a comic-book artist and alongside Bernardo Rincón – an academic and comic-book fan himself – created the cult magazine *ACME*, which has been hailed ever since its inception in 1993 as the most important point of reference for comics in Colombia (Suárez and Uribe-Jongbloed 2016, 55–6). Librería Francesa expanded its business and opened a shop called *The Hobby Store* in the mid-1990s, with more comic books, RPG books and sci-fi toys precisely to cater for this specific audience. Most books, including comics, were found in their English version, setting a high cultural capital barrier for consumption. Also, as these works were imports from European countries and the US, the prices were considerably higher than those of the kiosk comics of the 1980s. Most patrons were university-level students, many of whom were linked to a new hobby club called Trollhattan, founded by some of the regular customers. Trollhattan members met weekend nights at an old mill, which was a restaurant by day, near the city centre of Bogotá, where a number of private universi-ties are located. Trollhattan lasted two incarnations in as many sites in the city but always concentrated its activities around RPGs, with Librería Francesa acting as their site for acquiring new products. When Trollhattan closed its doors, Librería Francesa opened a new, larger locale, which included a back room – by 2018, an upper floor – for playing collectable card games (CCGs) such as Magic, the Gathering. In the late 1990s, a variety of coffee shops and bars near the universities started offering RPG nights to cater for this new interest. Simultaneously, in 2001, a new club was created, following Trollhattan's footsteps. Escrol was the new place to play board games, RPGs, CCGs, and it offered access to comics and other books lent or donated by members. Escrol also moved sites and eventually included MMORPGs as part of their entertainment offering, closing its doors for good in 2007. Librería Francesa ended up closing the Hobby Shop and the other branches, keeping only the larger one, which still houses large comic-book offerings, and spaces for playing different games. The activities of Librería Francesa with Trollhattan and Escrol highlight the intertwined experience of nerd culture with comics consumption.

In a similar fashion to the way Woo describes the context in the US, in Colombia too 'comic shops are indeed central to the practices of comic fans and collectors, but most are also game shops and toy stores and purveyors of t-shirts and miscellaneous licensed merchandise' (Woo 2011, 129). Hobby and comic-book stores, such as Too Geek in Bogotá, have become the sites for gatherings and small events, which also cater to the needs of the current 'nerd culture'. Librería Francesa was a space that allowed for the discussion of related hobbies, among them comic-book collection. Comic-book stores also 'act as a space for people to argue over the intricacies of their favourite heroes and villains, various plotlines and reboots, and to discuss how the comic-based movies are similar, but also different, than the original pulp publications' (Herrmann 2018, 4). In Colombia, clubs became spaces of interaction that, except for Librería Francesa, eventually started to distribute comic books, rather than the other way around. The heyday of RPGs at the end of the 1990s and the early 2000s went hand in hand with the expansion of 'nerd culture' in Colombia. Clubs have come and gone in all the cities, but today *Casa Friki* in Medellín and *Valkyrias y Dragones* in Barranquilla remain as evidence of the lasting effort of dedicated individuals who have brought together comic book fandom and other elements of 'nerd culture'.

Comics in events and festivals: Book and hobby fairs, universities and public libraries

At the beginning of the 1990s, in different universities in Bogotá, Medellín, Cali and Barranquilla, students, professors and graphic artists began to organise spaces to present and exhibit their own work. Gatherings with talks about comics and caricatures began to grow in number. Such events were important for increasing the visibility of comic fanzines sold independently without ISSN or ISBN identifiers, and whose existence is largely only documented from the testimony of those who read them at any given moment. As in Peru (see Carla Sagastegui Heredia's chapter in this volume) and Argentina (see Vazquez's chapter in this volume), self-published and informally distributed fanzines and single-issue comics became the norm in the 1990s (Suárez and Uribe-Jongbloed 2016).

In the late 1980s, the Cali Departmental Institute of Fine Arts – then called the School of Fine Arts – created a bi-annual exhibition of graphic art, consisting primarily of comics and caricature. One of the first of its kind, this event inaugurated the growing presence of comics in academic contexts. The exhibit was promoted and managed by the artists Ricardo Potes, León Octavio, Jorge Saavedra, Marco Aurelio Cárdenas, Wilson Ramirez, Hans Anderegg and Gilberto Parra, who organised the magazine *Click* in 1985 and 1986 (Ossa 2019, 242–3). Fernando Suárez remembers:

> I joined the School of Fine Arts [in Cali] in '87, and then I started to meet people. It was hard to know who the comic-book artists were, because you could pick up the comics, but there was no contact information.
>
> (Interview with Fernando Suárez, 2018)

This did not stop Suárez, who joined a group of eager students and alumni in 1994 to create the Salón de Historietas y Caricatura (The Comics and Caricature Assembly) in Cali, a yearly event that started with the support of the Cali Chamber of Commerce. Later, in the mid-2000s, it became Calicomix, an annual event that is still running. Originally an exhibition of artwork with a few talks by guest speakers from different countries and with a handful of comics being sold on site, it has grown in size and importance and is now one of Colombia's main comics events.

Medellín had a similar experience, with students of the Universidad Pontificia Bolivariana (UPB) and graphic artists working together to make their work visible through an event called *Visiones*. These events allowed artists to establish and collaborate on projects which were published years later, such as *Agente Naranja* and *Zape Pelele*. César Ramírez remembers finding these magazines:

[...] right there, at the Bolivariana [UPB], because the main artists graduated from there, after they'd studied Advertising and Design. So the group from *Zape Pelele* were the group that all came from Advertising, whereas those from *Agente* [*Naraja*] were from Advertising and Design.

(Interview with César Ramírez, 2018)

Zape Pelele lasted longer than other magazines and had a wider distribution in cities other than Medellín because it was more marketable, not least because its content was more family-friendly than the other publications. Although it contained some comic strips and pages of comics, it was rather like a Colombian version of *MAD* magazine.

In the late 2000s, Salón del Cómic started gaining prominence and relevance in Medellín and it became a permanent fixture that would be followed by other artists and event organisers in other cities of Colombia.

At that time, we had Salón del Cómic. Then I was organizing Salón de Cómic y Manga de Medellín [Medellín Comic and Manga Assembly] in the latest instalments of Fiesta del Libro [The Book Fest] . . . I joined Salón del Cómic around 2006 or 2007, the day I met Granda[2] and he invited me to work with them, but they had been at it for some time.

(Interview with César Ramirez, 2018)

Just like Fernando Suárez, César Ramírez grew up reading comics in the 1980s. They both support Bernardo Rincón's (2013) claim that the children who grew up reading comics in the 1970s and 1980s became the university students of the 1990s, and it was their dedication and interest which initiated some of the more interesting comics projects that developed subsequently. In fact, Jorge Peña, well known for his comic book *Maku* in 1967 and *Tukano*, released in the weekly publication *Los Monos*, lectured at the School of Graphic Design in the Universidad Nacional in Bogotá for over 25 years. Rincón has also lectured there since the early 1990s, having created a course on comics in 1993 (Peña 2000, 15). In 2009, the 29th exhibit of the School of Graphic Design focused on national comic-book artists, presenting honours to Jorge Peña for his contribution. This event was held at the Architecture Museum in the Universidad Nacional de Colombia in Bogotá.

In the early 1990s, Colcultura, the state institution in charge of promoting cultural production, started to support projects which eventually became volumes of comics compilations from a variety of national artists. It was one of those grants which allowed for the creation of *ACME*, the most popular and renowned comics publication of the period. In 1992, Bernardo Rincón, alongside Gilles Fauveau of Librería Francesa and other enthusiasts, collected the work of national and international comic-book artists into one magazine with high production standards. *ACME* quickly became the comic magazine that had the widest reach within the almost nonexistent comics market in Colombia, and it lasted for about four years (1992–6) (Suárez and Uribe-Jongbloed 2016, 55–6). *ACME* started by presenting the work of graphic artists from Colombia and some guest artists from Venezuela and Argentina, whose work was known via earlier publications that had limited distribution. *ACME* presented short stories by artists clearly influenced by Moebius, not only in the style of the drawings, but in the way the sci-fi stories were told. For many readers, *ACME* formed comics readers for whom other comic magazines, such as *Heavy Metal* or *Métal Hurlant*, were unaffordable as a result of the high prices at specialised bookstores.

Universities were fundamental as places to encounter the new generation of comic-book artists and enthusiasts. Schools of graphic design were hotbeds for these artists who, slowly but surely, began bringing comics back to the fore in the late 1990s and early 2000s, a trend that suggested that the 1990s marked a new future for comics in Colombia (Rabanal 2001). There has been a steady growth in the readership of comics, a change in the status of comic consumption and, though there is still no fully fledged Colombian comics industry, a significant change in momentum in terms of production, all of which has meant many more academics working on the subject (Suárez and Uribe-Jongbloed 2016). Just as in Peru (see Sagástegui Heredia's chapter in this volume), some comic-book artists became professionals, but there was no developed industry, in contrast to, for example, Argentina (see Vazquez's chapter in this volume).

The late 1990s also saw the creation of university guilds and clubs based around elements of 'nerd culture', including RPGs and comics, which also integrated patrons of the larger clubs mentioned above, such as Trollhattan and Escrol. Three former members of Escrol created El Cómic en Línea, which started as a website highlighting comic production, hoping to become a network of creators, and which eventually became a non-profit organisation that supported the creation of two of the *Exogen* comics. El Cómic en Línea also organised Los Monos de Oro at one of the Bogotá Chamber of Commerce offices, a contest and event that brought together local comic-book creators with international academics and artists, granting a symbolic prize to winners in several categories.

This period also saw growing interest in Japanese manga, which was introduced in Colombia in the 1970s through public television, which broadcast anime shows, such as Heidi, Doraemon (known in Colombia at that time as the Cosmic Cat), and Mazinger Z. During the 1980s, anime shows took up more TV screen time, particularly family-oriented shows like Tom Sawyer or the Tales of the Brothers Grimm. During the 1990s, with the appearance of national private TV channels and satellite TV, anime took over prime time, and small children became more and more interested in the anime aesthetic. By the start of the twenty-first century Colombia had a huge number of anime and manga enthusiasts who soon started to look for, and to create, spaces to share that particular type of art and comics. Manga and anime clubs started popping up in neighbourhoods in similar fashion to the trade-in shops of the late 1980s and early 1990s. These clubs started importing manga and pirated copies of anime videos, which would also be shown via small-scale video projections for a small fee. This growing interest has prompted events such as the Shinanime Festival (https://shinanimefestival.com) in Cali, the Matsuriken collective in Medellín, and the large gathering in Bogotá at the yearly SOFA (Showroom of Entertainment and Leisure), all of which gathered together many elements of 'nerd culture'. The success of *Two Aldos* could be predicated upon this interest in manga, and some bookstores – like Librería Nacional – also began importing manga books just as some national artists began to reproduce the aesthetics of manga comics in their artwork. On the whole, however, manga comics still do not have a large turnover in Colombia.

By the year 2012, there were collectives that focused on creating series of stories to secure continuity of publication. Examples include: *Bogotá Masacre Zombie*, produced by Go Up Comics; *Ana Crónica*, produced by the Greiff Brothers; or *Saic*, produced by Ave Negra, a company led by the García brothers. These collectives, though small, were designed to ensure that their comic books lasted more than one or two issues. At the same time, they managed to organise distribution channels that were strengthened using web sites and fan pages. The quality of such products was higher than it had been 20 years earlier, and their prices were more accessible, to the extent that even school-age students could afford the magazines. These works were almost always available at the national book and hobby fairs throughout the country and through direct sales via Facebook and Instagram fan pages.

Other events have also had an impact on the social milieu. Highbrow gatherings and events include El club de lectores de Cómic (started in 2009 in Armenia), a reading club sponsored by Banco de la República in its libraries, including the Luis Ángel Arango Library in Bogotá; and Entreviñetas, an academic and artistic gathering that started in 2010 focusing on comics and graphic novels (Correa 2010, 136–7). The brainchild of Daniel Jiménez Quiroz, the Entreviñetas festival started in Armenia, alongside the magazine *Larva* (Guerra 2010, 39), but is now held in Bogotá and Medellín as a yearly event that brings together renowned artists, publishers and academics, hosting discussions about comics to open audiences, and including talks, conferences, exhibitions and workshops. Although both El Club del Cómic and Entreviñetas are open to the general public, they tend to be attended by people with significant cultural capital and academic interests. Entreviñetas has become particularly relevant because it has helped to raise the perception of comics and graphic novels to a level and status approaching that of high-end prose literature.

A more commercially oriented event is Comic-Con Colombia. Comic-Con started in Medellín in 2013 in a shopping mall but also recently took place in Bogotá. Now Comic-Con has yearly events in both cities. Although this event tends to concentrate on many other aspects of entertainment, comics remain at the core of the event and César Ramírez makes certain that there is a comprehensive number of talks and workshops that focus on them.

Finally, we should mention recent work undertaken by Santiago Suescún and volunteers of the Festival de Cómic Colombiano, FICCO, which has started to gather momentum. Inaugurated in 2016, FICCO is a gathering place for young comic creators with regular bi-monthly meetings that include talks and comic-book sales. FICCO usually partners with public libraries and specialised shops, including Too Geek, and uses their spaces for the gatherings. Although originally established in Bogotá, FICCO meetings have also taken place in Medellín and Barranquilla, bringing together young artists and hosting talks that are free to attend. FICCO has also participated in the Bogotá International Book Fair (FILBO) and in SOFA, both of which are annual events that take place in the capital.

Final remarks: The Colombian comics scene

Several key elements emerge from the transformation of the comics scene in Colombia that we have described above. The disappearance of kiosks certainly changed the overall presence of comics in the streets. The impact of kiosks can perhaps now be seen in the extensive murals and graffiti that are present in most Colombian cities today. After the social action that led to the constitutional court reinstating comics as cultural goods in 2013, making them exempt from value-added taxes, high-end bookstores started selling more comics and including Colombian graphic novels as part of their stock. Nevertheless, the loss of kiosks is still deeply felt among certain sectors of society, not least as it has resulted in more limited access to comics as a form available to all, turning it instead into a more elitist manifestation of cultural consumption.

Perhaps in response to the aforementioned limitations in terms of access to comics, universities have emerged as key spaces for comics consumption and for making visible the work of local graphic artists, in many cases via events that are co-sponsored with private sector companies or local government bodies. University courses have also brought together students who subsequently became leading figures within such activities, working alongside specialist academics who also created and promoted many such initiatives. Simultaneously, the involvement of public libraries in fostering comic-book reading clubs and participating in or promoting events such as Entreviñetas and FICCO, indicates that some public institutions are realising how comics can be used to promote literacy.

While it is true that there is still no national Colombian comics industry as such, the country does have a long tradition of caricature, mainly of a political nature and with ample exposure in printed media. When academic spaces of exhibition and reflection around comics began to develop, it was, at least to begin with, linked to an interest in political cartoons and visual satire. Organisers also recognised that more people were familiar with caricature and that such familiarity would bring in larger numbers to the events. Caricature was used as a hook for attracting new enthusiasts into the world of comics and particularly national comic production. The lack of a comics industry has made it difficult for artists to make a living out of producing comics alone – a situation similar to what was happening in Peru (see Sagástegui Heredia's chapter in this volume). The fusion of comics and caricature has also meant some artists and followers moving from one field to the other. Cases like that of

Fernando Suárez, who drew single-panel cartoons in the Cali newspaper *El País*, but who is also a comic-book creator, is symptomatic of such movements. Many of the cartoonists of the 1980s and 1990s were also part of the comics movement, including Bernardo Rincón, Grosso, Jorge Peña, Ricardo Potes and others, and most were also involved in university teaching.

During the decades that followed, the demand for comics fell significantly and, at the same time, the number of anime programmes imported from Japan and with Mexican or Iberian-Spanish translation grew in number, and young people became increasingly focused on television series rather than reading comics. With the growing popularity of anime, however, came a growing demand for manga among young readers, a demand that was reflected by the decision of commercial bookstores to start importing manga books.

During the first decade of the twenty-first century, large publishing companies entered Colombia, distributing their collections in commercial bookstore chains. The high prices of comics meant that only a small number of buyers were able to afford volumes edited by DC Comics, Vertigo or Marvel. Stores also imported comics linked to major film series, such as X-Men, Iron Man, Spider-Man, etc., but as these are mostly only available in English they are also difficult to sell on a large scale.

In the 1990s, magazines such as *ACME, TNT, Zape Pelele* or *Agente Naranja*, among others, allowed middle-class readers to access national comics, developing a new type of habitus, in the sense set out by Pierre Bourdieu (2012), since few middle-class college students could afford to buy expensive French or North American comic books and magazines at the specialised book stores or hobby centres. Simultaneous to this growing demand for national comics, role-playing started to find a place with college and university students, partly due to the fact that both comics and RPGs were offered in the same places. Thus, playing games and reading comics turned into a manifestation of class habitus, and a material expression of a new type of cultural capital. They became the markers of a 'nerd culture' that was associated with a certain level of sophistication and a middle to upper-middle class of college-educated, bilingual (or even multilingual) consumers of foreign-language comic books. Such a trend highlights that the disappearance of kiosks and Mexican comics is not only a visual change in the city landscape but also a transformation in comics consumption from the working and lower-middle classes into a very bourgeois pastime. In a relatively short period of time, access to and consumption of comics went from being popular to being a means of distinction, to use Bourdieu's concept.

The cases of Librería Francesa – as the most important comic-book store for many years – and the clubs that now have a dual existence as gathering places and sources of novelty and collectable products, still show how exclusive this market is. Nowadays, even though people in Medellín can attend Casa Friki, where a wide range of national and foreign comics are available to be read on-site, and patrons at Valkyrias & Dragones in Barranquilla can acquire comics at reasonable prices, they are also indicative of how limited the comics scene has become in their respective cities.

The comic-book scene in Colombia has thus moved from the public space of street kiosks to a more private sphere. Although comics are evident in universities, bookstores and public libraries, comics are also associated with large-scale events that garner more and more international attention. In that sense, comics are not as widespread as they once were in the 1970s and 1980s. The cities discussed in this chapter range from 1.2 million inhabitants in Barranquilla to more than 2.4 million in Cali and Medellín and 8 million in Bogotá, according to the projections for 2018 (DANE 2018). If we compare these sizes to those undisclosed Canadian and US cities where Woo (2011, 2012) and Herrmann (2018), undertook their research,[3] then the presence of comics in Colombian cities is a small-scale phenomenon. As comics became targeted at the middle class, and Mexican comics disappeared along with the kiosks that stocked them, comics became an increasingly niche product. Nevertheless, the demand for comics in Colombia is starting to grow, due in part to the growth of that same middle class, and the concerted efforts of many artist collectives, events and festivals. The disappearance of the kiosks is symptomatic, in that sense, of wider urban transformations and, akin to what has happened with other media, suggests a shift in Colombian culture away from a Mexican-led influence, towards a more US-led one. It remains to be seen whether these recent expansions in the production of national comics manage to reach the same people who used to participate in trade-ins and sidewalk reading around kiosks.

Notes

1   The word *paquito* or *paco* became synonymous with the words 'lie' or 'con' in everyday slang in Barranquilla, and continues to be used to this day to refer to elaborate stories that no one believes.

2   Granda (full name Carlos Granda) is one of the most famous Colombian comic-book artists, known for his work for Marvel and other international comics publishers. He also has the largest collection of Superman comics and collectable figures in Colombia. He has been a big fan and supporter of many comics events in Colombia.

3   There is no direct reference in either of their articles to the cities where the stores they analyse are located. It seems that those mentioned by Woo are in the Burnaby/Vancouver area, but there is not enough information to make an estimated guess in the case of Herrmann, although it would seem to be in a smaller town.

References

Bourdieu, Pierre. 2012. *La Distinción*. Madrid: Editorial Taurus.

Correa, Jaime, ed. 2010. *El cómic, invitado a la biblioteca pública*. Bogotá: CERLALC.

DANE. 2018. 'Proyecciones de Población'. Last accessed 8 October 2019. https://www.dane.gov.co/index.php/estadisticas-por-tema/demografia-y-poblacion/proyecciones-de-poblacion.

Fernández, Laura Cristina and Sebastián Horacio Gago. 2012. 'Nuevos Soportes y Formatos: Los Cambios Editoriales En El Campo de La Historieta Argentina', *Cultura, Lenguaje y Representación* 10: 83–96.

Guerra, Pablo. 2010. 'Panorama de la historieta en Iberoamérica'. In *El cómic, invitado a la biblioteca pública*, edited by Jaime Correa, 36–53. Bogotá: CERLALC.

Herrmann, Andrew F. 2018. 'Communication and Ritual at the Comic Book Shop', *Journal of Organizational Ethnography* 7, no. 3: 285–301.

Merino, Ana. 2017. 'Comics in Latin America'. In *The Routledge Companion to Comics*, edited by Frank Bramlett, Roy T. Cook and Aaron Meskin, 70–8. New York: Routledge.

Ossa, Felipe. 1984. 'Felipe Ossa'. *El Tiempo*, 6 May 1984, Tiras Cómicas Section, 7.

Ossa, Felipe. 2019. *Cómic: La Aventura Infinita*. Bogotá: Planeta Cómic.

Pareja, Reynaldo. 1982. *El Nuevo Lenguaje Del Comic*. Bogotá: Ediciones Tercer Mundo.

Pareja, Reynaldo. 1985. 'El Nuevo Contenido Temático Del Cómic', *Chasqui* 16: 24–27.

Peña, Jorge. 2000. 'Cronología de la historieta en Colombia'. In *Comics 99*, 13–16. Cali: Tercer Milenio Comics.

Pustz, Matthew. 1999. *Comic Book Culture: Fanboys and True Believers*. Jackson: University Press of Mississippi.

Rabanal, Daniel. 2001. 'Panorama de La Historieta En Colombia', *Revista Latinoamericana de Estudios Sobre La Historieta* 1, no. 1: 15–30.

Rincón, Bernardo. 2013. 'Héroes Del Cotidiano: Los Protagonistas de La Historieta Bogotana de Los Años 90'. Master's thesis, Universidad Nacional de Colombia.

Suárez, Fernando and Enrique Uribe-Jongbloed. 2016. 'Making Comics as Artisans: Comic Book Production in Colombia.' In *Cultures of Comics Work*, edited by Casey Brienza and Paddy Johnston, 51–64. New York: Palgrave Macmillan.

Woo, Benjamin. 2011. 'The Android's Dungeon: Comic-Bookstores, Cultural Spaces, and the Social Practices of Audiences', *Journal of Graphic Novels and Comics* 2, no. 2: 125–136.

Woo, Benjamin. 2012. 'Alpha Nerds: Cultural Intermediaries in a Subcultural Scene', *European Journal of Cultural Studies* 15, no. 5: 659–76.

Woo, Benjamin, Jamie Rennie and Stuart R. Poyntz. 2015. 'Scene Thinking: Introduction', *Cultural Studies* 29, no. 3: 285–97.

5

The authors of Contracultura Publishing: Self-portrayal and the graphic novel

Carla Sagástegui Heredia
Translated by Mariana Casale

In Latin America, unlike Mexico, Chile, Brazil or Argentina, Peruvian comics have never been industrialised, only professionalised.[1] The comic-strip projects that gave us the first Peruvian characters became financially viable in the 1950s, but comics were a form of entertainment that never reached the levels of production needed for full financial autonomy from newspapers and magazines. In the past three decades, as the publishing of comics moved away from newspapers and magazines to books and fanzines, Peruvian comics have been incorporated in a process of novelisation similar to developments in countries more representative of the industrial comic strip, even if the local context means that Peruvian comics are still located within a very political tradition. This shift has come to the interest of literary, graphic and cultural academics and has given rise to projects such as that of Contracultura Publishing, founded in 2005 and the first publishing house to specialise in fanzine and graphic novel authors. This chapter will focus on how Contracultura's widening of authors' access to the publishing market has produced several 'author privileges' (Foucault 1991), including being able to display anarchism, success for women in a predominantly male medium, and participation in national and international author circles. The chapter also shows how the creation of small, local presses like Contracultura, which evidently do not provide financial stability, problematise the idea that author privileges should be considered solely in terms of the economic importance of copyright in comic production.

How do these circumstances in which authors find themselves affect the Peruvian graphic novel in thematic terms? To answer this crucial question, I will first review the concepts of novel and author. Second, I will focus on interviews with four Peruvian comics authors, looking at their relationship with Contracultura and the publication of their work in book form. Their accounts, I suggest, demonstrate that their author privileges, despite low profitability, have granted them a degree of political enterprise that is central in the struggle over human rights in Peru. To conclude, I look at how these four authors portray themselves in graphic form in their work and whether such portrayals account for their privileges.

Novelisation and the author

In *Epic and the Novel*, published in 1941, Russian critic Mikhail Bakhtin (1996) turned the study of the novel on its head as he considered it a genre devoid of operations or laws that dictate its inherent nature, unlike the epic, which is a genre tied to an absolute past, a model hero and a national epic language.[2] The graphic novel might also be described in opposition to the graphic epic of the heroes and superheroes of traditional comic books, which are tied to unreal temporal worlds and commanding nationalisms.

A product of transgressive and ironic laughter, Bakhtin refers to the novel as a runaway genre which incorporates a variety of artistic, everyday and ideological discourses in its prose with an open-ended present and a self-enquiring man; in short, the novel includes a combination of expressions typical of its *author*.

The possibilities of representation afforded to the author by the novel enumerated by Bakhtin make it possible to prevent the crystallisation of the genre. The author tends 'towards that which is uncompleted': the author can play any role he wants to in the work, playing out his life or alluding to a particular moment in it, taking part in the characters' conversations, arguing with other real authors. But also, as the 'author of the author's image' (Bakhtin 2000, 328), the author is part of that representation, who thinks differently from his characters or who is in dialogue with other works. Bakhtin reminds us that no author reaches that status in the epic. Adding the author to the main elements that determine the novelisation of a genre, it is evident that it becomes freer and more flexible, its language renewed by incorporating a range of languages. It becomes dialogised, rife with irony and self-parody, and incorporates an 'indeterminacy, a certain semantic open-endedness, a living contact with unfinished, still-evolving contemporary reality (the open-ended present)' (Bakhtin 2000, 323).

For Manuel Barrero, the author introduces characteristics that break with the model of comic books, which have no particular author and which are aimed at children:

> The graphic novel is a comic strip in book form which contains a strip by a single author created specifically for this publication, it deals with topics in depth (aimed at an adult readership) and develops an extended narrative, without editorial or previously imposed format constraints, where characters grow in complexity until a closed ending is reached.
>
> (Barrero 2013, 197)

This novelistic condition, derived from the author, is a slow and complex process of cultural transformation which presents tensions and the transgression of boundaries at a deep and structural level. For José Manuel Trabado (2013), there are four tensions produced by graphic novels, regardless of whether they are North American, European or Japanese: recognition of the author's creative freedom as a result of having a poetics of their own; insight into the character's slow reflectiveness; narrative as a source of memory, catharsis and liberation; and enough formal and symbolic complexity for self-portrayal.[3] Without heroic and epic comics, the graphic novel ironically rereads the 'cloak and dagger hero through introspection' (Trabado 2013, 43), replacing him with an imperfect hero. Eddie Campbell suggests that contemporary comics require real-life stories because they are 'more peculiar and intriguing' than the well-known stories about made-up heroes (2013, 37).

At such a deep level, real life splits man's epic integrity in comics. Bakhtin states that the novel disintegrates it in various ways. The first and fundamental one is between the external and internal man, since in the novel 'the subjectivity of an individual becomes an object of experimentation and representation'. Another more specific way is splitting man as seen by himself from man seen through the eyes of others. In this way, a newer and more complex integrity for man is created, just as endowing him with ideological or linguistic initiative also divides him.

The nature of his image changes, therefore, as it creates 'radical restruc-turing of the image of the individual' (Bakhtin 1996, 56).

The incorporation of comics into modern expressive writing by means of the book has produced new authors and a new positioning within the hierarchies and cultural values which transcend personal poetics. Understood in this way, writing is not restricted to the act of writing nor to the mere graphic manifestation of what somebody wishes to express; instead, following Foucault, the writing of our day – *ecriture* – entails a profound attempt to consider the general condition of a work, the space it occupies and the time in which it is deployed. Projected towards the psychodynamics of writing (Ong 1982), this attempt enables an increasingly articulated introspection which opens the psyche up to a world that is different to itself because it is objective and external to the inner self, as opposed to the world of subjectivity.

Writing as a producer of subjectivity is, then, the conditioning medium for the development of prose and of the silent reader and, as such, it restores the presence of the author. The novel is a product of writing. Foucault explains this transformation into book form as a relationship between writing and death, which the epic does not present due to its oral nature. The aim of the epic is to perpetuate the hero's immortality, repeatedly remembering his story, while written literature is designed to perpetuate the existence of its author. Writing is no longer linked to the sacrifice of the hero who obtains glory and remembrance in exchange for his death, but to the sacrifice of the real person writing the novel, so that they can be replaced by the produced author. In exchange for his disap-pearance, the flesh-and-blood author leaves his glory and remembrance to his 'author's name'. There was a time, then, when accounts, stories, epic poems and comedies were received and valued without questions over their authorship being posed, in much the same way as superhero comics. But literary and comic strip discourses conceived from writing and the book, from the novel, cannot be accepted without knowing who has written them and in what circumstances. In the case of industrially produced comics, among which epic genres predominated, anonymity was not a problem. The age of legends and epic poems was enough to guarantee its acceptance. As for comic books, characters' popularity, which created approval, was manipulated by press agencies and publishing houses and by the conventional codes of the works. With the emergence and consolidation of the author within the world of comics, the control of meaning, status and value moved from the syndicate to the individual, just as in literature the author replaced the character. Once established, the presence of the author accounts for the modifications and even the contradictions that arise between a series of texts, as can be seen in the various lines of Juan Acevedo's work or in the difference between Jesús Cossio's fanzines and documentaries (which is not to say that each of his works does not hold within it a certain number of signs which point to his authorship).

The authors, graphic novels and Contracultura Publishers

Hola Cuy was the first Peruvian comic-strip compilation published in book form, released in 1981. After that, in a context of social fracture, Peruvian comics were sustained by fanzines and political projects until the emergence of the first of the publishing houses that specialised in graphic novels and compilations for adults in 2005. I have selected four authors published by Contracultura as part of my analysis of their links with the graphic novel: Juan Acevedo (b. 1949), Jesús Cossio (b. 1970), David Galliquio (b. 1969) and Avril Filomeno (b. 1973). All of them have been interviewed because of their prominence in the publishing market (the first three boast the largest number of copies sold while Avril Filomeno, together with the publishers, set up the first all-female space for comics) and because of their historical position in relation to fanzines, which is key to understanding the Peruvian graphic novel and its authors.

Juan Acevedo is Peru's most important and representative comics writer; Jesús Cossio has developed, if not established, the documentary comic in the Andean region, if not in Latin America at large; one of the most prolific fanzine and graphic novel authors, David Galliquio has published the largest number of books with Contracultura; and Avril Filomeno has promoted and created comics and fanzines in La Paz and Lima and was in charge of Peru's first anthology of female comics authors. These four authors are well known to comics consumers, who readily associate their work with their names. Through this operation, not only does the consumer of the texts identify the authors but their names also describe them, placing them within a cultural hierarchy, in much the same way as they have been intentionally introduced in this paragraph.

Each author plays a clear role in relation to their works and their discourses: to begin with, they play a classifying role.[4] The way Juan Acevedo remembers the association of the work with its author is an example of this: 'In the case of *Paco Yunque* by César Vallejo, it's a short story which I adapt with a personal stamp that people recognise: *that's*

Juan's Paco Yunque. How is that character going to come to life, how is it different from the *Paco Yunque* drawn by Carlos Jiménez or from other *Paco Yunques* that might have been made? I gave it a personal stamp. In that case I am the filter through which it reaches people, especially children' (Acevedo 2018). Any of the names of these four authors would allow for a regrouping of a certain number of texts, defined in such a way that some are excluded, some placed in opposition to others. But though there may be several different ways of regrouping them, the typical one is by graphic style. In the case of Avril Filomeno, her name is associated with her own specific way of drawing characters, their eyes, their faces and their bodies. In Cossio's case, it is his documentary line; in Galliquio's his neighbourhoods. For the author themselves, their name establishes a relationship of homogeneity and graphic filiation between their comics, just as it does for their readers.

For this study, it is even more relevant that, while an author's name serves to characterise the artwork, it is their discourses that endow them with the *name of the author*. Benjamín Corzo, director of Contracultura, has said about Jesús Cossio and Juan Acevedo:

> In Juan's case, in Jesús's . . . they have a discourse. In other words, a combination of coherent ideas, which they can explain well. That is a fundamental aspect for everything, as in the recent book fairs, those who sell the most are those who, beyond their books, are themselves characters.
>
> (Corzo 2018)[5]

Jesús Cossio himself was clear in his interview about his professional responsibility over his discourse; when asked about his relationship with academic contexts, he said that they had influenced his preparation, reading, analysis and awareness of how to express himself (Cossio 2018). David Galliquio claims that he does not consider himself an author – although he knows that his main character, Lito the Dog, is well known (Galliquio 2018). It is not just about recognising the artwork but about identification with its marginal nature. In the case of Avril Filomeno, she feels acknowledged as a fine art author rather than an author of comics (Filomeno 2018). That is because, despite succeeding in creating a publishing space for comics by female authors, she earns her living as an artist, within painting, pottery and other forms of expression. The case of Juan Acevedo is unique because he had the awareness and intention to become an author of political and existentialist comic strips three decades before the birth of Contracultura and he managed to achieve recognition for his discourse. For the latter, he refers to the emotional element that his projects aimed at:

> I wanted to do humour, but I also wanted people to think, I wanted to move the reader. So that people could laugh, but so that they would be moved by what was being told. . . . [F]or the cartoonist it was enough to monkey around and make a joke, but I wanted to unsettle, to make misery felt.
>
> (Acevedo 2018)

Acevedo's discourse is, as described by Foucault, the discourse of an author and it is a long way from being indifferent or oppressed expression. These words must be received in the same way as, and in relation to, irony, and as a discourse that is given the status of political and social commitment in Peruvian culture. This is how Juan expresses the characteristic style of his comics which, at the same time, is associated with a certain combination of Latin American liberation discourses within Peruvian society and within a culture linked to art, the press and social critique (Kruijt 1991, 107). His name is not located within the narrative of his work but in the rupture that his uniqueness establishes. He is the oldest author in Corzo's publishing house. Ironically named and with this ironic profile in mind, Contracultura lay down acceptance criteria for graphic novels by young people interested in garnering enough appreciation as authors to gain access to the media and to the international festivals circuit. Contracultura's first requirement for publication is that whether written by young people or by established authors, the works should 'sound' like rock music, 'with a strong, anti-establishment personality, one which should move the reader' (Corzo 2018).

The authors were asked about this direct link that Corzo believes exists between book format and authorship, to find out the extent to which it had had an impact on the creation of their work and, in turn, on their discourses. The question was asked on several occasions during each interview, sometimes being rephrased by replacing the word 'book format' with 'graphic novel' or enquiring about the fanzine format. Juan Acevedo and Jesús Cossio agree that the book influences the design of their works, although not in a way that detracts from it. When Cossio was asked about the design for *Barbarie*,[6] about whether he first considered a book about the conflict or whether the seriousness of the conflict should be represented in a book, he replied that he thought both questions were inseparable. Acevedo took the same view when asked about the story of *Túpac Amaru II, Anotherman* or *Paco Yunque* itself. Both authors described format and story as a unit, suggesting a correspondence between discourse and format types. David Galliquio directly stated that the 'graphic novel comes out as a book'. The dissident response came from Avril Filomeno, who says that she has never stopped doing fanzines, even in the case of her graphic micro novel, *Qué ciudad de locos*, co-written with Bolivian author Alejandro Archondo (2006). Filomeno's replies show the extent to which she associates her ironic creation with fanzines.

Going through their published work with each of the authors and reviewing the book format, in most cases they were described as compilations, as in *El cuy* and *Pobre Diablo* by Juan Acevedo, which were published in magazines and newspapers for many years and whose strips and pages are grouped together by set characters in a book (Acevedo and Munive 2015); or as an anthology by different women authors such as *Venus ataca* (Various authors, 2010). In the cases of Cossio, Filomeno and Galliquio, the compilation maintains its links to the fanzine, a product of the photocopier, equivalent to Lima's underground comix. The transition from fanzine to graphic novel is the transition from the serialised novel to the book or, as Filomeno prefers to call it, the 'de-luxe fanzine'.

The fanzine poses the issue of length, close to that required by a book to merit a spine and a hard cover even if those elements are irrelevant to this particular format. Length is fundamental to the comic from its inception, as artists were paid by the strip or the page. In the era of the graphic novel, however, payment in Peru is by low-cost book rather than by page. Out of the authors interviewed, David Galliquio is renowned for his ability to write works of great length (160 pages, for example), while Acevedo and Cossio prefer long episodes or chapters more akin to the comic book or album, albeit longer than the fanzine preferred by Filomeno.

This fanzine format lacks a formal canon or established length because, before the book, it emerged when comix were tuning in to 'the radical sensibilities of the Vietnam-era counterculture' (Hatfield 2005, 11). The main irony of the underground comix movement was the way it imitated the format of comic books produced by large industries. Robert Crumb's Zap Comix proved that it was possible to produce comics outside of the industry and its self-censorship code (Magazine Association of America 1955). The emancipation of comix prior to the book paved the way to authorship for two reasons. The first is that, with 'the radical reassessment of the relationships among publishers, creators, and intellectual properties [. . .] it was the first movement of what came to be known among fans as "creator-owned" comic books – and creator ownership was prerequisite to the rise of alternative comics' (Hatfield 2005, 16). The second was the fact that comix valued the production of the solitary illustrator over team work or the assembly line. In essence, says Hatfeld, 'comix made comic books safe for auteur theory' as it fit 'with the idea that cartoonists were expected to express themselves singly, just as a poet is typically presumed to speak with a lone voice' (2005, 16). In time, alternative comics went over to direct market comic shops in the US, Canada and various European cities, which sell graphic novels and fanzines. That is how they became detached from the cultural and political preoccupations which brought them to life in the underground movement.

The Peruvian fanzine does not revolt against a prior industry but rather finds a model of protest in the North American underground movement, which in the 1980s was inextricably linked to violence. It must be added that the movement's actions and publications were endorsed by a group of young artists who intervened from concert stages and via the DIY aesthetic of flyers. The 'under' movement has been studied by Shane Greene in his punk book *Punk and Revolution: Seven More Interpretations of Peruvian Reality* (2016). In Interpretation #5, 'The Worth of Art in Three Stages of Underproduction', Greene offers a rather blunt description of the context of political chaos midst a 'total economic crisis' within which the movement broke out:

> Curbs were covered in trash and dog shit. Street recyclers rode around on three-wheeled carts, picking up junk and reselling to street venders that resold it as junk elsewhere on the street. Migrants erected thousands of precarious domestic structures on recently occupied sandy hills overlooking the city's colonial center. There was also hyperinflation upward of 2000 percent and a total liquidation of middle-class incomes after Alan García assumed the presidency in 1985. Indian cadavers were piling up in mass graves in the Andean provinces and showing up on daily newspaper covers. Executive-ordered military massacres of rioting political prisoners were something you learned to expect in Lima detention facilities. Disfigured corpses, once the bodies of journalists mistaken for militants, laid out in a line on a frigid mountain landscape: this image would be burned into your brain.
>
> (Greene 2016, 112–13)

Surrounded by death and violence, the Peruvian fanzine started as a profound form of protest with underground rock as its protagonist, followed by comics. Its creators could be professional or amateur artists, like David Galliquio. Up until the mid-1990s, this movement produced and exchanged fanzines in central Lima's countercultural spaces, such as the well-known Jirón Quilca. In his origins in the working-class quarter of La Victoria, Galliquio finds links to the work of Robert Crumb and Gilbert Shelton, the Mexican 1960s, and the Spanish 1980s, all of which led him to the discovery of the concept of the underground, subculture, punk and fanzines (Galliquio 2018).

The publishing journey of the fanzine from the late 1980s up until the appearance of Contracultura in the mid-2000s can be traced through the Galliquio and Corzo interviews (Galliquio 2018; Corzo 2018). In 1986, there was no internet and circumstances did not allow fanzine authors to get to know each other. It was on his own initiative and because he was attracted by urban music that Galliquio went to those places in Central Lima where he came across fanzines, a format that allows for writing and publication without erudition, out of interest or out of love (Galliquio 2018). In terms of acquisition and reading, the fanzine's circulation was limited because it would be quickly discarded, and its print run was small because photocopiers were still scarce and places with public reprographics services were few and far between. The first major change in the development of the fanzine occurred around 1994 when Peru's oldest and most prestigious newspaper, *El Comercio*, together with the Calandria Association, organised a comic-strip competition. This competition is how Galliquio met Cherman Kino, Jesús Cossio, Álvaro Portales, and Renso and Amadeo Gonzales. In this context, Cherman published *CRASH, BOOM, ZAP* (*CBZ*), the first professional fanzine: the print run was 10,000 copies and it was delivered for free in Peru's major cities, a mode of distribution that was true to the 'under' aesthetic. The criteria for publication was that each author should create and maintain a set character throughout the various issues.

Peruvian comics during this period never managed to become an industry, only a profession. The North American industrial model involved staff illustrators, syndicates, mass media, mass distribution and sales, as well as form and content codes and conventions. Such an industry did not materialise, only a sporadic professionalisation which produced the long-term financial viability of some comics projects.

Peruvian comic strips had begun, as in most cities worldwide, with localised entertainment humour in magazines with a large circulation, even though in Lima they did not manage to survive in the press (Sagástegui 2003, 9–13). Comics later reappeared not as strips but as political cartoons, which ironically relativises the conventional use of strips and of fiction to give way to satire, political context and art nouveau. *Monos y Monadas* (1905–8), for example, the most refined of ironic magazines at the time, lasted only three years and had a small print run.[7] As an attempt to create a magazine for children, the publication *Palomilla* appeared three decades later in 1940, a 'chiste' (joke, as the comic book was known in Peru). Young amateur authors who sent in their first homemade adventure comics formed a generation which later developed the two largest professional projects of nationalist comics: the newspaper *Última hora*'s 100 per cent Peruvian strips (1952–68) and the great Catholic children's magazine *Avanzada*. Rubén Osorio, Hernán Bartra, Javier Flórez del Águila, David Málaga and other illustrators were the authors of the first comic strips and of the sustained production of *chistes* for more than a decade. Peruvian readers had never before seen themselves stereotyped in early characters like Juan Santos, Serrucho, Boquellanta, Sampietri, Coco, Vicuñín or Tacachito. Without a doubt, these stereotypical male protagonists represented the political views of General Manuel Odría's regime, although they transcended it inasmuch as they embodied certain consequences of developmentalist thought which the US government had inculcated in Latin America after the Second World War: a first world country should have industrial self-sufficiency and a deep sense of national pride. Accordingly, the autochthonous Sampietri bid farewell to Disney characters and cleared a path for Peruvians from the city, the countryside and the jungle into comic strips. We know from the letters to *Última Hora* that Peruvians enjoyed laughing at their bad habits. Nowadays, these comic strips are studied as cultural representations from the point of view of contemporary political canons, but so far no study of how they themselves constituted cultural change has been carried out. The attention the comics received and readers' identification with nationalist tropes resulted in their sustainability over time. Even though these conventional comics authors went on to work freelance in newspapers and school magazines, which is close to an industrial model, it was never thought necessary to create an agency or for the publishing house or the press to be the owner of the characters. The authors owned their creations. Osorio and Bartra, for example, who signed as Osito and Monki, kept the rights to their comic strips so that, although they had been first paid for them by the Pontifical Missionary Organization, they were able to republish them in newspapers like *El Comercio* or *Expreso* during the Revolutionary Government of the Armed Forces.

Monos y Monadas (1978) was first published 20 years after the creation of the Peruvian character types, towards the end of the second of two military regimes (Villar 2016). A political project led by artists, writers and cartoonists, the publication considered the raising of political awareness through art and irony necessary for addressing various urgent social conflicts. This project was continued some 10 years later when several of its authors came together again, first with the magazine *El Idiota*, and later with *¡No!*, a supplement of *Sí* magazine. It was also at this time that Juan Acevedo led his popular comic-strip workshops in Lima and in Ayacucho, part of that same ideological project. The fanzine emerged following the decline of such aims, during the armed conflict. A photocopied, folded and stapled piece of paper without a cover, the fanzine criticises the wider social system, not everyday politics. It is an aggressive, countercultural medium which resents *costumbrista* traditions and political satire.[8] It is the art of urban culture and resistance. After the artistic exploration of the previous political project, *CBZ* was the first professionalisation of countercultural comics. Emerging within a growing concerts market, 10 years later it circulated in local fanzine fairs, and 10 years after that, international comics festivals. When *CBZ* lost its funding, marking the end of an era, the Gonzales brothers managed to turn the collective fanzine *Carboncito* (2001) into a magazine. The first of David Galliquio's books to be published by Contracultura was *Lito the Dog* (2009), a character developed in *CBZ* and in *Carboncito*.

The privileges of being a book author

An author is not just the owner or parent of a work. Foucault demonstrated that the term refers to diverse privileges in our book cultures. Author privileges are the modes of circulation, valuation, attribution and appropriation that a culture gives to their work. These manifest themselves directly, as well as in other ways, in financial terms. But in comics production, questions of copyright have produced a tension between low-profile authors with a regular income and more visible authors subject to the financial vicissitudes of the independent market. Within this context, and despite economic differences, the interviews show several common traits in the privileges which Peruvian book culture assigns comics authors.

Juan Acevedo is the only comic-strip author who claims to have been able to make a good living out of comics (Acevedo 2018). That was especially so when working as a magazine editor, such as for the *¡No!*

supplement, or when he was hired by institutions such as the Centro de Estudios para la Acción por la Paz (Centre for Peace Studies) or the Rädda Barnen foundation to put together anthologies or comic books on human rights topics. Despite not being paid enough to support him outright, signature works such as *Paco Yunque* and *Túpac Amaru* have provided a significant income. After studying history of art, his professional career began as a public employee at the San Marcos History and Art Museum, then at the National Institute for Culture, later as head of the Ayacucho School of Fine Art and finally at the Ministry of Education. With the support of these institutions, Acevedo managed to hold popular comic-strip workshops to develop spaces for political reflection. By the time these workshops came to an end, the Revolutionary Government of the Armed Forces was no longer under the leadership of General Juan Velasco Alvarado but under Francisco Morales Bermúdez, who set about dismantling the first administration's progressive national system. The methodology underpinning the popular workshops was published by the Ministry in the book *Para hacer historietas* (Acevedo 1978), though the book was immediately recalled when they realised that Acevedo was a dissident. Acevedo's five years in public administration came to an end in 1978, when he gave up being a bureaucrat and was taken on as editor of the culture section of *Marka* magazine. He managed to make a living from the daily strip *Aventuras del Cuy*, saving enough to buy a car. Shortly afterwards, Morales Bermúdez would become a character in the strip *Love Story*. The manual for the workshops has been translated into English, German and Portuguese and he repeated the workshops in various cities in Latin America, all of which have contributed to the universal intellectual and artistic recognition of his contributions to comics. Nowadays he thinks of himself as the author of the comic strip *El cuy* in the newspaper *El Comercio*, addressing history, different forms of abuse, and discrimination. He sees himself publishing more strips than books, as books tend to be compilations. At the 2018 Lima International Book Fair, Juan Acevedo was celebrated by the Peruvian Chamber of the Book, the general public and the comics authors of the *CBZ* generation for his oeuvre and his political irony.

Cossio's irony and privileges are different. Even though he cannot make a living from comic strips alone, his documentary comics are valued culturally and academically. He started his work at a time when Peruvian politics had changed radically after the armed conflict: socialist, left-wing ideological stances were no longer associated with just the causes but also with the terrorism of Sendero Luminoso, an association referred to as 'terruqueo' (Rivas 2018) by those who support the prevailing extractive economic model. Cossio's documentary comics are usually about the 'terruqeada' (terrorised) population, one which fights for the right to basic living conditions. Invited by various institutions dedicated to establishing reparations for victims of the armed conflict, Cossio facilitates workshops in villages and cities. He has made his name doing this kind of work, although he would like to be appreciated for the comics themselves: 'many things happened because of circumstances and it was something I had to do for economic, format or circulation reasons rather than artistic ones' (Cossio 2018). While he has no idea of the extent to which his work circulates in an academic context (see Milton 2014 and 2017), he recognises that it is one of the most fruitful spaces for him, as he is constantly being invited to give talks or interviews at universities and as part of comics discussion forums.

Avril Filomeno studied art at the Fine Art National Academy of La Paz. She witnessed how a group of French amateurs together with the Simón I. Patiño Foundation succeeded in opening a comics café ('c+c espacio'), which was later replaced by the city's comics library (Filomeno 2018). That process, which started in 2002, was furthered with the organisation of the international comics festival, 'Viñetas con altura', which attracted young artists and art students like Avril, as well as writers and intellectuals. The foundation adopted comics as a mode of expression for working with adolescents from marginal urban areas, and the first fanzine workshop took place in 2003 with Avril in charge. Renowned as an artist, her fanzines have always been included in the cultural circuit for their quality despite their discourse and aesthetics of protest. She has led two major projects as a comics author. The first was the exhibition *Fiesta pagana* held in La Paz (2007), an event for comics authors whose aim was to work on the *fiestas* of Western Bolivia in colour. The tenth anniversary of the publication of the accompanying book was celebrated with an exhibition in Colombia and with the publication of a new collective book about La Paz. The second was the first publication of women comics authors, *Venus ataca* (Various authors, 2010), which was published in Peru. Together with Contracultura she also organised Peru's first international festival of comics by women. She currently facilitates workshops for women in a community which confronted Sendero Luminoso.

David Galliquio does not offer art workshops; in fact he prefers not to work as a comic-strip writer as he would not be able to cover his expenses by doing so. He wants his work to be looked after and preserved, which is why he publishes his comics in books. 'Lito the Dog', an 'under' steeped in urban violence, is one of the 10 most renowned characters in Peruvian comics. He knows that his comics can be found in the School of Art and Design of the Universidad Católica. His readers, 'under' readers, fanzine readers, often ask to interview him. The representation of the city of Lima in his comics constitutes his author discourse. He does not feel he has any privileges: 'I know that here you won't get rich or become a millionaire making books. I would love for it to be so, I would give up my miserable job, but it isn't. We are in Peruland and reality is different, here those who make comics make them because they really like and enjoy it' (Galliquio 2018).

The four authors present a range of critical discourses and, when working in conjunction with the political focus of certain institutions and magazines, receive fair remuneration for their work as comic-strip creators. But publishing books does not significantly alter their income.

Contracultura constitutes a milestone in the evolution of Peruvian comic strips as the first graphic novel imprint and publishing agent. But it is only allowed to pay, by law, 10 per cent of author royalties. By means of a verbal agreement and not a written contract, the publisher pays an advance of 5 per cent and submits the remaining 5 per cent once sales conclude. The informality of publishers in the Peruvian sales system, whether international groups or small local ones, was pointed out by all interviewees. In the case of an anthology of 10 women authors, for example, none of them is paid enough to cover their weekly expenditure. Only by publishing weekly in the press, like Acevedo, can comic-strip authors make a living. The privileges which graphic novels grant Peruvian comics authors, therefore, are not economic but political: (i) they provide the author with the privilege to articulate a critical and radical discourse against conditions of poverty and violence without being censored; (ii) they provide the author with the ability to interact with national and international institutions related to comics, books and human rights; and (iii) they provide the author with the means to teach political reflection via graphic expression workshops to people affected by violence and poverty.

When these authors draw themselves, they may or may not draw these privileges. Whenever Juan Acevedo is closely related to the characters he draws, his hair appears untidy: Anotherman, Humberto the dog and Luchín González are three characters in political comic strips. *Anotherman* is a graphic novel in which the masked hero confronts his father, who turns out to be the Devil and the head of the infernal

Peruvian state. Humberto is Cuy's sidekick, an autobiographical comic not of Acevedo but of the Peruvian Left of the 1970s (Figure 5.1).

Figure 5.1 Humberto the dog, an untidy character associated with the author Juan Acevedo in his popular comic strip *El cuy*. © Juan Acevedo

Figure 5.2 The main character of *Mala Onda* who has the physical features of author Jesús Cossio. © Jesús Cossio

Luchín González is the first comic to narrate the armed conflict and the atrocities that took place. The dishevelled hair, therefore, represents Acevedo's political freedom, and he remembers it through a drawing: 'He's a guy with hair like this [gestures to indicate dishevelled hair], just a brushstroke, "they say I'm an anarchist" and then he adds, "they can all go to hell"' (Acevedo 2018). Jesús Cossio points out that he does not have an autobiographical character because he is interested in going beyond himself to create a more universal character (Cossio 2018). He cites *Mala Onda* (2016) as an example, in which the main character caricatures his physical features, as well as his way of mocking Facebook posts (Figure 5.2). It conveys the performance of an author who ridicules without being censored, who is not afraid of showing his antipathy. Rather than political, the context is outright psychological, as posts in that particular social network refer to 'statuses' and 'topics' which the participant claims to be feeling or thinking about. The humour mocks spoken behaviour on social networks.

David Galliquio does draw himself, creating a character of himself as a comic-strip illustrator (Figure 5.3). He describes the character 'as a fat fool, bored with problems, a bit neurotic and with a fear of society' (Galliquio 2018). The character laughs at himself and wants others to laugh with him. The author has the 'under' privilege of clumsiness, artisanship, untidiness and misshapenness.

Figure 5.3   David Galliquio as his own character. © David Galliquio

From the first time Avril drew herself, she depicted herself naked. The situation was not erotic; she just dispensed with drawing clothes. It was an act of liberation, given that in Bolivia 'she would appear as a stuffed turkey amongst jackets and scarves'. During the interview, Filomeno enumerates the details of the caricature: 'with my big nose, the little bags under my eyes, my tummy, my big calves, that image in which I have gradually fine-tuned my gestures'. She did not intend to be recognised but to reach maximum self-expression. The author did not say what she meant by maximum self-expression but later in the interview, referring to a poem in comic form by Carlos López Degregori, she remembered that he drew a man naked because that meant only thoughts remained (Figure 5.4). As this was how she realised that her naked characters were abstract ruminations, this may constitute the author's 'maximum self-expression', allowing her hidden privilege to emerge from under layers of censorship: the privilege to abstract.

Figure 5.4   Avril Filomeno's self-portrait for the anthology *Venus ataca*. © Avril Filomeno

Conclusions

In countries with a comics industry, the book brought with it copyright, which up until then had belonged to the syndicate, as well as the valuing of individual over assembly-line production. In that way the author's discourse and name became novelised. Authors left behind the epic or localised heroes of comic strips and became valued as creators of profound writing, joining a publishing market system similar to the literary market. In the Peruvian case, where comics authors always kept copyright and where very few of them were able to devote their professional lives to comics, the introduction of book format comics has not created a noticeable economic change (as with the literary market) but it has favoured the author's political value, something that comics authors prior to Juan Acevedo did not have.

None of the authors interviewed for this chapter have achieved financial sustainability with novelised comics turned into books. But they have managed to obtain three political privileges, namely: to critique without being censored; to connect comics to human rights struggles; and to expand comics as a political tool. However, when it comes to authors representing themselves, only Acevedo does so to any great extent, as a character with the privileges mentioned, even though he does not advertise the fact. The rest of the authors, while all of them recreate themselves in characters who reflect and criticise with complete freedom, focus on depicting their cultural privileges more than their political ones, relating comics to their own thoughts and sharing them as an expressive tool.

Thus, although the role played by Contracultura has not had the once-desired economic impact, it has contributed to the novelisation of authors who know themselves capable of representing the country's existential, social and political conflicts from their subjective point of view. And it has helped those authors participate in a wider community of festivals and exchanges with Latin American authors who share political discourses from the margins of art, testimony and Latin American culture.

Notes

1 For an overview of the disparity in comic production in Latin America, see the chapters by Laura Vazquez and by Enrique Uribe-Jongbloed and Daniel E. Aguilar-Rodríguez in this volume.

2 Genres are agreed categories of classification. Within the tradition of literary studies, it is possible to distinguish two main classifications. The first, which stems from Aristotle, divides literature according to its form of representation: epic, lyric, drama. The second classifies fiction according to theme and is contemporaneous with the book: horror, science fiction, Western. They often coincide: drama is divided into tragedy and comedy, for instance. In the case of comics studies, the second category is used as genre and the first as 'format' (Trabado 2013; Cossio 2018).

3 We might consider a fifth tension: several authors have referred to the discomfort produced by the resignification of certain comics as 'graphic novels' because they see the term as expressing a value judgment and as establishing indeterminate criteria for a superior comic format. The

arguments of Hatfield (2005), Jan Baetens (2008), Pascal Lefèvre (2013) and Barrero (2013) on this hierarchy have updated debates around *auteur* theory from the 1970s (Cuevas Álvarez 1994), which tried to establish structural criteria for film as a product of an author. Similar efforts to determine criteria in relation to comics can be found in the work of Scott McCloud (1993), Trabado (2013), Roger Sabin (2013), Santiago García (2013) and Eddie Campbell (2013).

4   Reviewing *auteur* theory, Michel Foucault displaces the search for structural and ideological patterns in the work of the author by looking at the instrumentalisation of the author as a means of classifying their works (Cuevas Álvarez 1994).

5   For more on the role that comic-book stores, festivals and other events can have in relation to the new scene of graphic novels and fanzines, see Uribe-Jongbloed and Aguilar-Rodríguez's chapter in this volume.

6   *Barbarie: Comics sobre violencia política en el Perú, 1985–1990* (2010) is Cossio's longest documentary about the clash between the Peruvian state and the communist organisation Shining Path that lasted from 1980 to 2000. He has also co-authored *Rupay: Historias gráficas de la violencia en el Perú 1980–1984* (2008).

7   The publication was made up of an elite group of visual and literary artists, notably Leonidas Yerovi, Abraham Valdelomar, Jorge Vinatea Reinoso and Julio Málaga Grenet.

8   There has been no study of the generational influence of this topic in the interpretation of the Internal Armed Conflict.

References

Acevedo, Juan. 1978. *Para hacer historietas*. Lima: Instituto Nacional de Investigación y Desarrollo de la Educación, Retablo de papel ediciones.

Acevedo, Juan. 2018. Interview with the author, 23 June.

Baetens, Jan. 2008. 'Graphic Novels: Literature Without Text?', *English Language Notes* 46, no. 2: 77–88.

Bakhtin, Mikhail. 1996. 'Epic and Novel: Towards a Methodology for the Study of the Novel'. In *Essentials of the Theory of Fiction*, edited by Michael J. Hoffman and Patrick D. Murphy, 43–62. London: Leicester University Press.

Bakhtin, Mikhail M. 2000. *The Dialogical Imagination: Four Essays*. Austin: University of Texas Press.

Barrero, Manuel. 2013. 'La novela gráfica: perversión genérica de una etiqueta editorial'. In *La novela gráfica: Poéticas y modelos narrativos*, edited by José Manuel Trabado, 191–223. Madrid: Arco/Libros.

Campbell, Eddie. 2013. 'La autobiografía en el cómic. Una muy breve introducción a un tema muy extenso, visto desde una bicicleta en marcha'. In *Supercómic: Mutaciones de la novela gráfica contemporánea*, edited by Santiago García, 25–38. Madrid: Errata Naturae Editores.

Corzo, Benjamín. 2018. Interview with the author, 7 June.

Cossio, David. 2018. Interview with the author, 15 June.

Cuevas Álvarez, Efrén. 1994. 'Notas sobre la Teoría del autor en ficciones audiovisuales', *Communication & Society* 7, no. 1: 155–64.

Filomeno, Avril. 2018. Interview with the author, 8 June.

Foucault, Michel. 1991. 'What is an Author?'. In *The Foucault Reader* edited by Paul Rabinow, 101–20. London: Penguin.

García, Santiago. 2013. 'Después del cómic: Una introducción'. In *Supercómic: Mutaciones de la novela gráfica contemporánea*, edited by Santiago García, 7–24. Madrid: Errata Naturae Editores.

Gilliquio, David. 2018. Interview with the author, 24 June.

Greene, Shane. 2016. *Punk and Revolution: 7 More Interpretations of Peruvian Reality*. Durham, NC: Duke University Press.

Hatfield, Charles. 2005. *Alternative Comics: An Emerging Literature*. Jackson: University Press of Mississippi.

Kruijt, Dirk. 1991. *La revolución por decreto: Perú durante el gobierno militar*. Lima: Facultad Latinoamericana de Ciencias Sociales, Mosca Azul Editores.

Lefèvre, Pascal. 2013. 'La importancia de ser publicado'. In *La novela gráfica: Poéticas y modelos narrativos*, edited by José Manuel Trabado, 83–102. Madrid: Arco/Libros.

Magazine Association of America, Inc. 1955. 'Code of the Comics Adopted October 26, 1954'. In *Comic Books and Juvenile Delinquency*, Interim Report of the Senate Committee on the Judiciary. Washington, DC: United States Government Printing Office.

McCloud, Scott. 1993. *Understanding Comics: The Invisible Art*. New York: Harper Collins Publishers.

Milton, Cynthia E., ed. 2014. *Art from a Fractured Past: Memory and Truth-Telling in Post-Shining Path Peru*. Durham, NC: Duke University Press.

Milton, Cynthia E. 2017. 'Death in the Andes: Comics as Means to Broach Stories of Political Violence in Peru'. In *Comics and Memory in Latin America*, edited by Jorge Catalá-Carrasco, Paulo Drinot and James Scorer, 166–96. Pittsburgh: University of Pittsburgh Press.

Ong, Walter. 1982. *Orality and Literacy: The Technologizing of the Word*. New York: Routledge.

Rivas, Jairo. 2018. 'Enfrentar el terruqueo'. *Columna de Opinión Noticias Ser. PE*, 30 May. Last accessed 23 July 2018. http://www.noticiasser.pe/opinion/enfrentar-el-terruqueo.

Sabin, Roger. 2013. 'La novela gráfica en su contexto'. In *La novela gráfica: Poéticas y modelos narrativos*, edited by José Manuel Trabado, 65–82. Madrid: ARCO/LIBROS.

Sagástegui, Carla. 2003. *La historieta peruana: Los primeros 80 años 1887–1957*. Lima: Instituto Cultural Peruano Norteamericano.

Trabado, José Manuel. 2013. 'La novela gráfica en el laberinto de los formatos del cómic'. In *La novela gráfica: Poéticas y modelos narrativos*, edited by José Manuel Trabado, 11–61. Madrid: Arco/Libros.

Various authors. 2010. *Venus Ataca: 10 historietistas peruanas*. Lima: Contracultura.

Villar, Alfredo, ed. 2016. *BÚMM! Historieta y humor gráfico en el Perú: 1978–1992*. Lima: Reservoir Books.

6

Expanded visual experiences and the expressive possibilities of the digital comic in the work of Alejandra Gámez

Carolina González Alvarado
Translated by Alana Jackson

One of the most significant characteristics of contemporary visual production is the hybridisation produced by the presence and combination of various resources and languages that were previously mutually exclusive. Today, works characterised by their multimodal nature are increasingly common. These works are created with diverse systems of signs and levels of communication and where the reader has the opportunity to interact with both visual and written codes, as happens with comics, or with visual and audio codes, as is the case with digital animation. Such hybridisation and transformation of expressive approaches is not the result of a centralised process but of a gradual transformation that is constantly subject to change. Even though comics are, by their very nature, a hybrid form of art, the interactions between comics and other artistic expressions, as well as the use of digital tools when creating comics, have both gradually transformed the way we define comics and also expanded their expressive possibilities.

The means and tools of production have always been important in the evolution and diffusion of comics. Advances in printing techniques, for example, allowed for the publication of caricatures and comics in magazines and newspapers in the nineteenth century. With the growing visibility of graphic narratives and low-cost printing came regular publications and magazines that included caricatures and short comics, as is the case with the Mexican magazine *El hijo del Ahuizote*, a satirical publication which opposed the regime of the then President of Mexico, Porfirio Díaz. Later, the serial publication of comics would allow for the creation of works which would be published and developed piecemeal. In the 1960s and 1970s in Latin America, examples of such works include *Mafalda* by the Argentine artist Quino, the pseudonym of Joaquín Salvador Lavado, which was made up of sequential comic strips that collectively constructed a single narrative world and which would later be compiled in albums. Though addressing different themes, in Mexico the comic *Kalimán*, initially created for Mexican radio by Rafael Cutberto Navarro and Modesto Vázquez González in 1963, was produced by Clemente Uribe Ugarte and sold weekly across the region.

More recently, however, comics in Latin America are increasingly created with digital tools and disseminated via the internet. Tablets for digital drawing and specialised programmes and platforms for publishing comics are common and have transformed graphic narratives. Such transformations are not just an example of moving techniques and publishing formats to a digital world; they have also transformed and expanded the concept of comics itself.

The complex dynamic present in digital comics implies the integration of elements from other digital languages. In this sense, readers must possess far more complex reception mechanisms as, in addition to the components of the semantic code, elements of visual grammar are essential. Readers must not only process more than one mode or language, but must also identify the interconnections between them, including reader reception and publication processes. As a result, digital comics must be positioned at the convergence between medium, structure and discourse, given that each of these instances restructure the language of the comic. Digital comics offer a multiplicity in which the way a work is made is integral to what is talked about.

In many cases, some of which are analysed below, the presence of elements from other forms of visual narratives – such as animation, sound effects, and music, among others – relate specifically to the comic, the characters or the plot, and do not imply significant changes to the structure of comics. In other cases, however, the presence of these elements does suggest a shift in the structure of comics and alters the way they should be interpreted.

Technological developments and the use of digital platforms have also transformed the way comics are edited, published and distributed. The diffusion of comics via the internet has resulted in greater cultural visibility of the form, and there has been significant growth in the self-publishing of comics on digital platforms such as Tumblr, blogs, social networks such as Facebook and Instagram, and applications such as Webtoon. Such platforms have allowed for a closer relationship between creator and reader. As well as readers commenting on works, artists can demonstrate in real time the development and advancement of the creative process, or they can answer questions through videos or video conferencing applications. Such formats allow independent artists to disseminate their work without the need for a publishing house, disrupting the long-standing role of publishing houses as the exclusive representatives of the institutionalisation and validation of a work.

The contemporary Mexican graphic narrative scene has also been transformed by the presence of artists using digital platforms to publish and disseminate their work. The work of the artist Edkkar, for example, has become known mainly via Facebook. Working with fantasy and science fiction, Edkkar has developed his own style that has made him something of an icon. Like other authors, he has published independently a volume entitled *Aleatorio: Un pequeño universo de cómics*, which gives continuity to his comic strips published online. Even though contemporary comics artists tend to develop their careers and presence via the internet, the publication of a printed book continues to lend the artist prestige and status. Despite advances in digital technologies, therefore, the publication of a printed book is still an important output within the world of comics, even for artists who are predominantly webcomic artists.

There are several other well-known creators of Mexican digital graphic narratives who have a very successful presence online but who have also published their work in printed editions. Alberto Nieto, for example, publishes and disseminates his webcomic *Betinorama* on Facebook. Nieto has a large number of online followers and readers, but he has also published *El mapa de mi lonja* (Betinorama 2017), using Betinorama as the author's name, co-edited by the major publishing houses Grijalbo and Random House Mondadori. Another example is the comics artist Jonathan Rosas, the winner of various awards related to graphic design and who has been included in the Catalogue of Illustrators of Children's and Youth Publications created by CONACULTA (National Council for Culture and Arts). Rosas has published his work in digital format on platforms such as Issu, Facebook and Bahence, a platform dedicated to making the creative work of various artists public. He also owns a Tumblr page called *El curioso mundo de Nathan y Joo*, where he publishes an eponymous webcomic. Though his works still achieve wider circulation through social networks, he has also independently published his works in printed versions as fanzines, which can be acquired at special events, and in illustrated children's books. Rosas is not the only example of a self-publishing Mexican author; others have even created their own publishing houses, as is the case of Augusto Mora and his publishing house Muerte Querida or Héctor Germán Santarriaga, one of the founders of the independent publishing house Nostromo. Both Mora and Santarriaga are authors and editors, and the majority of the graphic novels that they have published have been released under the label of their own publishing houses, which gives cohesion and unity to their whole corpus.

These artists, working on both digital and print platforms, form a new generation of Mexican comics artists. Born in the 1980s and 1990s, this generation is not only transforming the themes and discourses of Mexican comics, which previously centred fundamentally on satire and political caricature, but also modifying the processes of creation, publication and reception of comics. The result is a resurgence in Mexican comics that is consolidating the national artistic scene and appealing to an increasingly demanding public.

One example that clearly illustrates this transformation is the comic *Bunsen: ciencia y chocolate* by the Mexican artist Jorge Pinto. This work narrates the unexpected turn of events that affects a diverse group of researchers and scientists in the physics faculty of a university. The characters include research professors, a rebellious monkey, a recent young graduate whose work is devalued, along with other incidental characters who appear throughout the story and who, as a whole, make up a parodic portrait of contradictions, difficulties and dynamics in the university sciences. The comic is narrated episodically in strips of an average of five to eight vignettes. This format, though continuing the tradition of the comic strip, developed its own humorous and ironic tone and visual style which made it easily recognisable in the field of Mexican comics, in large part thanks to the exposure it had on the internet. *Bunsen* was originally published on the internet, on different platforms such as blogs and even on an application available on iOS devices, over a period of 10 years. Since its creation, the project was under the Creative Commons licence, which allowed readers to share the comics freely and create their own stories based on and around the original, thus establishing a kind of open work subject to change at the hands of its readers.

In 2011, when the *Bunsen* comics app was released for sale for iOS devices, a pirate version was launched almost simultaneously with the slogan 'now Dr Mono is a pirate too'. The author saw this version as an opportunity for new readers to discover his work and, in fact, shortly after the pirated version was available on the internet, sales of the original application increased, which suggests that the pirate version encouraged new readers to support the author by buying the official app through the App Store.

In this sense, *Bunsen* formed part of a new model of circulation, and the absence of copyright meant that the comic could be printed, modified and reproduced in different formats and media over the course of a decade. Not having copyright was a decision by the author to consent to free use of the work. Aware that it was inevitable that it would be modified and shared online, he voluntarily freed up the use of the work.

In 2018, the more than 1,000 comics that formed *Bunsen* were compiled in a printed edition, prepared by the independent publishing house La Cifra, to commemorate the conclusion of this work (Pinto 2018). This collection was put on sale inside a case which also contained collectable picture cards, printouts of the characters in formats suitable for framing, as well as a certificate, signed by the author, which gave authenticity and legitimacy to the work. Though the comic strips that make up the printed volume can also be found on the web page of the author, the printed collection forms a physical archive and a tangible example of the work carried out by the author. Here again it is clear that artists feel it is important to have a tangible and concrete sample of their work. In turn, such products become desirable for readers, circulating in the market not just as a form of representation but also as a collectable product.

The care and attention that the editor dedicated to publishing this compilation provides a certain cohesion and structure to a work created with different tools and techniques over the course of several years. Here the publishing house retains a significant role in terms of the configuration of the final product, consolidating the creative heterogeneity of the artist into a coherent volume in which the comic strips are in dialogue with each other. The final product also commemorates the conclusion to *Bunsen*, providing a means to satisfy both established and new readers.

Bunsen's dissemination on the internet was rhizomatic, facilitating dialogue with the public, allowing its entry into the national graphic narrative scene and contributing to its subsequent publication with a publishing company. The process of notoriety happened inversely: the publication in print was the result of the recognition and trajectory that it already had in digital form, such that the publication in physical format is material evidence of the importance of digital comics in the Latin American field. The process of reception and publication of *Bunsen* is similar to the work of various Mexican comics artists, whose success online has allowed them to finance the printed publication of their work through crowdfunding campaigns or by securing grants or awards.

Despite the global reach artists can achieve by publishing their work online, interest in publishing printed versions persists. The average print run of comics publications in Latin America is around 1,000 copies, a number that represents the possible profits for the publishing houses in this type of artistic expression, as well as indicating high levels of reader interest. That is compounded by the fact that, even though the entire print run usually does not sell out very quickly, the cost of the publication itself is usually expensive since a special paper is generally used to obtain high-quality image resolution, many of the works are in colour, and the editing process is more complex than in standard fictional texts.

An example such as *Bunsen* demonstrates how the processes of comics publication are changing and how that affects other facets of the comics world, such as reader reception, the circulation of digital comics on the internet, authors' rights and costs (which, in the case of online publishing, are reduced). These modify the reception of comics in an environment where digital platforms have increased the cultural visibility of comics and encouraged a growth in self-publishing.

In the world of Mexican publishing, publishers dedicated to graphic narratives are facing difficulties such as the reduced number of spaces where works can be sold, as well as difficulties in securing funds to enable the publication of larger print runs or to expand their catalogue of works. The presence of North American comics, especially superhero comics, which are very popular among graphic narrative readers in Mexico, hinders the dissemination and sale of more independent or experimental works. That said, the creation of festivals such as Pixelalt, an annual event that aims to publicise the work of independent artists through conferences, presentations and prizes; the establishment of publishers specialising in graphic narrative, such as La Cifra or Resistencia; and institutional initiatives such as the creation of a grant focused on graphic narrative awarded through the FONCA (National Fund for Culture and the Arts) are promoting and boosting the creation of graphic narratives in Mexico. So though we might talk of a crisis in terms of the conflicts and difficulties that both artists and independent publishers face in Mexico, we can also talk of a revival in the creative scene of comics and an expansion in artistic and cultural possibilities.

Given this context, I will explore how technological developments have transformed the way we understand and study comics in terms of processes of adaptation and intermediality and the relationship between comics and other visual narratives. To address these issues I focus on the work of the artist Alejandra Gámez, whose presence in the field of Latin American graphic narrative has gained in prominence in recent years, due both to the quality of her work and to the growing popularity she has gained through her use of social networks and self-publication in digital and physical formats.

That Gámez's work is published both online and in hard copy places demands on the artist to produce comics that can be replicated on different platforms, whether that be social networks, a web page, physical books or even merchandise, given that the author also has an online shop selling badges, patches for clothes, a soft toy of Lucía, the peculiar protagonist of her comic strips, along with other products with designs taken from her comics. In this sense, the work of Alejandra Gámez stands out due to the originality of her work within the world of Mexican graphic narrative, and, at the same time, illustrates the processes of remediation and reception to which her work is subject.

Gámez has become one of the most representative voices of Mexican comics precisely because of her work within the broad panorama of digital graphic narrative, as well as her engagement with the growing trend in visual and transmedial readings. Within the wider context of Latin American comics, Gámez's career has been extremely successful. As well as publishing several books, winning grants, and running very successful co-funding campaigns, she has developed a strong and close relationship with her readers. Her fictional universe, populated by specific characters, scenarios and rules, a space where the quotidian encounters the sinister aspects of fantasy, means that she has developed a clearly recognisable visual and narrative style. Her combination of tender and cute characters who nonetheless have disturbing elements lends her stories a metaphorical power that moves beyond individual comic strips to construct a narrative world.

Gámez's work is also a clear example of how digital comics have developed in Mexico in recent years and how technology and social media have transformed the creation and circulation of comics and the relationship between author and readers. Gámez's digital output highlights the tensions between the potential loss of aura, as understood by Walter Benjamin (2009), that circulates around the physical object, and the production of communities that consume her work online. And yet, the fact that Gámez recently published a graphic novel entitled *Más allá de las ciudades* (Gámez and Eneas 2018), a collaboration between Axul Eneas and the Spanish-language publisher Océano, and because her previous works are available in physical format (*The mountain with teeth* (Gámez, 2014, 2015, 2017) and *Un claro en el bosque* (Gámez 2016) are both collectable objects among comics readers), suggests that she nonetheless values the aura and prestige of the hard copy.

In the following section I provide a more focused discussion and definition of digital comics, before going on to analyse the artistic and formal qualities of Gámez's work, as well as its reception and publication process.

Digital comics and online comics

The publishing of literary and visual content on the internet is also transforming the publishing industry and the modes of circulation of comics. The internet also allows for a particular interaction between creator and reader such that the form of creating and reading the language of comics has contributed to a creative transformation which goes beyond technique and means, also establishing a new way of reading and interpreting comics. These new interactions, which often include visual and narrative elements from other media, especially cinema and digital animation, has expanded the very concept of the comic, to the point that the term 'online comic' refers to a type of comic published online. In this sense, I believe that online comics question what a comic actually is. For the purpose of this initial reflection, I take the online comic, also called webcomic, as a comic published online or whose sales, distribution and reading is primarily dependent on the internet. I use the term digital comic to refer to works whose format and reading depends on a digital medium, whether an application on a mobile device, an internet webpage, or a blog, etc.

In the comic, visual and written codes have a dynamic, non-hierarchical relationship that constructs a particular language. However, the incursion of elements from other visual grammars transforms what we usually refer to as the language of comics. In his book *Reinventing Comics*, Scott McCloud picks up various arguments from his previous work, *Understanding Comics*, and gives us one of the fundamental critical tools for this study. McCloud focuses on the manner in which time and space are related, describing it in the following way: 'In relying on *visual sequence*, comics substitutes *space* for *time*' (2000, 2; original emphasis); in this sense, 'moving through time requires moving through space' (217). McCloud's proposal directs our attention towards the manner in which the language of comics establishes a relation between space, visually represented, and time, the intangible but fundamental basis for the development of narrative. In the last decade or so, online comics have altered notions of time within comics by incorporating elements of digital animation in such a way that movement is given not just by the ordering of elements in the visual space but also by the alteration of the image.

Discussing digital comics, even given today's diverse visual languages, is problematic. The study of digital comics is a relatively recent field that is developing alongside the swift evolution of online platforms and tools. The study of online comics is not without areas of controversy, especially around their expressive capacity and the innovations that they may or may not bring to the language of comics. The academic Thierry Groensteen, for example, in his book *Comics and Narration* (2013), argues that digital tools do not bring about significant changes to the 'system of comics', as he calls it, given that online comics maintain the structure and essential basic distribution of the comic page. Groensteen describes the reading experience of a comic in digital format as a limited practice in which the reader's body is subject to statism. If in the reading of a comic in physical format the reader must use their upper body to hold a work and interact with it physically, when reading a piece of work in digital format this experience 'is replaced by intermittent pressure on the mouse from the reader's index finger' (Groensteen 2013, 66). Groensteen even highlights that the difficulty of retaining specific content is detrimental to the process of reception 'apart from the fact that digital media are characterised by the removal of content from a surrounding context, when a comic is read on the screen, as each page succeeds the next it also replaces and effaces it, precluding the mental retention of the arrangement of panels' (2013, 67). In general, then, Groensteen believes that the reading experience of digital comics is simply the 'viewing of contents online'.

In his analysis, Groensteen refers to comics which were originally published in print format and subsequently adapted to digital formats through applications on portable electronic devices, which are easy to download and transport but that essentially did not transform the language of comics, as is the case with apps by DC Comics, Marvel or Dark Horse. Another example of an application for mobile devices including tablets is Web Toon, a free app which offers an extensive and varied catalogue of styles, authors and themes in such a way that the reader can access a wide range of narrative and visual styles. Though the comics are created to be read on a mobile phone or a tablet, the reading experience is limited to the space offered by the screen and the narrative progresses by scrolling the touchscreen.

I would argue, however, that Groensteen underplays the importance of another type of comics artist who creates works expressly to be read online. These works have sufficient malleability to be published in physical/paper format and to function effectively in both mediums. In that sense, apart from a growth in accessibility, Groensteen also ignores the interaction that is enabled between readers and authors via webcomics. The reader is no longer limited to being a mere recipient of content but is now an active subject who can intervene in the creative process via comments, or even through both formal and discursive modifications, as with the hybrid comic *Framed* discussed below. In that sense, contrary to Groensteen's position, I would suggest that digital comics do indeed expand the expressive possibilities of the language of comics.

Although in appearance the differentiation appears obvious, within the wider panorama of graphic narrative digital comics present a high degree of structural and discursive complexity which requires us, as critical readers, to undertake a theoretical and methodological exploration tailored to this object of study. Digital comics have allowed for the hybridisation of different mediums including digital animation, auditory games, music, reader interactivity, colour changes, as well as the incorporation of tools that allow for displacement between vignettes and pages, all of which have contributed to experimentation and the development of a set of dynamics in which the word and the image have expanded their expressive capacity.

Contrary to Groensteen's standpoint, elements brought into comics from other visual disciplines, such as cinema and animation, are not unnecessary impositions: 'these add-ons tend to curb the reader's imagination and, in any case, to impose an extraneous rhythm on the reading process' (Groensteen 2013, 71). They are an aesthetic response to an environment in which the digital is transforming ways of creating and reading content. In this sense, comics artists are not limiting themselves to conventional means of creation but are delving into their role as creators of sequential visual narratives, developing new strategies and broadening the limits of the language of comics. Here I highlight two prevailing characteristics of digital comics: hybridisation and experimentation.

Digital comics offer the possibility of a multisensorial reading experience in which the reader is recipient and interpreter, as well as an active and transformative agent. At the same time, artists face the challenge of not only offering plots which are attractive and capable of capturing the attention of readers but also developing narrative strategies which respond to the constant transformations that characterise the digital setting. As a result, the limits of the concept of the comic are becoming blurred.

The dialogue between word and image and the blurring of the boundaries between digital animation and comics force us to reassess the very nature of these cultural forms and their forms of expression, insofar as they are linked to the culture of the image. In this sense, we can offer a more accurate and complete definition of digital comics as an intercultural construction comprising heterogeneous narrative devices that also facilitate and, in many cases, promote a direct and active relationship with the reader, while expanding the aesthetic and narrative qualities of the comic. Within what I call digital comics we can also find 'expanded comics', 'video comics', 'painting in virtual reality' and 'motion comics'. These terms are intimately related but have differences with regard to the narrative effects that each of them pursues and their discursive and structural qualities.

The term 'expanded comic' refers to a variant of digital comics, in that such comics maintain the use of vignettes and speech bubbles, as well as the use of the visual space of traditional comics, but they also incorporate elements such as movement, music, dialogue, scenes, sound effects, among others, from other media, such as cinema, both in the creative process as well as in the final product. The transitions from one vignette to the next conserve the essential character of the language of comics, that is to say, the sequence and disposition of space in relation to time and movement. But each vignette is animated and possesses elements that approximate cinematographic narrative. In the expanded comic the movement between pages occurs as it does with a printed comic, emulating the physical journey that the reader would otherwise undertake with a print comic. As the name implies, these comics expand the experience of comics: the digital is not just a medium but a tool for modifying the way the comic is read.

One of the most representative examples of expanded comics in Latin America is *Dark Pulsar*, created by a team of illustrators, digital artists, composers, translators, sculptors and digital developers, all directed by Diego Escalada, director of the 7th Art Studio located in Buenos Aires, Argentina (Escalada 2015). The studio has also created digital animation and content development spanning education, publicity, illustration, 3D packaging, and they also have an education programme called *Art Land Escuela de Arte*, which trains new artists and professionals in the field of the creative arts and industries.

Dark Pulsar can be read using the expanded comics app for iOS devices, specifically the iPad, and is available in five different languages.

Dark Pulsar forms part of a series of comics with the studio's aesthetic style, drawing on science fiction and the presence of robots and human-technological bodies that inhabit a dystopian and hypertechnologised city. It is a product which conserves, in essential terms, the structure of a traditional comic, as previously mentioned, such as the linearity and use of vignettes, but obliges us to decode a moving image while discerning a meaningful unity with the rest of the vignettes, which are in constant dynamism, and their relationship with the development of the narrative action.

The comic's movement produces a particular experience in the reader, obliging them to focus their attention on the development of the story. In this sense, *Dark Pulsar* positions itself in the liminal space between comics and cinema. The reader can pause for as long as they like when reading a vignette, or they can move through the pages with the speed of an action film, avoiding the temporal pace associated with reading a traditional comic. The presence of music and sound effects designed specifically for this work conveys a particular atmosphere and meaning for each individual image. The root menu also has sound and animation effects. While the reader advances through the pages, the sound and music also change, expanding the sensorial experience of reading and giving each page a specific atmosphere. And yet vignettes are preserved, as is the use of onomatopoeia and speech bubbles. As a result, reading a work such as *Dark Pulsar* presents us with a multidimensional process characterised by simultaneity. Reading this work implies a complex exercise in decodification which requires us to carry out a revision of our basic visual strategies.

One other example of expanded comics is *Framed*, a hybrid device between a video game, digital comic and puzzle. Developed by the Australian studio Loveshack and available in various languages, *Framed* is a digital app available for mobiles and electronic tablets, compatible with both iOS and Android (Loveshack 2012). It has won various awards, including best game at the Freeplay Independent Games Festival (2013), best narrative at the Brazil Independent Games Festival (2014), and best visual design at Indiecade (2014), among other awards. *Framed* might be described as a game whose pieces (the vignettes) are mobile. With a style associated with detective and suspense literature, the reader not only decides the fate of the character but must also work out a mystery. In this way, the narrative is transformed by the choices made by the reader-player, ultimately modifying the ending of the story.

Motion comics, video comics and virtual reality are also moving visual narratives. Motion comics, also called multimedia comics, alter the elements that make up the semiotics of comics by incorporating elements from digital animation. Motion comics are directly related to video comics, a discursive form in which digital animation allows for the creation of short videos, like microfilms, in which a microfiction is narrated by means of moving images and the incorporation of components of cinematography such as sound effects and visual displacements. It is important to differentiate these expressions from expanded comics since multimedia comics, despite their shared characteristics, are closer to digital animation and cinema, whereas expanded comics maintain, without modifications, the 'traditional' semantic elements of comics, such as the use of panels and balloons.

To date, there are no examples within Mexican digital graphic narrative of these large-scale projects, but there are many works that incorporate elements of the traits I have referred to above. In Jonathan Rosas's webcomic *El curioso mundo ilustrado de Nathan y Joo*, for example, some of the characters and visual elements that make up the page are animated, adding dynamism to the work and expanding the reading experience. The use of gifs – animated images on a static background – is also common practice among many artists, including Alejandra Gámez.

The borrowings that comics have made from other cultural forms have converted them into an intertextual network of diverse references. The flow of elements belonging to other visual media has widened the aesthetic and conceptual repertoire of the comic to blur the boundaries between institutional art and the popular, and the local and the global, enriching the aesthetic language of the form. Motion comics in particular call into question the understanding of the language of comics as being a series of juxtaposed images that represent a succession of events in a set time, as proposed by McCloud. In this modality of digital comics, time is disrupted when these images acquire movement, whether as a result of the animation effects present in each vignette, or due to the distribution of the elements with which they are composed. Due to both their origin and development, the reception of digital comics is complicated due to the demands they exert on the reader. Digital comics are not a substitute for, or an answer to, the growing demand for visual sources of entertainment since they possess stylistic qualities that are quite complex. Digital comics have progressively reached a high level of structural and discursive complexity that means they are increasingly directed at a public with high levels of (comics) reading competence, a shift that is exacerbated with digital narratives.

Motion comics and Alejandra Gámez's creation of a visual language

Alejandra Gámez has been publishing weekly comics on her Tumblr page *The mountain with teeth* for over four years. The artist's work has been received very positively, owing both to the quality of her work and to the active relationship that she maintains with her readers on social networks. Thanks to this interaction, which includes voluntary donations from her readers, she published the first volume of her comic in 2014 with the title *The mountain with teeth* (Gámez 2014), followed shortly after in 2015 with a second volume entitled *The mountain with teeth 2* (Gámez 2015a), and a further volume entitled *The mountain with teeth, historias de piedra* in 2017 (Gámez 2017). Her graphic novel *Un claro en el bosque* won first prize in the SecuenciArte (2015) competition, organised as part of the Festival Pixelatl and, thanks to this award, this work was released in print format the following year (Gámez 2016b). The annual Festival Pixelatl promotes the creation and dissemination of multimedia narratives and content, with the aim of generating strategies to encourage the development of creative and multimedia industries in Mexico and to make the work of artists and creators better known at a national and international level. Since its beginnings, the Festival Pixelalt has managed to generate a community of creators in different cultural industries, promoting the development of cultural creation in Mexico, as well as offering a global vision by extending invitations to internationally recognised figures. Artists who win one of the festival's prizes not only earn the recognition that goes with the award but are helped with the publication of their work in physical format, as was the case with Gámez. Once again, even though some of the comics included in her books are also published on her Tumblr page, the artist's interest in publishing work in printed versions is clear.

Over time, Gámez has used the digital platform of *The mountain with teeth* to publicise brief comments, messages for her readers, invitations to conventions or conferences and also brief reflections on her publications. These comics are replicated on other platforms like Instagram and Facebook where the use of hashtags not only describes the publication but lends it an identity. In that way readers can familiarise themselves with the artist by following her announcements, updates and messages. In these ways the role of the author becomes more explicitly both creator and self-promoter. This practice shows how Gámez builds an active and close relationship with her readers, further indication of, as Edward King puts it in his chapter in this volume (136), the way that 'digital comics have developed in close connection with social media platforms'.

Another attribute of this active dialogue with her readers is that Gámez frequently creates illustrations or short comics about a popular movie or recent television series. By using images or visual narrative devices, she expresses her opinion or, in some cases, presents a different version of a specific scene. In that sense, her images are related to different types of visual material so the reader must consider 'the different information – social, historical, imaginary – each type of image communicates alone and in combination with other types of images in a comics universe. In these instances, readers are asked to engage multiple visual literacies, to integrate them in the construction of the storyworld, and to synthesize them into a coherent narrative meaning' (Pedri 2017). In addition, readers take part in the conversation not only by commenting via posts but also by expanding the story or adding more images by using emoticons or, sometimes, even an original illustration. What started as a single publication in a social media context is transformed into an open and interactive design space.

The reader not only makes connections to other visual narratives but also has to be familiar with the plot and be able to interpret it, writing opinions or, as suggested above, expanding the story. Thus, 'the reader must be able to understand the semiotic interplay of all these modes and often of visual modes and verbal discourse in particular, so that reading becomes a multi-literate act based on the capacity to integrate a range of single literacies' (Hallet, cited in Pedri 2017).

Given this multiliteracy, it is perhaps unsurprising that the artist is interested in other kinds of visual expression, such as digital animation. Gámez is currently working on a series of short films based on some of her comics. She has a MicroToon on the YouTube channel Atomo Network Channel, a network made up of a community of Spanish-speaking digital animators and creators. Atomo Network Channel is the product of a collaboration between Channel Frederator Network in the US and Ánima Estudios in Mexico and Spain, and its purpose is to support and disseminate the work of artists and increase visibility. Gámez recently published a short animation on this channel entitled 'El lugar correcto', a minifiction that maintains the aesthetic and theme of the comics that she publishes on her Tumblr page but that is enhanced by sound effects and moving images, as well as opening and closing curtains.

Gámez's interest in animation projects is indicative of the way that flashes of such techniques are visible in some of her comics, especially with her use of gifs. In the motion comic entitled 'Proceso creativo'

(Figure 6.1), Gámez (2016a) depicts herself as a character in the company of fellow artist Axur Eneas. By means of simple animations and short sequences, the characters converse about the creative process of the comic. As the dialogue advances, the expressions of the characters also change with their comments, echoing animation scene by scene. Here digital comics involve 'multiple (often interwoven) modes of expression' that demand of the reader 'the mastery of a number of different literacies' (Leber-Cook and Cook 2013). The reader must follow the rhythm of the story and move forward by observing and reading a panel that is constantly moving and transforming. In this particular example the theme of the motion comic is the creative process itself. By mixing different visual expressions, Gámez reflects on the artistic process and, simultaneously, explores the expressive possibilities of comics. This is an example of how 'in comics that narrate across different types of images, readers join aesthetic considerations with considerations of how a particular type of image communicates and what meanings are implied in its mode of production, its history, and its familiarity to readers' (Pedri 2017).

Figure 6.1   'Proceso creativo'. © Alejandra Gámez

In one further case, the author describes another untitled example (Figure 6.2) in the following way: 'This week there was no comic . . . or rather maybe there was, because I don't really know what to call it, but I hope you like it. Something along the lines of a winter story' (Gámez 2015b). The doubt introduced by the artist when describing this piece highlights the border zone in which motion comics, as an artistic manifestation of the blend between the language of comics and digital animation, are located. The image shows a young woman with her back to the viewer against a snowy backdrop, along with a small sign that translates her thoughts as the snow falls and begins to settle on her. The animation is accompanied by music and the scene can be interpreted as the condensation of time in visual space. In this motion comic the elements of the image, both due to their disposition as well as the movement and the music, are transformed into visual symbols. As Pedri suggests, 'the mixing of visual images in comics thus orchestrates a unique reading experience, one that draws on the preconceived notion of readers, accentuates the mechanisms of visual storytelling, instates complex multimodal reading practices, and distinguishes comics as a highly malleable and experimental multimodal form' (Pedri 2017). Cases like these show how, in motion comics, the music, the movement and the image itself are part of the same expressive unit.

Figure 6.2   *Sin título*. © Alejandra Gámez

These examples highlight how the digital comic is an intercultural construction in which heterogeneous narrative devices both facilitate and often promote a direct and active relationship with the reader, while expanding the aesthetic and narrative qualities of the comic. This digital and media textuality, a discursive reality consisting of the interaction of elements taken from the wide spectrum of expressive media, has consolidated the popularity of the artist's work. At the same time, Gámez's textual landscape of hybrid and transmedia practices demands a revision of the traditional concept of the comic. The work of Gámez constitutes a symbolic construct that requires a transversal and peripheral reading process, as its elements do not follow a linear narrative but a multidirectional one produced by moving visual components.

Gámez frequently experiments with the virtual space of the author and the mechanisms of fiction that are involved in the production of the 'self', as can be seen in the untitled comic, which centres on self-worth. In this comic, the difficulties the artist faces in recognising the quality of her work are narrated with autobiographical overtones. Gámez unfolds her voice and image to represent an internal, personal conflict. In this sense, the use and construction of the 'self' are implicated in the fiction and the visual scenario that constitutes the digital comic.

The comic 'Sombra azul' (Gámez 2018; Figure 6.3) is a further example in which the author uses the first person to narrate an emotional state – represented by a little blue man resembling a small flame – of the protagonist narrator. Later on, as the narrative advances, we discover that this phantasmagorical figure is the symbolic duplication of the author. With graphic narrations such as these, Gámez situates herself within the field of autobiographical comics, in which the distinction between the poetic 'self' and the creator is blurred. She undertakes a similar approach in the comic 'Órganos' in which the fictional image of the author is recovering from cramps. The setting is very much everyday but, through reflections focused on her anatomy, the author's soliloquy expresses an awareness of being mortal. As in the previous examples, the author constantly interweaves the sinister and the disturbing with characters whose appearance is tender and friendly. Nevertheless, her comics do not indulge in excesses or gratuitous violence but rather create their own symbolic universe.

Figure 6.3   'Sombra azul'. © Alejandra Gámez

Over the past decade, discussions of autobiographical aesthetic qualities have focused on the construction of the 'self' in writing and its role in auto-fiction. Phoebe Gloeckner (2011) has questioned the possibilities of auto-fictional writing, suggesting that the term itself contradicts its own nature. The word auto-fiction implies the union of two concepts to construct a new one: on the one hand, the prefix auto-, which refers to the self; on the other, the term fiction, which refers to a story that did not take place exactly in the manner described. Such narratives imply a contract between the speaker, the creator of the narrative, and the reader. The pact of verisimilitude, by which the reader renounces the need for evidence to verify the narrative, allows the fiction to acquire a degree of truth.

Language allows this dynamic because, as Gloeckner indicates, the game is permitted via word play:

> I am not writing about myself – I am delivering myself of myself, and that is not what I'd call autobiography – it is, rather, a form of suicide.
>
> I aspire to create characters who can be universally understood despite being constructed with details so numerous that they could only refer to a particular situation. The process is destructive – I must die so that Minnie can live. I don't want her to be me – she must be all girls, anyone. I am the source of Minnie, but I am depleted in creating her. This is not history or documentary or a confession, and memories will be altered or sacrificed, for factual truth has little significance in the pursuit of emotional truth.
>
> (Gloeckner 2011, 179)

As Gloeckner notes, artifice is essential in auto-fictional writing as language is focused on aesthetic creation, such that this apparent confusion of the real and the fictional is nothing other than a mechanism that makes the narrative possible.

In the case of Gámez's work this device is even more complex due to the synergy between word and image and the autobiographical character of a number of her comics. It would be easy to assume that, because the main character in a number of her comics shares not only the name but also the physical appearance of the author, these comics are autobiographical. However, despite such correspondence, it would be inappropriate to jump to the conclusion that these are life stories of the author, either in part or in their entirety. Even if the author had made an accurate account of her experiences, the mediation of the language and the literary construct would be creating a fictional construct. That said, the author deliberately creates a close association between herself and her textual persona, which creates the impression that the reader is actually reading a true experience lived by the author. The presence of fantastic and symbolic elements creates a tension, a sleight of hand that, on the one hand, puts the reader closer to the author but, on the other, simultaneously distances them from the real figure of the artist. This dynamic creates a further set of complexities around the notion of the author discussed by Carla Sagástegui Heredia in this volume precisely because here the reader is invited to become part of the symbolic life created by the author.

Since most of the work of Alejandra Gámez is published on the internet, it is very easy for the reader to comment, share and like her work. Gámez often answers comments in a friendly manner, joking with her followers and, in so doing, creates a digital community comprising her and her readers. Sometimes she even creates comics strips to please her readers or make announcements. For example, when she announced the publication of her new book *Más allá de las ciudades* on Facebook, she created a short comic and wrote a very brief story related to this graphic novel.

The digital works of Alejandra Gámez, whether her illustrations, motion comics or digital comics, create an integral and complex visual and narrative discourse that interacts with other media expressions or with characters or short stories created by the artist herself. In this way, Gamez's digital expressions develop the reader's multimodal competence, that is to say, their capacity to choose, to develop connecting and interrelating skills, and to acquire the knowledge necessary for the reception of texts constructed of different codes and means. As a result, Gámez is developing an oeuvre that produces meaning out of a unifying perspective. As well as her unique style, the digital platforms where she publishes her work connect to each other, forming a unit that is constantly evolving in tune with the very platforms and digital tools themselves, which makes for an extremely dynamic output. As an artform in constant transformation, digital comics require us to constantly reconsider their diverse elements and the way they operate. These changes take place structurally due to the presence of animation, sound effects and the arrangement of other technical elements; semantically, due to the articulation of these elements and the way they question the intrinsic relationship between content and form; and also discursively, in terms of new linguistic forms of presenting narrative. The digital in digital comics is not only a tool or support but also a fundamental part of the composition of the work. In this sense, digital comics are made up of different codes that together create an aesthetic, visual and narrative relationship.

In the particular case of Mexico, the world of digital comics is still developing. That many contemporary comics authors and artists publish their work online and, following favourable reception by readers and at specialised events, fairs, conventions and contests, then publish their work in print format, raises the question as to where an author's standing within national graphic narrative lies. Without devaluing the quality of their work, it is noteworthy that, though the majority of comics artists use online spaces and social networks to make their work public, publication by a print publisher still grants them a legitimacy that is otherwise difficult to obtain. Alejandra Gámez started publishing her work online and, after she obtained recognition from both readers and cultural institutions, she then published her work in printed formats. Even today, with a very active online presence and with her more experimental work being published on the internet, she still looks to printed publications as material support for her artistic work and, quite possibly, to formalise her career and output.

Though many Mexican comics artists want to publish their work in printed format, the free distribution of digital content online is now an essential part of the comics world. In fact, artists design a large part of their creative production to be released online. Thus, though printed editions are important, digital comics have established more direct relationships between author and consumer, resulting in greater reader participation at the point of creation. In the case of Alejandra Gámez, despite having published content both independently and with a publishing house with wide circulation, she continues to publish content, on her Tumblr page and on social networks, that establishes and develops out of creative dialogues with her readers, which has enabled her to construct visual symbols that give her comics a specific identity.

As I have suggested in this chapter, the work of Alejandra Gámez not only illustrates how digital comics transform the language of comics but also demonstrates the speed and adaptability needed by artists in an environment in constant transformation, with such a diverse range of material available for consumption and with the continuing need to publish work in printed editions. The study of digital comics themselves is also subject to such constant changes, and we must be open to analysing works that do not fit with conventional models but that demand new analytical strategies of us.

References

Benjamin, Walter. 2009. *One-Way Street*. London: Penguin.

Betinorama. 2017. *El mapa de mi lonja*. Mexico City: Grijalbo/Penguin Random House.

Esclada, Diego. 2015. *Dark Pulsar*. Digital application. Last accessed 8 October 2019. https://itunes.apple.com/us/app/expanded-comics/id962204800?mt=8.

Gámez, Alejandra. 2014. *The mountain with teeth*. Author's self-published edition.

Gámez, Alejandra. 2015a. *The mountain with teeth 2*. Author's self-published edition.

Gámez, Alejandra. 2015b. 'Sin título'. From *The mountain with teeth*, 18 December. Last accessed 8 October 2019. http://mountainwithteeth.com/post/135480267663/esta-semana-no-hubo-c%C3%B3mic-o-bueno-a-lo-mejor-s%C3%AD.

Gámez, Alejandra. 2016a. 'Proceso creativo'. From *The mountain with teeth*, 6 June. Last accessed 8 October 2019. https://mountainwithteeth.com/post/145536416670/el-fin-de-semana-dimos-una-conferencia-sobre-el.

Gámez, Alejandra. 2016b. *Un claro en el bosque*. Mexico City: Pixelatl.

Gámez, Alejandra. 2017. *The mountain with teeth, historias de piedra*. Author's self-published edition.

Gámez, Alejandra. 2018. 'Sombra azul'. From *The mountain with teeth*, 8 August. Last accessed 8 October 2019. http://mountainwithteeth.com/post/176776843700/sombra-azul-una-peque%C3%B1a-historia-para-este.

Gámez, Alejandra and Axur Eneas. 2018. *Más allá de las ciudades*. Mexico City: Océano Historias Gráficas.

Gloeckner, Phoebe. 2011. 'Autobiography: The Process Negates the Term'. In *Graphic Subjects: Critical Essays on Autobiography and Graphic Novels*, edited by Mitchel A. Chaney, 178–9. Madison: University of Wisconsin Press.

Groensteen, Thierry. 2013. *Comics and Narration*. Jackson: University Press of Mississippi.

Leber-Cook Alice and Roy Cook. 2013. 'Stigmatization, Multimodality and Metaphor: Comics in the Adult English as a Second Language Classroom'. In *Graphic Novels and Comics in the Classroom: Essays on the Educational Power of Sequential Art*, edited by Carrye Kay Syma and Robert G. Weiner, 23–34. Jefferson, NC: McFarland.

Loveshack Studio. 2012. *Framed*. Digital application. Last accessed 8 October 2019. https://itunes.apple.com/us/app/framed/id886565180?mt=8.

McCloud, Scott. 2000. *Reinventing Comics: The Evolution of an Art Form*. New York: Harper Collins.

Pedri, Nancy. 2017. 'Mixing Visual Media in Comics', *ImageTexT: Interdisciplinary Comic Studies* 9, no. 2. Last accessed 23 October 2019. http://imagetext.english.ufl.edu/archives/v9_2/introduction/introduction.shtml.

Pinto, Jorge. 2018. *Bunsen: Un comic de ciencia y chocolate*. Mexico City: La Cifra.

7

Autographic selfies: Digital comics, social media and networked photography

Edward King

In a post-internet age, in which access to online information is increasingly controlled by a small number of gatekeepers, digital comics have developed in close connection with social media platforms. After years of debate as to what digital comics actually are – whether an extension of print comics or an entirely distinct medium (see Wilde 2015) – there has been little discussion of the role played by social media in the production of comics both constructed with digital technologies and consumed through digital interfaces. This, despite the fact that sites such as Facebook, Instagram, Twitter and Tumblr have become the primary means by which comics find their readers, whether it be through social media campaign battles between industrial giants Marvel and DC (see Brundige 2015), or their use by emerging independent artists to develop a style in dialogue with readers (see, for example, Carolina González Alvarado's chapter in this volume). Rather than the potential of what Scott McCloud termed the 'infinite canvas' (2000, 200–42) (in which the computer monitor is converted into a 'window' onto an infinitely vast comic-book page) or the ability to divide the page into dynamic individual panels that the reader must click through (an approach performed by French cartoonist Yves 'Balak' Bigerel in his 2009 comic-manifesto 'About Digital Comics'), it is the interface provided by the social media giants that is proving the most influential on contemporary comic-book production. While the affordances and constraints of sites such as Instagram contain elements of both of these approaches, depending on whether you view a profile on one potentially endless scroll or as individual images that you click through one at a time, the use of social media also foregrounds an aspect of digital comics less often invoked to describe them as either a distinct medium or an organic development of print comics: their status as networked objects.

This confluence of digital comics and the networked logic of social media has been nowhere more in evidence than in Brazil. In part, this is due to the dominant role of social media sites in the country. Following a period of economic growth, coupled with government-led digital dissemination initiatives (see Oram 2016), Brazil experienced an unusually abrupt social media uptake during the mid-2000s to become the home of the second-most active population on social media in the world after the US. The spread of information and formation of opinion made possible by social media played a key role in the ensuing social and political crisis that, at the time of writing, continues to grip the country. Citizen journalist organisations such as Mídia Ninja turned their preferred platforms (Instagram and Facebook) into the prime sources of information during the anti-government protests of 2013 as well as the subsequent state-driven repression. During these same events, both ends of the political spectrum harnessed the viral spread of internet memes to mobilise and manipulate public opinion while, following the decree of Federal Law No. 12.034, official political candidates standing for election attempted to secure votes through social media sites that held the promise of more direct connections to voters than afforded by the broadcast media of radio and TV (see Arnaudo 2017). In many ways, the instrumental role of social media websites in the 2014 presidential elections in Brazil provided a precedent and model for the much more heavily publicised manipulation of user information during the US elections of 2016. Social media in Brazil has become the stage on which individuals position themselves in relation to the latest developments and declare political affiliations and oppositions. It is where social divisions are performed, reaffirmed, and sometimes contested.

The booming domestic comic-book industry in Brazil has also harnessed this abrupt social media uptake. This encounter has taken a number of forms, whether it be the use of online platforms by individual practitioners for crowdfunding campaigns, publicity pushes by established corporations such as Maurício de Sousa Produções, or the diffusion of satirical cartoons, or 'tiras', in online commentary on political debates (such as the work of Laerte or Angeli). One of the most striking trends in this convergence of social media and digital comics has been the focus on the individual: the use of the form for creative and self-reflexive re-imaginings of the self. In many ways, this is a tendency specific neither to the Brazilian context nor to the digital turn in comic-book cultures. In her chapter in this volume, Carla Sagástegui Heredia discusses the strategies of self-representation carried out by Peruvian comics artists, including Juan Acevedo and David Galliquio. Jan Baetens and Hugo Frey, meanwhile, identify autobiography as one of the dominant narrative modes behind the rise of the long-form genre sometimes, though never without caveats, referred to as the graphic novel. Certainly, 'graphic memoirs', such as Art Spiegelman's *Maus*, first published between 1980 and 1991, and later released as *The Complete Maus* (1996), and Alison Bechdel's *Fun Home* (2006), have garnered the most sustained critical attention among the various comic-book forms and tendencies. In her study of Spiegelman's *In the Shadow of No Towers* (2004) and Marjane Satrapi's *Persepolis: The Story of a Childhood* (2003) and *Persepolis 2: The Story of a Return* (2004), Gillian Whitlock (2006) coins the term 'autographics' to describe the formal design strategies and narrative techniques that set graphic memoirs apart from autobiographic narratives in other media. The first of these specificities is the critical distance introduced by what Marianne Hirsch (2004) described as the 'biocularity' of the form, the demands on the reader made by the 'distinctive verbal-visual conjunctions that occur in comics' (Whitlock 2006, 966). The second specificity mentioned by Whitlock is the idea, developed from McCloud's landmark study *Understanding Comics* (1993), that 'iconic drawings of the human face are particularly powerful in promoting identification between reader/viewer and image' (Whitlock 2006, 976), which means that graphic memoirs possess an ability to elicit a higher degree of empathy than film and prose.

However, whereas the dominant points of reference for Spiegelman, Bechdel and Satrapi's long-form memoirs are cinematic and literary (explicitly so in Bechdel's highly intertextual work), the mode of narrativising or performing the self that provides the main point of reference for digital comics is that which takes place through online social networks. Rather than autobiography, these tend to consist of snapshots of the self, fragments of textual-visual information that can fit on the screen of a mobile phone one piece at a time, even if these pieces are part of a longer series bound together by a common aesthetic, characters or narrative point of view. Wes Nunes's 'Manifesto dos Quadrinhos', for instance, is a memoir that first appeared on Tumblr in four-panel sections and was subsequently published in print. Deborah Salles's series 'Quadrinista de Ocasião' was published through the online magazine medium.com in single pages, excerpts of which – mainly individual panels – were also posted on her Instagram account. At the level of theme, a recurrent focus has been the modes of presenting the self to others, the forms of subjectivity and inter-subjectivity, specific to the digital age. Artists such as Nunes and Salles reflect a number of tendencies informing the political crisis that provides the backdrop to their work. They register the shifting forms of relating the self to wider national, regional and civic communities as well as the political causes and identity categories that have been shaped by the crisis. The work of Wes Nunes, the more explicitly political of the two artists, confronts readers with the often-violent reality of growing up as gay or transsexual and black in an authoritarian society such as Brazil's. Nunes shows how digital communications both serve to reinforce the prejudices that legitimise violence against LGBTQ+ communities and offer alternative avenues for the expression of self and the construction of alternative modes of belonging or connection. More generally, by developing what Carolina González Alvarado describes as the reader's 'multimodal competence' (see her chapter in this volume), 'autographic' digital comics such as these provide a space of reflection on the ways in which social media platforms articulate individual subjectivities with the networks of technologies, images and discourses that bind these subjectivities together.

One of the dominant ways in which recent narrativisations of the self through online digital comics have reflected on the social affordances of networked communications technology is through a focus on the centrality of the photographic image to social media. A particular focus has been the role of what Edgar Gómez Cruz and Eric Meyer (2012) describe as 'networked' photography produced by the conjunction between camera phones and social media in both the ongoing processes of constructing the self and articulating connections between bodies, images and technologies. Gómez Cruz and Meyer argue that the conditions of production, storage and distribution enabled by camera phones and social media sites has brought with it a new stage in the history of the medium in which photography should be understood not as a mode of representation or a particular media technology but as a 'socio-technical network' (Gómez Cruz and Meyer 2012, 2). The photographic object is 'nothing but the materialization of a series of assemblages' (ibid.), interlacing ideological discourses concerning what merits visibility, technologies that inscribe and reproduce these ideologies, and bodies that are conditioned by but also resist them. Digital comics in Brazil have engaged with networked photography in a manner that has been both 'explicit' and 'implicit', to borrow a distinction made by Baetens in his work on intermediality in photo novels (Baetens 2017, 3). That is to say, on the one hand, digital comics have referenced networked photography explicitly at a thematic level while maintaining the purity of the recognised medium they are working within. A good example of this is Salles' 'Quadrinhista de Ocasião', a comic that was hand-drawn and only subsequently uploaded onto a digital platform, but which thematises the centrality of digital photography to the artist's life. Other comics that do not thematise networked photography nevertheless mobilise its affordances in an implicit way. The artist Lovelove6, whose work centres on themes of gender and sexuality, uploads photographs of her work to the Instagram account @odiozinho. The networked interactions enabled by the platform are the element in which her work exists without being an explicit focus of the comics themselves.

The focus of this chapter is a Brazil-based comics artist whose work blurs the distinction between 'explicit' and 'implicit' treatment of networked photography through a prolonged engagement with the genre of photographic self-representation known as the selfie. Éff is a design student from São Cristóvão in the state of Sergipe in the North East of Brazil who has been producing a series of comics and distributing them through Instagram, Twitter and Tumbler since 2015. His Instagram account (eff.eff.eff) is subtitled in a way that draws attention to its interplay between one-page autobiographical comics, painted self-portraits and selfie photographs: 'Éff Alguém que registra a vida em quadrinhos, pinturas e uma ou outra cara sem muita expressão nas fotos [Éff somebody who records his life in comics, paintings and the occasional expressionless face in photographs]'. The highly curated Instagram stream combines the implicit engagement with networked photography through the use of the image-sharing site as an interface with readers, with an explicit thematisation of the modes of selfhood and intersubjectivity produced in their mediation by social media photography. The comics contain a striking number of cartoon drawings of smart phone screens, a feature that is indicative of the central role they play in the artist's emotional life. In some ways, the account can be seen as a narrative of the artist's ongoing love affair with his mobile phone. A four-panel comic posted on Instagram on 21 April 2018 narrates the artist's struggle to decide how frequently to text somebody he is dating (see Figure 7.1).

Figure 7.1 A comic exploring Éff's affective relationship with his mobile phone, posted on Instagram on 21 April 2018. © Fernando Caldas (Éff)

The first panel appears beneath a text box written in the first person: 'Se mando mensagem sempre me sinto sufocando a pessoa [If I send a message I always feel like I'm suffocating the person]'. The image shows an anthropomorphised mobile phone, whose eyes are bulging under the suffocating grip being exerted by a hand the reader assumes belongs to the artist. The mobile phone here is made to stand in metonymically for the social relations it enables. The comic ends by concluding that what is needed is a middle way between bombarding somebody with messages and leaving them alone. The final panel shows the artist peacefully asleep in his bed still holding a phone, which is displaying a similar level of contentment to its owner. The one-page comic introduces the thematic focus that runs through the work as a whole: the affective assemblages between bodies, images and networked technologies, and the potential critical role of autographic comics in relation to these assemblages.

In what remains of this chapter, I will examine the encounter between the digital comic form and social media photography in the work of Éff. I use the term 'autographic selfies' to describe the meeting point, represented in his work, between the graphic memoir genre and the aesthetic regime of the selfie. The selfie has proved to be a particularly fruitful focus for the analysis of the socio-technical assemblages enabled by networked photography. Often critically or dismissively described in the popular press as being symptomatic of a narcissistic culture, selfies have been attracting increasingly sophisticated critical attention for the light they shed on the complex forms of intersubjectivity of the digital age. Rather than reflective of the technology-driven atomisation of communities, they can be more productively viewed as socio-technological assemblages. I will start by placing Éff's use of the selfie in a longer history of interconnections between the comics medium and photography, before analysing the work itself through a focus on two themes: the staging of intimacy and the changing modalities of touch. Through an in-depth analysis of this individual body of work, I will explore the critical role the form of digital comics can perform in relation to the changing modes of selfhood and intersubjectivity bound up with social media. While, unlike Nunes, Éff's work is not political in an explicit sense, I will end by considering the light it sheds on the political implications of the vernacular hybrid visualities of the digital age.

Scholarly discussion of the use of photographic media in comic books has centred on questions of authenticity and truth. This has been most clearly the case in works of graphic journalism (or graphic reportage) that employ combinations of photographic and drawn images. In her comparative study of Joe Sacco's *The Fixer: A Story from Sarajevo* (2014) and *The Photographer: Into War-Torn Afghanistan with Doctors Without Borders* (first published in French between 2003 and 2006), Katalin Orbán focuses on the tension, central to both works, between the use of photographic images as 'the twentieth century's primary medium of documentary evidence' and the emphasis of first-person reportage on 'the presence, perspective and representational choices of the person(s) representing' without any 'assumption of unmediated reality' (Orbán 2015, 124). In a digital technological context in which photographic images are increasingly recognised as being subject to manipulation (and even if this was always the case even with 'analogue'), photographs, Orbán points out, 'have arguably come closer to being "drawn"' (Orbán 2015, 125). In other words, there should be nothing jarring about the presence of photographic images in graphic narrative since both are equally mediated. And yet, the form of graphic reportage is testament to a 'disjunction or lag' between our 'knowledge' of the manipulability of photography and our cultural 'response' to this knowledge. Even if the emplacement of photographs within graphic narrative draws attention to their subjective nature (an argument also made by Roy Cook, 2012), they still carry with them a lingering sense of a privileged connection to the real.[1] This association has also become central in works of graphic memoir that either reproduce photographic images or remediate them through drawing. In an analysis of the work of Swedish and Finnish graphic memoirists, Nina Ernst argues that 'intrusions' of photographic images in their 'storyworlds' function both as 'narrative strategies for forming authenticity' and 'to convey a sense of process in the creation of identity' (2015, 65–6). As I will go on to demonstrate, these associations have been self-reflexively problematised and complexified in a number of texts that position themselves within the genre of graphic memoir.

These tensions between graphic narrative and photographic media have been particularly pronounced in Latin American comic-book production. Debates surrounding memories of state-sponsored violence in the region have provided a particularly fertile ground for this encounter between photography and comics. In Argentina, this meeting point was marked by the publication of *Historietas por la identidad* (Gociol 2015), the result of a collaborative project between the Mariano Morelo National Library and the Abuelas de la Plaza de Mayo, a human rights organisation whose aim is to track down the children stolen or illegally adopted during the Argentine dictatorship of 1976–83. The aim of the book, which is based on work used in a travelling exhibit, is to employ the comics medium as an instrument in this search. In all of the short narratives – each produced by a different artist and focusing on the search carried out by a different family or families – photographs occupy a central position. The stories evidence the tension that Ernst ascribes to the role played by photography in graphic memoir: namely between authenticity and process. The story produced by Andy Riva (2015), on behalf of the families of Mónica Eleonora Delgado and Eduardo Benito

Francisco Corvalán, who were both kidnapped and killed by military police in July 1976, is exemplary in this regard. The two-page comic takes the form of a series of strips of photographic negatives. Each frame in the script is turned into a panel in the unfolding narrative, which narrates the birth of Mónica and Eduardo's children Mariana and Gabriel in 1973 and 1964 respectively (before the kidnapping) and, over a sun-bleached frame of an eye closing, tells the reader that Mónica was three months pregnant at the time of her 'disappearance'. The narrative ends with a plea to the reader: 'Tal vez vos sepas dónde está [Perhaps you know where he/she is]' (Riva 2015, 9). The comic brings to life the reason why the connection between photography and documentary truth 'lingers' in a particularly powerful way in social contexts coming to terms with past conflict. The reader learns in a postscript written by Gabriel that the photographs used in the comic were taken by the couple shortly before the kidnapping and were only revealed in 2000 when the roll of film was discovered by a friend. So, the photographs perform two main functions. On the one hand, they stand in for the memories of the children Mariana and Gabriel and draw attention to the formative role of media in the active construction of memory (a process documented by Marianne Hirsch in her account of the 'post-memories' of the children of Holocaust victims). On the other hand, they fulfil the more pragmatic function of displaying the faces of the two children for a reader to identify family resemblances between them and their missing sibling.

The post-dictatorship context has also been the focus of a number of comics in Brazil, especially after the establishment of the truth commission in 2011. One of the most interesting comic-book approaches to the subject is *Ditadura no ar* (2016), scripted by Raphael Fernandes with art from Abel (Rafael Vasconcellos), which was first published online in 2011 before appearing in print. The comic focuses on a freelance photographer searching for his girlfriend who has been kidnapped by the military regime. Although not as conceptually complex as the *Historietas por la identidad* collection, the inter-medial inclusion of photographs in the comic book serves to question the epistemological discourses surrounding photography, especially in the context of a repressive regime, while interrogating the role of media in the constitution of individual identity in relation to collective modes of belonging.[2] In both *Historietas por la identidad* and *Ditadura no ar*, identity is presented as a process and a search, at the centre of which is an absence. Individual identity is constituted through the network of forces, discourses and technologies that determine it.

Recent scholars writing about the role of photography in graphic memoirs have shifted the focus of debate from the documentary function of photographic images in establishing truth and authenticity, to the layering of different media as a way of presenting the self as the epiphenomenon of assemblages of forces, discourses and technologies. The work of Nancy Pedri has been central here. In her analysis of a number of works, including *Mendel's Daughter* (2006) by Martin Lemelman and *Mallko y papa* (2014) by Argentine illustrator Gusti, Pedri argues that photography is increasingly used in graphic memoirs not only as 'evidence or proof, aide-memoires, or markers of the passage of time' but also in the name of a 'critical engagement with questions of self and its representation' (2017, 7). For Pedri, the inclusion of photographs – whether they be reproduced from familial or public archives, cuttings from newspapers and magazines, or taken by the authors themselves expressly for inclusion in the work – introduces a 'complex layering of perspectives' into graphic memoirs (2017, 20). These multiple perspectives are presented as co-constitutive of the self that is under examination. Through their use of hand-drawn cartoon versions of photographic portraits, Lemelman and Gusti present 'understanding[s] of the self and experience as embodied, shared, relational' (2017, 34). Furthermore, because they are constituted by 'crossing, overlapping, complementary, and competing perspectives', these understandings are 'always in the making' (2017, 20). Although Pedri lists a number of what she terms 'photo-comics' that were produced specifically for online digital platforms, she does not explore the implications of the networked interface on the 'embodied, shared, and relational' experience of selfhood produced through the layering of photographic media and comic book form. Nevertheless, Pedri's work provides a useful critical frame through which to explore the nature of the self and subjectivity that is emerging from the convergence between digital comics and social media.

The centrality of the genre of the selfie to Éff's work is illustrative here, as it foregrounds both the modes of selfhood emerging from the conjunction of social media and digital comics more widely and the role of the comic form in providing a critical frame for the ways in which social media facilitates increasingly complex entanglements between the self and the networks of bodies, images and computational systems that produce it. Recent critics of the selfie have moved away from viewing the genre as evidence of a collective cultural self-obsession or as an indication of the reduction of public discourse to what Zygmunt

Bauman terms 'life politics', in which the subject, stripped of any real political agency and unable to connect his or her experience to that of the wider social field, is reduced to maintaining an illusion of agency through the exercise of market-driven lifestyle choices (2000, 51–2). Aaron Hess, for example, focuses on how selfies illuminate emerging and evolving 'relationships between technology, the self, materiality, and networks' of the digital age (2015, 1630). The 'selfie assemblage', as he terms it, gives expression to 'the affective tensions of networked identity: the longing for authenticity through digitality, the conflicted need for fleeting connection with others, the compulsion to document ourselves in spaces and places, and the relational intimacy found with our devices' (2015, 1631). Selfies both 'announce' these tensions and act as ways of 'coping' with or reconciling them. The tensions identified by Hess provide a useful starting point for examining the role of selfies in Éff's work.

The dominant theme of Éff's Instagram account is a tension between the author's feelings of loneliness and solitude and the cultural imperative to constantly connect with others through online networks. This tension is eloquently captured in a one-page comic posted on 13 June 2018, which narrates the painful process of overcoming a break-up. The first two panels show the author at home gazing down at his mobile phone, while first-person text boxes addressed to his former lover explain that he 'unfollowed' him as soon as they had broken up, but nevertheless continued to check every day to see whether 'se pensava sobre mim [you were thinking about me]'. However, despite this constant albeit clandestine online contact, when the author sees him by the beach the former lovers ignore each other. A possible conservative reading of Éff's critique of social media culture would be that online contact is presented as a replacement for affection in real life. The more that attracting 'likes' and 'follows' online becomes the focus, the less the artist is likely to make any real 'human' contact. There is plenty of evidence to support this reading. There is a tension that runs through Éff's work between frantic activity and movement online and a lack of movement offline. The artist repeatedly presents himself as 'lazy' or overcome by tiredness. The most frequent pose in which Éff depicts himself is lying sprawled in bed, often with his mobile phone gripped in an outstretched hand. And yet, the upkeep of the various platforms and the production of new artwork requires a prodigious amount of activity. Mobility through online networks makes up for a lack of mobility in real life. A two-panel comic posted on 27 June 2017 but with a title 'Mood (2016)', indicating that it was published the previous year, lampoons this contradiction (see Figure 7.2).

Figure 7.2 Éff confessing his inertia in a comic posted on Instagram on 27 June 2018. © Fernando Caldas (Éff)

The first panel displays a close-up of the artist's head resting against a pillow. Two connected speech bubbles read: 'Aparecendo pouco nas redes sociais / pra criar um mistério sobre o que tenho feito da vida [Appearing infrequently on social media / to create a mystery about what I have been doing with my life]'. The second panel is a zoom-out of the first and reveals that the artist is lying on a worn-out sofa with a bag of crisps. A one-word thought panel states: 'Nada [Nothing]'. The object of satire is the fact that social media is often used to produce the illusion of an active and fulfilling social life, which belies a reality that is more disconnected.

And yet, when taken as a whole, the staging of Éff's work through social media platforms presents a much more complex picture in which online connection and embodied affective life are inextricably intercon-nected. A further tension that runs through Éff's work in a less explicit way is between the author's embodied emotional life and the algorithmic systems that govern the ordering, storage and display of information on the sites used as the primary interface with his readers. Firstly, the fragmented sequentiality of the platform Instagram dictates the manner in which the autobiographical narrative reaches its readers. Rather than a linear chronological narrative, Éff's life story is focused on the present and broken down into brief 'hits' of textual-visual information. A post on 15 June 2018 acknowledges the state of the online information ecology in which Éff's work is competing for attention. Three images collated in a slide show contain split screens of a well-known meme on one side and Éff role-playing the meme on the other. The title reads: 'Incluindo cosplay de memes como habilidades extras no meu currículo [Including cosplaying memes as extra skills on my CV]'. The parody strips the memes of their communicational content, drawing attention to both their composition and their intended effect of cutting through the imagistic 'noise' of social media. One is a version of the 'Is this a pigeon?' meme, adapted from the 1990s Japanese anime series *The Brave Fighter of Sun Fighbird*, used on social networks to express total confusion. The original image is a still from the anime showing an android pointing to a butterfly while the subtitle shows him as saying 'Is this a pigeon?'. As the image went viral, the three elements – humanoid, butterfly, subtitle – were adapted to express situations in which something is misun-derstood. The parody of the meme draws attention to a parallel with the communicational intent of many of Éff's comic pages, which are intended both as snapshots of the artist's life and as pithy observations on digital existence. The 'appearing infrequently on social media' post, for instance, received a number of comments expressing identification: 'Muito eu isso [That's so me]'.

In a post that appeared on 22 January 2018 Éff openly addresses the fact that, at the level of distribution, he is forced to negotiate the constraints of the platform. The post was composed in reaction to a change to the Instagram algorithms which meant that his 'tirinhas' (comic strips) would not appear automatically on the timelines of his followers. To ensure maximum exposure of his work Éff, appearing in front of a blackboard displaying instructions, encourages his follows to click on the 'Ativar notificações de publicação' option on the drop-down menu of the Settings tab. A long comment from Éff assures his readers that 'não é culpa minha e sim do algoritimo [sic] do instagram que vai mudar [it's not my fault but that of Instagram's algorithms, which are changing]'. The agency behind the distribution and display of his work – the order and frequency with which it reaches its readers – is divided between the artist, the algorithmic infrastructure of the platform and the social media habits of subscribers. This algorithmic infrastructure affects not only distribution and ordering but also the composition of the images themselves. The drawn photographs that appear frequently in Éff's work draw attention to the algorithmic mediation of the photographic images that are constitutive of networked visual cultures. The layering of the textual-visual nature of the comic form over the networked photographic images that fuel Instagram draws attention to what Daniel Rubinstein and Katrina Sluis (2013) identify as a key paradox of the digital age: namely, the fact that the profusion of images in digital cultures is bound up with a shift away from the visual. The fact that in digital image platforms the close connection between storage and display that was inextricable for analogue photography has been disconnected (stored as 1s and 0s, displayed as pixels) 'suggests that the digital image cannot be fully understood through the premises of indexicality and ocularcentrism as its final appearance is the result of computation rather than the direct agency of light' (Rubinstein and Sluis 2013, 29). In networked cultures, Martin Lister points out, photography has become 'informational': 'Computational software and algorithms that carry out specific tasks and operations are now not only built into cameras but also into the extended apparatus of photography: the online organisations, social media sites, data-bases and post-production "lightrooms" where photographs are made, stored, organized, classified and shared' (Lister 2013, 13).

The 'informational' status of the photographic image is foregrounded in a number of ways by social media. Instagram, the main focus in this analysis, was one of the first platforms to popularise the use of stylistic filters that give the user the ability to create the impression of having used a variety of film stocks. At the time of writing, Instagram enables users to employ an extensive range of filters, including 'face filters' that allow you to add 'virtual koala ears' or 'nerd glasses' to photographic images, and software that enables you to write over images and videos by hand. The addition of hand-written text produced through touch-screen software to photographic images has become a dominant mode of vernacular expression on social media. To use Orbán's phrase, Instagram makes a feature of the manipulable 'drawn' quality of the digital image. In Éff's work, the cartoon versions of networked images, reproduced in the context of comic-book form, draw attention to their preexisting 'drawn' quality. A comic posted on 28 September 2017 merges the visual vernaculars of comic-book culture with selfie filters (see Figure 7.3).

Figure 7.3 A blend of comic-book syntax with selfie filters popular on social media, posted on Instagram on 28 September 2017. © Fernando Caldas (Éff)

The comic is composed of four drawn versions of photographic portraits of the artist, which are overlaid by both the visual techniques that identify the image as a comic (speech bubbles) and typical filters used in Instagram and Snapchat (emojis). The whimsical aesthetic of the four portraits clashes with the content of the speech bubbles in their expression of despair: 'Que Deus elimine todos nós [May God obliterate us all]'. Again, the satirical aim of the comic is to expose the gap between appearance and reality. This message supports the critical self-reflexive perspective Éff's digital comics provide on their use of photography. While Éff's work does foreground a continuity between photographic image and comic-book form (both being highly mediated), rather than an aesthetic of disjuncture between the two, the result is not to naturalise the algorithmic mediation of networked images. Rather, the comics draw attention to the effects of this mediation on the hybrid vernacular languages that they produce and the modes of connection that they encourage.

The foregrounding of filters draws attention to another aspect of 'informational' photography in networked culture: the fact that the metadata produced in the act of photographic capture and distribution – from tagging to recording the time and place of upload – is becoming equally if not more important than the content of the images themselves. As indicated by the post exhorting readers to enable the notification function on their timeline, the success of the comics is measured by how many readers they reach, how many 'likes' and comments they generate. In his analysis of what he describes as the 'rhetoric' of JPEG software, which is still the most common image software used by social media, Daniel Palmer argues that the practice of tagging, by enabling photographs to be 'catalogued, searched, shared and used', has replaced the caption as the dominant mode of textual accompaniment to photographic images (2013, 156). The use of hashtags by Éff – more frequent on his Twitter account than on Instagram, and even then only employed sparingly and ironically – provides searchers with alternate trajectories through points of contact with his work. For instance, a selfie posted across a number of platforms simultaneously on 18 July 2018, showing Éff perfecting his latest carefully cultivated 'look', was accompanied by the hashtag #NewProfilePic. If a Twitter user ran a search for this hashtag they would find Éff's image alongside a range of other selfies and profile photographs, using the hashtag either to mark a new phase in their online existence or as an ironic comment on a portrait (often of a celebrity) that is deemed awkward or inappropri-ate in some way. Éff's tagged profile photo – accompanied on Instagram by a long comment on the centrality of performance to both his identity and his work – might then become a point of entry to the work as a whole. The text that appears on the comics themselves can be viewed as an extension of the connective logic of tagging. In the competition with memes in the online attention economy, cartoon versions of the buzzwords of social media culture such as 'Bloquear' and 'Decontinuar' work as communicational channels that cut through the noise (see Figure 7.4).

Figure 7.4   Detail of a comic posted on 15 March 2018 exploring the buzzwords of connective digital culture. © Fernando Caldas (Éff)

Followers can immediately see that the comic is attempting, through a particular life experience, to articulate a wider truth about current cultures of connectivity. These drawn buzzwords are also nodes in what Thierry Groensteen describes as the 'plurivectorial' paths that readers take back and forth across panels and pages, often against the linear flow of the narrative (2007, 108).

These networks of connections are constitutive of both the mode of selfhood staged in Éff's comics and the dominant vehicle for this selfhood, the 'autographic selfie'. The connection between self and networks evidences one of the tensions described by Hess in his account of selfie assemblages: namely, between a desire for authenticity and meaningful interpersonal connection and an ecstatic embrace of the reduction of life to information and the production of connective metadata. On the one hand, the primacy of connection in his work positions Éff in relation to the dominant modes of what Grant Bollmer terms 'nodal citizenship' in digital cultures. For Bollmer, a 'nodal citizen' is one who 'relates to others by connecting and maintaining flows' of data (2016, 7). The rise of nodality as a measure of citizenship erodes 'the ability to distinguish between human and technology [. . .] producing humans as objects that serve as imagined material relays supposedly interchangeable with infrastructure' (Bollmer 2016, 8). On the other hand, as we have seen, the themes of disconnection, solitude and laziness are central to the narrative of many of the comics. Key to the development of these themes are depictions of the artists' body, whether stood in front of a camera phone at the end of an outstretched arm or positioned in front of a camera on a timer or operated by a friend. One of the repeated claims that Éff makes on behalf of his work is the exposure it subjects him to. The 22 January 2018 post begins by telling readers that 'vocês sabem como coloco meu coração e minha alma nas coisas que faço [you know how I put my heart and soul into what I do]'. His posed performative selfies alternate with unglamorous insights into his often lonely existence.

The selfies that appear in Éff's work are an attempt to reconcile these two desires caught in tension. Paul Frosh's (2015) description of the selfie as a 'gestural image' is a useful conceptual tool for identifying the specificities of the autographic selfie. Like Hess, Frosh argues that selfies should not be understood purely in visual terms, but rather for the ways in which they integrate photographic images into 'a techno-cultural circuit of corporeal social energy' that he terms 'kinesthetic sociability' (Frosh 2015, 1608). A key technological innovation that has enabled the selfie boom is the design of the smartphone. That they can be easily held and operated with the same hand, that they display an image of the 'pre-photographic scene' large enough to be viewed at arm's length, and that they have lenses on both the front and back mean that, unlike traditional cameras, smartphones no longer function as a 'barrier between visible photographed spaces and undepicted locations of photographing and viewing' (ibid., 1611). The two main consequences of this are that 'the space of photographic production or enunciation is effortlessly unified with the space of the picture itself' and that 'the unified space of production and depiction becomes a field of embodied inhabitation' since the camera is 'literally incorporated' as 'part of a hand-camera assemblage' (ibid., 1612). Selfies mobilise the indexical aura surrounding photography as part of a 'connective performance' between gestural images and their habituated embodied responses (whether tapping the screen in approval or swiping in dismissal) rather than to authenticate 'semantic reference' (ibid., 1609). Éff's selfies are bound up with this 'gestural economy of affection' (ibid., 1622) in that they routinely elicit hundreds of 'likes' from followers and are matched by the countless selfies of friends and followers that the artist 'retweets' in his Twitter account.

The 'technocultural circuits of corporeal social energy' of Éff's selfie networks are echoed by the modes of reading demanded by the comic-book form in two ways. Firstly, the type of engagement demanded by comics, whether print or digital, reflexively draws attention to the embodied dimensions of reading and viewing. As a range of scholars have pointed out, through their multimodal structures, comic books produce a broad range of sensory responses. Karin Kukkonen (2015), for instance, argues that the 'compositional lines' that determine page and panel layouts produce particular embodied responses that intervene into the reader's body schema (the use of the body to orient oneself in space).[3] Digital comics, in their various modes, bring with them their own set of habituated body responses. Some of these responses map onto those demanded by print (the compositional lines described by Kukkonen, for example), while others are specific to the interface (whether clicking through to the next page on a desktop computer or swiping on a touchscreen). Secondly, the relational construction of meaning in comic books echoes the relational constitution of selfhood in selfie culture. Just as the construction of meaning in comics is the production of a 'dynamic interaction between panel and page; word and image; book, reader and environment' (King and Page 2017, 12), in selfie networks, as Katie Warfield points out drawing on the agential realist philosophy of Karen Barad, self-portrait photographs posted on social media 'do not involve photos interacting with an a priori self, but rather the boundaries of the self are agentially cut and demarcated within the material-discursive entanglement of body, image, technology, photo, and place' (Warfield 2016, 3). While the formation of any identity is always already the product of a dynamic intra-action between mutually constituting elements rather than an inter-action between a priori entities, selfies, Warfield argues, enable a reflexive perspective on this process and therefore give selfie-takers a degree of control over it. Focusing on the role of gendered discourses, Warfield argues that selfie production often 'reveals a kind of agency that emerges as the result of small shifts and reconfigurations' of the ideologically dominant apparatuses of bodily production (Warfield 2016, 7). However, the potentially self-reflexive critical role of selfies identified in Warfield's optimistic reading is more often than not occluded by the sheer banality of this mode of image-making. The repositioning of the self within the comic form restores some of this critical potential. Éff's autographic selfies are critical interventions into contemporary selfie culture that perform the role of digital comics in both the formation of and critical reflection on emerging forms of networked techno-cultural sociability.

Éff's conflation of social-media selfie aesthetics with the genre of the graphic memoir draws attention to the networked nature of digital comics, a dimension that is often elided in discussions of the form that focus on definitions and questions of medium specificity. The parallel between the networked construction of meaning within the comics and the networked nature of the techno-cultural ecology in which they are constructed and circulate does not serve to simply naturalise the latter. Rather, the points of contact between the two open up a space for a critique of emerging modes of digitally mediated sociality. The specific form of the autographic selfie mobilised by Éff draws attention to the imbrication of networked photography in regimes of power. As Jill Rettberg argues in her discussion of female teen selfies and the public censure they often receive, '[t]his is about power and about who has the right to speak in public or share images in public' (2014, 17). By framing his selfies within a comic-book aesthetic Éff's work draws attention to their role in negotiating dominant regimes of representation, to the connection between the individual and techno-cultural assemblages of social media culture, as well as to the limits of the dominant doxa of connectivity. Furthermore, the networked digital comics analysed in this chapter provide an insight into the overlaps between comic-book form and the vernacular visualities of social media culture, from the combination of text and image to the merging of drawn and photographic imagery, in a way that draws attention to possibilities of multimodal expression that undergird these emerging practices of digital sociality.

Emerging research is pointing to the ways in which the increasing mediation of social life by online platforms in Brazil is not reducible simply to increased individualisation and atomisation. In his ethnographic study of social media usage in low-income informal settlements in Brazil, which have grown in number and density during the crisis despite being the object of mounting state repression, Juliano Spyer argues that digital platforms that use predominantly visual forms of communication (photographs and memes) enable communities to 'retain the type of dense social relations that migration and new modalities of work are diluting' (Spyer 2017, 1). Rather than another force of modernisation that is fragmenting communities, Spyer argues, in practice social media platforms are being used to reconstruct 'dense' forms of sociality. An analysis of digital comics in Brazil contributes to this picture of how social media is rapidly changing practices and conceptions of how individuals connect with one another. Rather than merely naturalising neoliberal dreams of connectivity and its dominant modes of 'nodal citizenship' or reflecting a return to 'traditional' modes of 'dense' sociality, the encounter between digital comics and social media creates a space of self-reflexive negotiation between the two.

Notes

1 For an overview of debates surrounding the 'truth claims' made for photographic image technologies, see Gunning (2008).
2 For similar approaches to the issue of post-conflict memory using combinations of photography and the comic-book form, see *Rupay: Historias de la violencia política en Perú, 1980–1984*, a dramatisation of the *Informe Final* (Final Report) published by the Comisión de la Verdad y Reconciliación (Truth and Reconciliation Commission) in 2003. For a discussion of this and other related works in Peru, see Milton (2017).
3 For a fuller discussion of the 'haptic turn' in comics scholarship, see King and Page (2017, 8–9).

References

Arnaudo, Dan. 2017. *Computational Propaganda in Brazil: Social Bots during Elections*. Working Paper No. 2017.8, Computational Propaganda Research Project, University of Oxford. Last accessed 8 October 2019. http://www.philosophyofinformation.net/wp-content/uploads/sites/93/2017/06/Brazil-Ready.pdf.
Baetens, Jan. 2017. 'Drawing Photo Novels, *ImageText: Interdisciplinary Comics Studies* 9, no. 2: 1–19. Last accessed 10 July 2018. http://www.english.ufl.edu/imagetext/archives/v9_2/baetens/.
Bauman, Zygmunt. 2000. *Liquid Modernity*. Cambridge: Polity Press.
Bechdel, Alison. 2006. *Fun Home*. Boston: Houghton Mifflin.
Bigerel, Yves. 2009. 'About Digital Comics'. Last accessed 10 July 2018. https://www.deviantart.com/balak01/art/about-DIGITAL-COMICS-111966969.
Bollmer, Grant. 2016. *Inhuman Networks: Social Media and the Archaeology of Connection*. London: Bloomsbury.
Brundige, Alex. 2015. 'The Rise of Marvel and DC's Transmedia Superheroes: Comic Book Adaptations, Fanboy Auteurs, and Guiding Fan Reception', PhD Thesis, Western University. Last accessed 10 July 2018. https://ir.lib.uwo.ca/etd/3104/.
Cook, Roy. T. 2012. 'Drawings of Photographs in Comics', *The Journal of Aesthetics and Art Criticism* 70, no. 1: 129–38.

Ernst, Nina. 2015. 'Authenticity in Graphic Memoirs: Two Nordic Examples', *Image & Narrative* 16, no. 2: 65–83.

Fernandes, Raphael and Rafael Vasconcellos. 2016. *Ditadura no ar*. São Paulo: Editora Draco.

Frosh, Paul. 2015. 'The Gestural Image: The Selfie, Photography Theory, and Kinesthetic Sociability', *International Journal of Communication* 9: 1607–28.

Gociol, Judith, ed. 2015. *Historietas por la identidad*. Buenos Aires: Biblioteca National.

Gómez Cruz, Edgar and Eric T. Meyer. 2012. 'Creation and Control in the Photographic Process: iPhones and the Emerging Fifth Moment of Photography, *Photographies* 5, no. 2: 1–19.

Groensteen, Thierry. 2007. *The System of Comics*. Jackson: University Press of Mississippi.

Gunning, Tom. 2008. 'What's the Point of an Index? or, Faking Photographs'. In *Still Moving: Between Cinema and Photography*, edited by Karen Beckman and Jean Ma, 23–40. Durham, NC: Duke University Press.

Hess, Aaron. 2015. 'The Selfie Assemblage', *International Journal of Communication* 9: 1629–46.

Hirsch, Marianne. 2004. 'Editor's Column: Collateral Damage', *PMLA* 119: 1209–15.

King, Edward and Joanna Page. 2017. *Posthumanism and the Graphic Novel in Latin America*. London: UCL Press.

Kukkonen, Karin. 2015. 'Space, Time and Causality in Graphic Narratives: An Embodied Approach'. In *From Comic Strips to Graphic Novels: Contributions to the Theory and History of Graphic Narrative*, edited by Daniel Stein and Jan-Noël Thon, 49–66. Berlin and Boston: Walter de Gruyter.

Lister, Martin. 2013. 'Introduction'. In *The Photographic Image in Digital Culture*, 2nd edition, edited by Martin Lister, 1–21. London: UCL Press.

McCloud, Scott. 1993. *Understanding Comics*. Northampton, MA: Kitchen Sink Press.

McCloud, Scott. 2000. *Reinventing Comics: How Imagination and Technology are Revolutionizing an Art Form*. New York: HarperCollins.

Milton, Cynthia. 2017. 'Death in the Andes: Comics as Means to Broach Stories of Political Violence in Peru'. In *Comics and Memory in Latin America*, edited by Jorge Catalá Carrasco, Paulo Drinot and James Scorer. Pittsburgh: University of Pittsburgh Press.

Oram, Andy. 2016. *Open Source in Brazil: Growing Despite Barriers*. Boston: O'Reilly.

Orbán, Katalin. 2015. 'Mediating Distant Violence: Reports on Non-Photographic Reporting in *The Fixer* and *The Photographer*', *Journal of Graphic Novels and Comics* 6, no. 2: 122–37.

Palmer, Daniel. 2013. 'The Rhetoric of the JPEG'. In *The Photographic Image in Digital Culture*, 2nd edition, edited by Martin Lister, 149–64. London: Routledge.

Pedri, Nancy. 2017. 'Photography and the Layering of Perspective in Graphic Memoir', *ImageText* 9, no. 2: 1–34.

Rettberg, Jill Walker. 2014. *Seeing Ourselves Through Technology: How We Use Selfies, Blogs and Wearable Devices to See and Shape Ourselves*. New York: Palgrave.

Riva, Andy. 2015. 'Familias Corvalán Delgado'. In *Historietas por la identidad*, edited by Judith Gociol. Buenos Aires: Abuelas de Plaza de Mayo and Biblioteca Nacional.

Rubinstein, Daniel and Katrina Sluis. 2013. 'The Digital Image in Photographic Culture: Algorithmic Photography and the Crisis of Representation'. In *The Photographic Image in Digital Culture*, 2nd edition, edited by Martin Lister, 22–40. London: Routledge.

Satrapi, Marjane. 2003. *Persepolis: The Story of a Childhood*. New York: Pantheon Books.

Satrapi, Marjane. 2004. *Persepolis 2: The Story of a Return*. New York: Pantheon Books.

Spiegelman, Art. 1996. *The Complete Maus*. New York: Pantheon Books.

Spiegelman, Art. 2004. *In the Shadow of No Towers*. New York: Pantheon Books.

Spyer, Juliano. 2017. *Social Media in Emergent Brazil: How the Internet Affects Social Change*. London: UCL Press.

Warfield, Katie. 2016. 'Making the Cut: An Agential Realist Examination of Selfies and Touch', *Social Media + Society* 2, no. 2: 1–10.

Whitlock, Gillian. 2006. 'Autographics: The Seeing "I" of the Comics, *Modern Fiction Studies* 52, no. 4: 965–79.

Wilde, Lukas. 2015. 'Distinguishing Mediality: The Problem of Identifying Forms and Features of Digital Comics', *Networking Knowledge* 8, no. 4: 1–14.

8

Comics on the walls: The *Zé Ninguém* street comics and the experience of the outsider view of Rio de Janeiro

Ivan Lima Gomes
Translated by Sarah Rebecca Kersley

Introduction

The streets and landscapes of Rio de Janeiro have long inspired painters, musicians and poets who have made their mark on the Rio scene with their respective arts. This relationship between art and the urban landscape dates back at least to the arrival of the Portuguese royal family in Brazil in 1808, at the time of the Napoleonic Wars. During the almost 15-year period when the Portuguese Court was moved to South America, Rio de Janeiro went from being a small city of just over 40 streets to the capital of the Portuguese Empire. A group of artists and scholars were recruited by the newly installed nobility to record the landscape and daily life of Rio de Janeiro, in what became known as the 'French mission' in Brazil (Pereira 2013, 65–110). Among these artists was the French painter Jean-Baptiste Debret (1768–1848), pupil and cousin of Jacques-Louis David (1748–1825). Academically trained in neoclassical art, he had gained attention at the beginning of the nineteenth century for his celebratory paintings of Napoleon's victories. However, following the French defeat of 1815, Debret lost his main source of income and he went, along with other artists, to Brazil, which by that time had been elevated to the status of part of the United Kingdom of Portugal, Brazil and the Algarves. As well as contributing to the establishment of the Imperial Academy of Fine Arts and the institutionalisation of academic art in the recently established court in Brazil, Debret produced a series of works representing nature and the daily life of the country, in particular of Rio de Janeiro. The series is entitled *Voyage Pittoresque et Historique au Brésil, ou séjour d'un artiste française au Brésil, depuis 1816 jusqu'en 1831 inclusivement*. The work contains 153 illustrations, accompanied by explanatory texts, and was published between 1834 and 1839 in Paris (Dias 2001, 35–46). Debret's work focused on highlighting Rio de Janeiro not only as the new and luxurious capital of the court but also as having very distinct urban rhythms and sensibilities, evident in everyday life on the city's streets, depicted as privileged sites of popular sociability. Slaves, musicians, cooks and merchants were key features of Debret's watercolours (Domingues 2018, 194–7).

Representations of the city from the point of view of the outsider have varied widely since those early images, as have the techniques and aesthetic processes used in such portraits. A history of imaginaries of the city can be traced from the aforementioned neoclassical paintings of the French Artistic Mission, to the lithographs produced in the latter half of the nineteenth century by the Italian journalist and illustrator Angelo Agostini, addressing themes such as the Carnival, the abolition of slavery, and the urban chaos of the Republic (Balaban 2009), through to the links between the US and Brazil suggested in the 1933 Hollywood musical *Flying Down to Rio*. More recently, the French comics artist Jano in his work *Rio de Jano* depicted a city beyond the exuberant landscapes and beaches celebrated by Hollywood and the musicians of Bossa Nova: his work shows a suburban city alive with funk dancers and street vendors. A vision of Rio de Janeiro by a foreign observer, *Rio de Jano* reinvents the city by showing this other face, highlighting how traditional tourist hotspots, of which Copacabana is certainly the best-known example (O'Donnell 2013), are the result of historically localised interpretations and circumstances.

Works such as these propose an urban landscape of the city from the perspective of a kind of displacement of the viewpoint of those born in the city. They are like a game of mirrors in which the foreigner, taking on the condition of external observer and, to some extent, the outsider, seeks to identify with the city. Being an outsider allows them to seize the city in a privileged way, often exposing contradictions, diversities, exaggerations and limits, at the same time as entering the public sphere of debate about meanings in and of the city.

In this chapter, I read *Zé Ninguém*, created by Alberto 'Tito na Rua' Serrano, from precisely this notion of foreign viewpoints resignifying the experience of belonging in Rio de Janeiro via cultural production and knowledge. As Serrano has said: 'I was a foreigner trying to adapt. In six months, I managed to walk into a snack bar and order a *joelho* [a type of ham and cheese roll] and a drink. But I was trying to understand the city, and I needed a character who was going through the same as I was, a guy who had come from somewhere else' (Thomé 2015). Nevertheless, while artists like Debret and Nicolas-Antoine Taunay (1755–1830) mobilised academic painting conventions learned in art schools, Alberto Serrano is an urban artist, closer to what Becker (1976, 9–26) classifies as the 'maverick', that is, an artist whose work does not fall into the established logic of art, perceived as too restrictive, but who nonetheless often desires to adhere – albeit partially – to that logic.

Born and raised in The Bronx, New York, the son of Puerto Rican parents, Serrano adopted the pseudonym Tito na Rua – which is how I will refer to him in the remainder of this chapter – in 2001, after moving from the US to Brazil following 9/11 in search of better work opportunities in his wife's native country. In Brazil, he trained as an artist, studying on various courses before, encouraged by graffiti artist friends, he started using the walls of the city, eventually developing *Zé Ninguém*, a series of graffiti works that narrate the saga of a man and his dog on the streets of Rio de Janeiro. With *Zé Ninguém*, classified by the artist himself as a 'street comic', Tito na Rua gained public and critical recognition, receiving requests for interviews and invitations to adapt his work for art galleries, animations and books. A graphic novel was developed, presenting a linear narrative of the saga of the eponymous protagonist. Though I am aware of the problems of adapting a street comic to the graphic novel format, I refer to the book here because, as pointed out by Tito na Rua, many of the original graffiti pieces created to tell the story of *Zé Ninguém* have now disappeared due to the impermanent nature of graffiti.

What, then, is the meaning of the term 'street comics'? To answer that question I will look at how Tito na Rua has developed his aesthetic approach to comics on and through the streets of Rio de Janeiro. I will analyse the ways in which he has engaged with Rio's landscape by expressing his experiences as a reader of several comics in different styles, genres and formats – from Franco-Belgian *bande dessinée* to Japanese manga, through the superhero genre and other graphic novels – and his experiences of graffiti in New York, all shot through by his status as a newcomer in the Brazilian city. A parallel can be drawn between my chapter and Jorge Tuset's chapter in this volume. Tuset shows how the language and aesthetics of comics establish distinct ways of representing cities that lie between the creativity of artistic expression and concrete graphic representations of abstract concepts. He shows how comics are a valuable resource for teaching architecture and urban history. Here, though, *Zé Ninguém* is embodied in the urban landscape: he follows everyday streets, walls and scenarios that are part of the daily life of local residents to develop a conceptual – but also creative – reading of the city of Rio de Janeiro.

Street comics: 'comics about the street, on the street'

Street comics have been defined by the author himself in interviews as 'comics about the street, on the street' (Vartanian 2009), a nod to a new way of narrating the geography of Rio de Janeiro. Despite street comics being relatively unexplored, compared with fields such as film studies or studies about graffiti itself, some research has analysed the significance of narrating the city through the artistic language of graphic novels. Researchers have discussed how these narratives produce new meanings of urban space, focusing on the eminently urban nature of the first comics published in newspaper supplements, in the elaboration of urban logics or in the graphic adaptation of cities such as New York and Paris, among other subjects (Ahrens and Meteling 2010). Case studies following the work of artists like Chris Ware demonstrate the possibilities of the relationship between comics and the city, analysing how their formalist aesthetics allow for the development of an urban and graphic architecture based on memories of ways of life in the US in the early twentieth century (Dittmer 2014, 477–503; Ball and Kuhlman 2010).

These dialogues between the language of graphic novels and the language of the urban landscape, something also seen in Cristian Palacios's chapter in this volume, are explored by Tito na Rua in *Zé Ninguém*. To begin with the work prioritises comics over graffiti, the art with which *Zé Ninguém* is traditionally more closely linked. When asked in interviews about which of the arts came first in his life, Tito na Rua makes clear that his first interest was not so much graffiti as comics. To reinforce his point, he recalls his early experiences as a reader of comic books, and how he grew up reading superhero comic books as well as *Tintin*, *Calvin and Hobbes* and *Lone Wolf and Cub* – all but the former cited as direct influences for *Zé Ninguém* (Rodriguez 2011).

Graffiti would have been a natural part of his life due to the fact that he lived in The Bronx in the 1980s, a fertile period for graffiti in New York. In an interview about the beginning of his activities in Brazil, the author points out that, in contrast to his native New York, he perceived that in Rio there was even more widespread public support for the practice of the urban art of graffiti:

> By the time I became a teenager, Giuliani, the mayor, was already on his mission to stop graffiti. Whatever you did, you got caught. There was no way you could be doing graffiti and not get caught. I said to myself: 'Forget it, what I really like is comics'. I saw graffiti and thought it was 'cool', but I felt that it lacked continuity, it was just letters and characters back then. I never imagined I would end up doing graffiti one day. When I came – and here everyone's good at graffiti – they invited me [to come and do graffiti]. I went along for the fun of it because I was bored just staying in the studio. I bought two spray cans and went along with one of the guys, doing a frog. Then I bought two more cans, and I practiced with a cardboard stencil. Then I started trying out more realistic [*designs*], reproducing photos. I got fed up of that – I was using photos taken by other people. I took some time out to think. Then I had this idea of street comics with Zé Ninguém. I thought about doing something Brazilian, and I looked to Latin influences, from Puerto Rico. I was here as an immigrant, so I used this factor as well. The bus station was the perfect place to start, and I did my first piece of graffiti on a pillar. It was a time when we could do anything. Everyone was doing stuff on the walls, and the police celebrated it too. Coming from New York, it was really odd. There, if you so much as spit in the street, you get fined.
>
> (Rodriguez, 2011)

These experiences demonstrate how the city of Rio de Janeiro effectively mobilised a New Yorker with little previous interest in graffiti to become 'Tito na Rua' and a graffiti artist. In this sense, it was the experience of displacement provoked by having a foreign viewpoint in a new reality that allowed Tito na Rua to reexamine his own trajectory, incorporating the urban art forms that had previously been a part of his upbringing. To a certain extent, therefore, in seeking to understand Rio de Janeiro, Tito na Rua is simultaneously rereading his memories of New York.

The idea of thinking about Rio de Janeiro and its early twenty-first-century urban graffiti culture in comparison with that of New York in the 1980s (Vartanian 2009) makes sense in the context of Decree 38.307 (Prefeitura da Cidade do Rio de Janeiro, 2014), a law approved on 18 February 2014. Known as the 'graffiti decree', it guarantees legal protection to a series of practices related to graffiti in Rio de Janeiro. Based on recognising local production as street art – evidenced by critical acclaim, awards, international visits of other graffiti artists to the city and through the emergence of a 'singular identity' of graffiti from Rio – the law establishes the sites where graffiti is permitted:

> [...] lampposts, pillars, grey walls (as long as they are not considered as being of historical heritage), blind walls (no doors, windows or other openings), skating rinks and construction hoardings [. . .] as long as it does not damage public or historical property, and does not constitute publicity (references to brands or products), is free of pornographic, racist or otherwise prejudiced content, does not condone anything illegal or contain religious offence [. . .] [and is] recognized as an artistic cultural manifestation that brings value to the city and prevents tagging.
>
> (Prefeitura da Cidade do Rio de Janeiro 2014)

The new law sparked different reactions among graffiti professionals, in part because of government interference in the creative freedom of graffiti artists and the political uses that could influence creative production.[1] It also represented a dispute over the spaces of the city, an attempt to reconfigure the landscape and occupy previously rundown areas. The beginnings of the 2010s was a period of profound urban transformation in Rio de Janeiro with urban interventions preparing the city for the forthcoming Olympic Games and the FIFA World Cup. The mayor at the time, Eduardo Paes, presented himself as a kind of twenty-first-century Pereira Passos.[2] Many of the city's *favelas* were occupied by a truculent military police force, specifically the Pacifying Police Units (Unidades de Polícia Pacificadora – UPP), symbols of a security policy that aimed to expel drug traffickers from the *favelas* through militarised occupation in strategic areas of the city. The result was an intensified process of gentrification in certain neighbourhoods, leading part of the population to feel excluded from having a say in the urban politics of Rio de Janeiro. The idea of 'the right to the city' (Harvey 2008, 23–40) began to gain strength and, not by accident, Rio was one of the epicentres of the protests that took hold of the country in 2013. These marches, which became known as the 'June Days', called for improvements in urban mobility and other rights related to urban life. They started up again in 2014 in protest over exorbitant public spending for the World Cup.

This was the context in which Tito na Rua developed his work with *Zé Ninguém*. Encouraged by public policy that supported urban art and by an intense debate on the meanings of the city, the moment also coincided with critical protests and the decree establishing the 'Rio condition' and the 'nature of Rio' as 'Cultural Commodities in the Intangible Cultural Heritage of the City of Rio de Janeiro' (Prefeitura da Cidade do Rio de Janeiro 2015). *Zé Ninguém* invites the city's population to discover this Rio together with him as he wanders its walls, viaducts and alleyways. In 2011, the saga of the eponymous character on the streets of Rio de Janeiro had around 50 graffiti pieces, making up half of the full narrative originally planned by Tito na Rua. By 2015, the total number of illustrations spread across the city had reached 200 (Sartori 2015), indicating not only how well the city had received the arrival of this new inhabitant who sought to interpret its landscape, but also how this very landscape reinvented the foreign viewpoint of Tito na Rua, positioning his career path in this new and hybrid urban art – that of 'street comics'.

The influences Tito na Rua cites for the development of *Zé Ninguém* help us understand the profile of the series and the specificities of the work. To begin with, the aforementioned *Tintin*, *Lone Wolf and Cub* and *Calvin and Hobbes* are representative of three schools or forms of producing comics: the Franco-Belgian tradition of *ligne claire*, manga, and the comic-strip format more directly associated with the North American newspaper context. In that way, it is as though *Zé Ninguém* generates a global synthesis of comic traditions to embody this saga of a character in a context as local and specific as Rio de Janeiro. And it is also a sign of the maturity of Tito na Rua as a comics reader. Growing up in the wake of the underground comix boom that helped develop a clearer awareness of comics as a language (Hatfield 2005), Tito dives into very distinct comics languages and combines them with a traditionally underground form of artistic cultural expression (graffiti) to create a street comic that lies at the intersection of the languages of comics and graffiti.

These three comics all have protagonists whose respective sagas mean that they discover their worlds through adventure. *Tintin* is a reporter who, through his profession, travels the world to write journalistic reports, ending up in, among other places, the Soviet Union, the Belgian Congo, Tibet and the US. Rather than being a journalist, Zé Ninguém is a professor and researcher, and his geographic repertoire is initially limited to the city of Rio de Janeiro, although he does end up going to other metropolises, like London and New York. However, as with *Tintin*, the narrative of the series plays itself out based on the character's constant peripatetic interaction with his new reality, in this case where his previous experience as a researcher comes face to face with the diverse and changing urban contexts of Rio de Janeiro.

The similarities between *Zé Ninguém* and *Tintin* are also evident in the aesthetic of *ligne claire*, which *Tintin* helped to popularise and which became a signature of Franco-Belgian *bande dessinées*. As Laurence Grove (2010) points out, *ligne claire* emphasises the use of strong black outlines, the use of primary colours and the avoidance of out-of-focus images. This ensures that places and objects are easily recognisable (Grove 2010, 122–3). Strong outlines, primary colours and well-defined images are traits of *Zé Ninguém* and mean that, to a large extent, the series can be adapted to all available walls, façades, steps and gates, regardless of material. This factor is fundamental for enabling *Zé Ninguém* to spread over the city, to be readily recognisable, and for readers to be able to accompany him in his narrative.

The links between Tito na Rua's series and the manga of Kazuo Koike and Goseki Kojima are evident in the relationships between the respective protagonists and the forms of violence exercised on their female companions. In *Lone Wolf and Cub* the brutal murder of the wife of protagonist Ogami Itto and the conspiracy to banish him are processed via the samurai narrative. From that point on, *Lone Wolf and Cub* portrays Itto's pilgrimage through Japan, together with his new-born son, in search of his wife's killers. We are introduced to a historical Japanese landscape through the eyes of the pilgrim, who filters reality through his thirst for revenge. Though *Zé Ninguém* is urban art aimed at a diverse public travelling through the city and avoids, therefore, the violence and ethics of justice present in the manga, the stories of lies and subsequent kidnapping suffered by Ana, the protagonist's girlfriend, are also forms of violence. These are indeed key elements that drive the plot of this 'street comic', with Zé Ninguém making the journey to Rio de Janeiro in search of Ana, where he confronts the villain who had also attacked him at the start of the narrative and steals his secret formula. It is also worth noting that, in the Brazilian case, the reading of manga requires other kinds of reading practices, not least reading in the opposite direction to comics produced in the West. Just as manga requires the Western reader to learn new reading practices, directing the reader's eye from right to left and from top to bottom, *Zé Ninguém* also disrupts the reader's experience of serialised graphic novels. By using walls and façades as a medium for the page, the possibility of reading in pre-established directions – from one side to the other, from top to bottom and vice-versa – is removed, instead putting the reading experience in tune with the urban space itself. In this space what matters is not only a static representation or a linear narrative within the city but also the flow, urban layout and discontinuity of the work. As a result, we are presented with a fragmented reading of the urban text of *Zé Ninguém*, where each reader who finds the character in alleyways, walls and back streets can construct their own graphic novel and think about the relationship between the character and the city.[3]

Finally, Bill Watterson's famous comic strip is connected to *Zé Ninguém* in its oneiric and creative dimension, in which a world of adventures in a restricted location is opened up via dreams and the imagination, bringing about all kinds of absurd situations. In *Calvin and Hobbes* many of the adventures alternate between interior spaces – at school, in the principal's office at school, in the protagonist's bedroom – and outdoor areas, such as the backyard or snow-covered hills. And it is through specific aspects of each space that the adventure develops: when Calvin is sitting in the principal's office waiting to get told off, he imagines that he has been imprisoned by a terrible alien monster; when playing with Hobbes in the yard, the grass becomes a dense and dangerous forest. *Zé Ninguém* also works to a large extent with the idea of interaction with specific spaces, such as in a *mise en scène*: part of the series is placed on a school, for example, positioning the narrative in such a way that it relates to the main character acting as a scientist (Tito na Rua 2015, 68–9); and the series begins with the character being placed in the region of the Novo Rio Bus Station, introducing the story with an image of Zé Ninguém lost and looking for his girlfriend, Ana (Tito na Rua 2015, 12–21). Moreover, comic strips in general, including *Zé Ninguém*, are historically recognised as being ephemeral – sometimes published in the sports or children's supplements of daily newspapers – and characteristically display discontinuity in their narratives, requiring an active reader who fills in the meaning in the gaps between the images or who appreciates the serial nature and the 'open' style of these comic strip narratives (see Figure 8.1).[4]

Zé Ninguém is also similar to the ways that Tintin and Itto carry out their respective journeys in *Tintin* and *Lone Wolf and Cub*. In the former, the protagonist deals with the landscapes he encounters from the viewpoint of his role as a travelling reporter – and also, it should be noted, as a traveller in dialogue with the tradition of travel narratives in the framework of an imperialist project (Dunnet 2009, 587–90). Itto, by falling into disgrace within the power structures that led to the death of his wife and his dishonour as a samurai, becomes a kind of foreigner in his own land, wandering Japan as if he were a pilgrim. *Zé Ninguém* similarly focuses on the experience of transit and displacement, bringing new meaning to spaces because, as well as searching for his loved one, which brings the necessary touch of adventure to the series, he is also marked out by his condition as an immigrant.

Figure 8.1 The character of Zé Ninguém interacts with the urban environment (Tito na Rua 2015, 78). © Tito na Rua

These examples set out a specific categorisation of the ways in which the respective protagonists relate to unknown spaces encountered when moving from their homelands, namely that the travellers construct their realities in the places they find themselves from the viewpoint of pragmatic questions associated with work, tourism or cultural interest. The pilgrim has a more perennial relationship with what he/she finds in front of him/herself, since the landscape figures in the background as he/she moves to a particular destination, establishing almost fleeting relations with the given reality – after all, the very condition of being a pilgrim forces displacement. The immigrant, however, has to develop connections to all new elements of their new landscape very quickly, so they can adapt themselves to the new reality in which they are inserted. By contrast to travellers and pilgrims, the immigrant's aim is to establish themselves in their new home and make it identifiable. It is within this dynamic, motivated by the search for his girlfriend, that Zé Ninguém migrates to Rio de Janeiro.

Scenes and characters of *Zé Ninguém*'s Rio de Janeiro

The city of Rio de Janeiro itself is a major character in *Zé Ninguém*. We are introduced to a complex city, which spreads out way beyond the tourist hotspots often associated with the city. In fact, beaches and other famous landscapes are scarce in this work. The medium used for the *Zé Ninguém* comics are the walls and façades of the city present in the daily lives of many ordinary people, a factor that reinforces the links between the protagonist and many average people living in Rio de Janeiro.

The beginning of *Zé Ninguém* sets the tone in relation to places chosen by Tito na Rua as the backdrop to the saga of the protagonist in his search for his beloved (see Figure 8.2).

Figure 8.2   The character of Zé Ninguém arrives at the bus station in Rio de Janeiro. This photograph was originally taken in 2008. Reproductions are included in the 'Tito' *Portfolio* (Tito na Rua 2014, 18) and the *Zé Ninguém* graphic novel (Tito na Rua 2015, 12). © Tito na Rua

A place of transit for people and vehicles, the Novo Rio Bus Station is the main point of arrival and departure in Rio de Janeiro. It is a very rundown area, permeated by viaducts and occupied by homeless people, drug addicts, prostitutes, police and illegal transport drivers. The choice of the Novo Rio Bus Station dialogues simultaneously with three important elements that make up *Zé Ninguém*: the production of comics in the framework of underground comix; the traits of urban graffiti; and the city of Rio de Janeiro, taken in a complex and fragmented way, and constructed as the 'wonderful city – purgatory of beauty and chaos', as expressed by the critical lyrics of the song written by Fausto Fawcett, Fernanda Abreu and Laufer.[5]

By inaugurating the piece in the bus station, Tito na Rua approximates his work visually to another figure who became a symbol of the city because of his urban interventions: the artist known as Profeta Gentileza. There are clear points of contact between the work of Gentileza and *Zé Ninguém* and this is certainly apparent to Tito na Rua, whose first illustration is located on one of the many pillars of the Gasômetro Viaduct, directly underneath one of the many messages written by Gentileza. At the same time, the interaction between Zé Ninguém and the work of Gentileza also suggests a reflection on the latter as an urban artist concerned with bringing new aesthetic meaning to the city. If we focus on the lettering used by Gentileza, for example, we can perceive an effective work of authorship which, just as in graphic novels, structures image and text as inextricably linked, something that also happens with other paratextual elements, such as colours, letter format, and the medium used. Within two dimensions, the boundaries between image and text, paratext and content, typography and illustration, are blurred (Kannenberg 2001, 165–92; Bredehoft 2014, 130–56).

Figure 8.3 Development process of a page/graffiti of *Zé Ninguém* (CDURP 2015). © CDURP

In *Zé Ninguém*, the materiality of comics can be considered in relation to the attention given to the publication formats of graphic novels, important elements when discussing material culture and the paratextual dimensions of all literary works. At times, the scenes in *Zé Ninguém* are thought out like magazine pages, with entire page layouts being prominent elements of the creative process (see Figure 8.3).

Graffiti such as this incorporates a metalinguistic discursive level in the published book version, such as in a passage where the reader finds a slightly folded page inside the graphic novel (Tito na Rua 2015, 139). The idea of taking *Zé Ninguém* as a comic published in specific formats is reinforced in a particular scene in the work – one which has been erased from the book – where a comic-book cover for the character is highlighted (see Figure 8.4).

Figure 8.4   Graffiti showing the cover for a comic book of *Zé Ninguém*, eventually excluded from the published version (Tito na Rua 2014, 19). © Tito na Rua

The places visited by Zé Ninguém during his odyssey in search of Ana are notable for their diversity, even surprising locals familiar with the city. His visits to the well-known tourist area of the city's South Zone are limited to the *favelas* located in the region, and references abound to abandoned areas of the centre, peripheral suburban neighbourhoods and *morros* considered dangerous for being occupied by drug traffickers. The only beach area visited by the character is the Ramos beach, popular with the poorer local community. At the end of the book, there is a map with a brief guide to the neighbourhoods visited by Zé Ninguém.

The places visited are not always obvious to the reader, as Tito na Rua is not concerned with making direct references or even pointing them out visually via references identifiable in Rio's cultural imaginary. Instead, there are references to places such as alleys, viaducts, expressways, deserted streets, etc. This process of deterritorialisation is an invitation to the reader to reterritorialise the city, seeking new meaning from the directions taken by the character.

The city of Rio de Janeiro is also visible throughout the work via the profusion of characters spread out across the story: rubbish collectors, residents, beachgoers and workers come and go along the pages/walls and help to place *Zé Ninguém* into a popular and typical Rio de Janeiro context. Perhaps the clearest example is the inclusion of the employees of the Municipal Urban Cleaning Company of Rio de Janeiro (Comlurb) – known as 'garis'[6] – in some episodes of *Zé Ninguém*. Part of Rio's community, recognisable for their orange uniform and well respected for the difficult work they carry out in the streets of the city, these cleaners are associated with many of the values considered typical of Rio de Janeiro, such as spontaneity and good humour in the face of adversity – to the point that one of the company employees, who goes by the nickname 'Renato Sorriso' (Renato Smile), is considered one of the symbols of the Rio Carnival. The orange colour of the rubbish collection company uniforms dialogues well with the work of Os Gêmeos, as the brothers Otávio e Augusto Pandolfo (1974–) are known. Os Gêmeos are one of Tito na Rua's cited graffiti influences and their work is also hybrid, in that they work with both graffiti and fine art in their process of international artistic recognition.

Besides the spontaneity and good humour associated with the *garis*, in *Zé Ninguém* they are black, with the exception of one blonde female *gari* called Ana. Many of the characters who appear in the series are black, introducing an element of racial representation still relatively uncommon in the production of Brazilian graphic novels.[7] The racial identity of the characters is important for thinking about the composition of *Zé Ninguém* as a transnational graphic novel, which developed from the migratory condition not only of the eponymous character but also of the work's creator. Tito na Rua has said on several occasions that the inspiration for the protagonist came from his Puerto Rican father, who had a moustache, wore open sandals and bore a close resemblance to many Rio de Janeiro locals he encountered on arrival in Rio. This kind of popular and subaltern identification helps the character of Zé Ninguém and his girlfriend Ana to settle quickly in the city: the locals warm to them and they visit many areas of the city with great ease. It should be noted, however, that Ana is not always well liked in the places she visits. Due to her blue uniform, she is sometimes confused with the Rio de Janeiro military police, which makes some inhabitants uncomfortable.

Conclusion: Two tales of one city

In a recent study dedicated to analysing post-humanistic aesthetic inflections in Latin American graphic novels, Edward King and Joanna Page (2017) point out that in general such works are marked by a strong inter-media dimension. That is, their discourse incorporates countless narratives from other artistic forms such as photography, music and fine art. *Zé Ninguém* is one of the works mentioned that use this approach. King and Page point out how the interplay between the artistic language of graffiti and that of graphic novels results in complex hybrid works, enabling the development of three-dimensional work at the intersections between the artistic languages of graffiti, comic books and graphic novels (King and Page 2017, 217).

I would stress two further elements to these reflections. First, that the intermediality present in Latin American graphic novels should incorporate two important elements: (1) that we should recognise the original intermedial nature of comics, something that led Thierry Smolderen to consider twentieth-century comics to be not only a continuity of the comic art tradition of the eighteenth and nineteenth centuries but also an effective 'semiotic laboratory' of graphic experiences (Smolderen 2009); and (2) that in Brazil such works should be linked to the peculiarities of the history of the introduction and diffusion of comics in the region, where they were endowed with a hybrid character predating today's graphic novels because they blended graphic and visual traditions as diverse as that of the *littérature en estampes* from

European-style illustrated magazines from the early twentieth century and of photo novels.

The second point I want to make is related to a suggestion made by the author Tito na Rua himself: that he is constructing a dialogue not only between his work and the history of comics but also with the historiography of comics, at least if we recall those interpretations that associate the graphic language of comics with expressions as far removed as the Bayeux Tapestry or prehistoric cave paintings. He makes this point in the following passage:

> It's a different artistic language, but at the same time, it isn't. What I did was take comics and graffiti back to their origins, which was a caveman writing on the wall that he had killed a buffalo. It was a story he graffitied, so I'm returning to that but using the resources we have today, like spray-paint, sharing on the internet and via the printed book.
>
> (Sartori 2015)

I would argue that this awareness of different formats for the publication of comics is a trademark characteristic of Tito na Rua's work, associated with his trajectory as a comic-book reader in the US and as an outsider artist. Contrary to the deep awareness of the limits and possibilities that marked this artistic language very clearly in terms of the diffusion of the underground comix (Hatfield 2005), I would argue that such expressions have different nuances in the Brazilian case. *Zé Ninguém* helps us understand comics as a language open to new influences from the standpoint of Brazilian reality, bringing new perspectives on comics and enabling us to think about the circulations and cultural appropriations that configure this artistic language. From the author's experience as a writer and reader of comic books in the US, it also becomes possible to think about the history of comics in Brazil as a history written by outsiders and creative artists who produced comics as a mixture of influences and languages. As a material and social practice, the idea of contemporary comics as a *co-mix* (Mitchell 2004, 255–65) is reinforced in *Zé Ninguém* through the fragmented readings carried out by urban dwellers on the city's walls and façades.

The publication of the graffiti pieces that make up this love story in book format has not meant the end of the adventures of *Zé Ninguém*. This is an ongoing work, one already forged from the language of the graphic narrative and adapted to fit both book form and graffiti form.

In the case of the book, the author opts not to give the work a closed ending but instead leaves the narrative open, encouraging the reader to imagine that there is more to come. The language of graffiti, in turn, reshapes the aesthetics of the superhero, positioned between the fixed image of the archetypal myth and a reading that leans towards the idea of continuous ongoing narrative developments, a style common in the nineteenth-century novel, which breaks away from the model of a linear narrative in which the character accumulates experiences and memories, imprinting upon them an inevitably mortal temporality, and instead passes into the eternal consumption of narrative in the present (Eco 1972, 14–22). Rather than a superhero renewing themselves in each new magazine edition, we are presented here with a changeable hero who renews himself as the city around him changes and requires his occupation. His superpower not only serves to 'bring value to the city and prevent tagging', as stipulated by the 'graffiti law', but also and more importantly reintroduces the city's inhabitants to each other as part of the construction of meaning that makes up the urban labyrinth of cities such as Rio de Janeiro.

Notes

1 Christina Cunha's study about Rio de Janeiro graffiti is ongoing and has yet to present specific conclusions on this issue (Cunha 2017, 505).

2 Pereira Passos (1836–1913) was an engineer and politician whose role in public life is mainly known due to his years as the mayor of Rio de Janeiro between 1902 and 1906. Inspired by the construction work carried out by Georges-Eugène Haussmann (1809–91) in Paris, he was responsible for widening streets, opening new broadways, and demolishing slum housing seen as unfit for habitation. These measures led to an increase in the cost of living in the urban centres, causing increased occupation of suburban peripheral and hill areas which were previously scarcely populated (Benchimol 1990).

3 For a more in-depth analysis of the relationship between graphic novels, specifically Chris Ware's *Building Stories* (2012), and the city via the concept of the 'urban assemblage', see Dittmer (2014).

4 Reflections inspired by studies on seriality in media are present in Hayward (1997) and Mayer (2014, 119–54).

5 This lyric is considered a classic of Brazilian pop music for the way it mixes hip-hop, funk and pop to address the contradictions of the city from the point of view of urban violence and politics (see Abreu 1992).

6 The name 'gari' to designate rubbish collectors in Rio de Janeiro and other Brazilian cities can be traced back to the French businessman Aleixo Gary, who set up a contract for the urban cleaning of Rio de Janeiro in the last decades of the nineteenth century. On seeing the rubbish that should have been cleaned up after horses passed through the city, the Rio locals informally spoke about calling 'Gary's people' (Prefeitura da Cidade do Rio de Janeiro 2010).

7 Only more recently has the production of comics in Brazil started to address blackness, the result of centuries of slavery and a liberation process that did not enable the exercising of citizenship for newly freed slaves. One exception is Marcelo D'Salete's recent graphic novels about Brazilian slavery (see, for example, D'Salete 2017).

References

Abreu, Fernanda. 1992. *SLA 2 Be Sample*. Rio de Janeiro: EMI-Odeon.

Ahrens, Jörn and Arno Meteling, eds. 2010. *Comics and the City: Urban Space in Print, Picture and Sequence*. New York and London: Continuum.

Balaban, Marcelo. 2009. *Poeta do Lápis. Sátira e Política na Trajetória de Angelo Agostini no Brasil Imperial (1864–1888)*. Campinas: Editora da Unicamp.

Ball, David and Martha Kuhlman, eds. 2010. *The Comics of Chris Ware: Drawing Is a Way of Thinking*. Jackson: University Press of Mississippi.

Becker, Howard. 1976. 'Art Worlds and Social Types', *American Behavioral Scientist* 19, no. 6: 703–18.

Benchimol, Jaime. 1990. *Pereira Passos, um Haussmann Tropical: A Renovação Urbana da Cidade do Rio de Janeiro no Início do Século XX*. Rio de Janeiro: Secretaria Municipal de Cultura, Turismo e Esportes.

Bredehoft, Thomas. 2014. *The Visible Text: Textual Production and Reproduction From* Beowulf *to* Maus. Oxford: Oxford University Press.

CDURP. 2015. 'Notícias: Zé Ninguém'. *Porto Maravilha*, 1 April. Last accessed 8 October 2019. https://www.portomaravilha.com.br/noticiasdetalhe/3720-ze-ninguem.

Cunha, Christina Vital da. 2017. 'Grafites do Amor, da Paz e da Alegria na Cidade Olímpica: Interfaces entre Política, Arte e Religião no Rio 2016', *Ciências Sociais Unisinos*, 53, no. 3: 499–507.

D'Salete, Marcelo. 2017. *Angola Janga: Uma História de Palmares*. São Paulo: Veneta.

Dias, Elaine. 2001. *Debret, A Pintura de História e as Ilustrações de Corte da 'Viagem Pitoresca e Histórica ao Brasil'*. Dissertation (Masters in History) – Campinas, Instituto de Filosofia e Ciências Humanas, Universidade Estadual de Campinas.

Dittmer, Jason. 2014. 'Narrating Urban Assemblages: Chris Ware and Building Stories', *Social & Cultural Geography* 15, no. 5: 477–503.

Domingues, Bruno. 2018. *A Cidade das Aquarelas: O Rio de Janeiro nos Registros de Jean-Baptiste Debret*. Dissertation (Master's in Social History), São Paulo, Pontifícia Universidade Católica de São Paulo.

Dunnet, Oliver. 2009. 'Identity and geopolitics in Hergé's *Adventures of Tintin*', *Social & Cultural Geography*, 10, no. 5: 583–98.

Eco, Umberto. 1972. 'The Myth of Superman'. *Diacritics* 2, no. 1: 14–22.

Grove, Laurence. 2010. *Comics in French: The European Bande Dessinée in Context*. Oxford and New York: Berghahn Books.

Harvey, David. 2008. 'The Right to the City', *New Left Review* 53: 23–40.

Hatfield, Charles. 2005. *Alternative Comics: An Emerging Literature*. Jackson: University Press of Mississippi.

Hayward, Jennifer. 1997. *Consuming Pleasures: Active Audiences and Serial Fictions, From Dickens to Soap Opera*. Lexington: University Press of Kentucky.

Kannenberg, Gene. 2001. 'Graphic Text, Graphic Context: Interpreting Custom Fonts and Hands in Contemporary Comics'. In *Illuminating Letters: Typography and Literary Interpretation*, edited by Paul C. Gutjahr and Megan L. Benton, 165–92. Boston: University of Massachusetts Press.

King, Edward and Joanna Page. 2017. *Posthumanism and the Graphic Novel in Latin America*. London: UCL Press.

Mayer, Ruth. 2014. *Serial Fu Manchu: The Chinese Supervillain and The Spread of Yellow Peril Ideology*. Philadelphia: Temple University Press.

Mitchell, W.J.T. 2014. 'Comics and Media: Afterwords', *Critical Inquiry* 40: 255–65.

O'Donnell, Júlia. 2013. *A Invenção de Copacabana: Culturas Urbanas e Estilos de Vida no Rio de Janeiro*. Rio de Janeiro: Editora Zahar.

Pereira, Sonia Gomes. 2013. 'Arte no Brasil no Século XIX e Início do XX'. In *História da Arte no Brasil: Textos de Síntese*, 3rd edition, edited by Myriam Oliveira, 65–110. Rio de Janeiro: Ed. UFRJ.

Prefeitura da Cidade do Rio de Janeiro. 2010. 'História. Conheça a história da Comlurb'. *Comlurb*, 4 May. Last accessed 8 October 2019. http://www.rio.rj.gov.br/web/comlurb/exibeconteudo?id=2815129.

Prefeitura da Cidade do Rio de Janeiro. 2014. Decreto Rio n° 38.307 de 18 de fevereiro de 2014: Dispõe sobre a limpeza e a manutenção dos bens públicos da Cidade do Rio de Janeiro e a relação entre Órgãos e Entidades Municipais e as atividades de GRAFFITI, STREET ART, com respectivas ocupações urbanas. Diário Oficial da Cidade do Rio de Janeiro. Last accessed 8 October 2019. https://leismunicipais.com.br/a/rj/r/rio-de-janeiro/decreto/2014/3831/38307/decreto-n-38307-2014-dispoe-sobre-a-limpeza-e-a-manutencao-dos-bens-publicos-da-cidade-do-rio-de-janeiro-e-a-relacao-entre-orgaos-e-entidades-municipais-e-as-atividades-de-graffiti-street-art-com-respectivas-ocupacoes-urbanas.

Prefeitura da Cidade do Rio de Janeiro. 2015. Decreto Rio n° 39.797, de 1° de março de 2015. Declara A 'Condição Carioca', A 'Carioquice', Como Bem Cultural Imaterial da Cidade do Rio de Janeiro. Diário Oficial da Cidade do Rio de Janeiro. Last accessed 8 October 2019. https://leismunicipais.com.br/a1/rj/r/rio-de-janeiro/decreto/2015/3980/39797/decreto-n-39797-2015-declara-a-condicao-carioca-a-carioquice-como-bem-cultural-imaterial-da-cidade-do-rio-de-janeiro.

Rodriguez, Diego. 2011. 'Quadrinhos de Rua', *Revista Trip*. Last accessed 8 October 2019. https://revistatrip.uol.com.br/trip/quadrinhos-de-rua.

Sartori, Caio. 2015. 'Palestra Conta História de Personagem Famoso nas Ruas do Rio'. *Jornal da PUC*. Last accessed 8 October 2019. http://jornaldapuc.vrc.puc-rio.br/cgi/cgilua.exe/sys/start.htm?infoid=3909&sid=29.

Smolderen, Thierry. 2009. *Naissances de la Bande Dessinée: De William Hogarth à Winsor McCay*. Bruxelles: Les Impressions Nouvelles.

Thomé, Clarissa. 2015. '"Zé Ninguém", personagem de 150 grafites, vira livro'. *O Estado de São Paulo*. Last accessed 8 October 2019. https://brasil.estadao.com.br/blogs/estadao-rio/ze-ninguem-personagem-de-150-grafites-vira-livro/.

Tito na Rua. 2014. *Portfolio Alberto Serrano 'Tito'*. Last accessed 10 June 2019. https://issuu.com/flioliveira/docs/tito_portfolio.

Tito na Rua. 2015. *Zé Ninguém*. Rio de Janeiro: Edições de Janeiro.

Vartanian, Hrag. 2009. 'Rio's Street Graphic Novelist: an Interview with Tito na Rua', *BrazilNYC*. Last accessed 8 October 2019. https://web.archive.org/web/20110803144410/http://www.brazilnyc.com/2009/06/rios-street-graphic-novelist-an-interview-with-tito-na-rua/.

Ware, Chris. 2012. *Building Stories*. New York: Pantheon Books.

9

'The Nestornaut', or how a president becomes a comic superhero

Cristian Palacios
Translated by Mariana Casale

Written by Héctor Germán Oesterheld and drawn by Francisco Solano López and first published in 1957, *El Eternauta* (*The Eternaut*) was an unprecedented success in the history of Argentine comic strips (Oesterheld and Solano López 2008).[1] The local comics industry was in the final stages of what would later become known as a veritable Golden Age, which largely coincided with the heyday of cultural industries as well as with a period of general expansion in the national industry (Vazquez 2010, 25–43; see also Vazquez's chapter in this volume). This success, which would continue to grow until it gained a prestige reserved only for great works of literature, could be explained by its exceptional quality, the use of intrigue as the main driver of the plot, the representation of the protagonist's stream of consciousness (who keeps repeating that it is 'best not to think', even as we readers witness the uninterrupted flow of his thoughts), but also, and above all, by the fact that the main events are set in some of the most iconic locations of the city of Buenos Aires (Avenida General Paz, the River Plate football stadium, Plaza de los dos Congresos). Until then, the 'home of the adventure story', as Juan Sasturain would rightly define it, had been European or US cities. It was the first time that Argentine readers witnessed a full alien invasion in the streets they walked through every day (Sasturain 1995). As in the *Zé Ninguém* street comics analysed in Ivan Lima Gomes's chapter in this volume, the city had itself become a character.

Many years later, that invasion would be reinterpreted allegorically as a representation of the numerous coups that would throw the country's precarious social balance into turmoil, between President Juan Domingo Perón's overthrow on 16 September 1955 (two years before the publication of the first *El Eternauta*) up until the definitive return to democracy on 10 December 1983. It is important to remember that, more broadly, the metaphor of invasion had been used in literature to represent the opposing forces (in Julio Cortázar's 'Casa tomada' ('House Taken Over'), for example).[2] But Peronist political allegory was a far cry from that first version of *El Eternauta* in which the army appear as allies and the petit bourgeois Juan Salvo manages to survive, first and foremost, thanks to the advantages afforded to him by his class. These advantages, he insists, are attributable to luck and not for one minute to the injustices of an unequal class system. In that sense, insufficient attention has been paid to the clue that Oesterheld himself offered in the prologue to the first reissue of the strip: '*El Eternauta* was my version of Robinson Crusoe, alone, surrounded, a prisoner, not of the sea but of death'. In the same way as Robinson, Juan Salvo was preparing to survive on his particular desert island, stripped of time and space. The deadly snow that falls at the start of the story and which kills anyone who touches it was the perfect symbol for the solitude surrounding his family and his friends in the middle-class suburb of Vicente López. Isolation – turning the house into a fortress – was the solution. But also, much like Robinson, his later aim would be to return to civilisation, to the comfort of his home and attic. The circular ending of *El Eternauta* closes the Robinsonian loop because ultimately it is about regaining lost class privileges.

> Juan Salvo, middle-class man, does not have a social conscience. He does not have a conscience of change and restructuring of the world. Like his friends, he seeks a return to a status quo: Elena wishes to return to her home, Juan wishes to be back in his wife's arms, in his property in Vicente López, his job in the business. And he does so. He actually does it. And on that return to the past, he not only builds his future tragedy, but also that of the whole of humanity.
>
> (Vazquez 2005)

One year before this first release of *El Eternauta,* the 'use of symbols, signs, meaningful expressions, doctrines, articles and artwork for Peronist ideological affirmation or for Peronist propaganda which may claim such nature or might be taken as such, belonging to or used by individuals representing Peronism or organisations thereof' had been banned under penalty of imprisonment by presidential decree on 9 March 1956 (Executive Decree number 4161 9/03/1956). This law inaugurated an extended period of proscription of the main national political force. This crucial interdiction would feed a Peronist imagery that would later acquire almost legendary status. Certainly the deliberate use of 'symbols, signs, meaningful expressions' that the decree refers to had been a trademark of early Peronism. And the visual imaginary of Perón and of Evita had been used for propaganda to a degree that surpassed all previous Argentine political movements (see, for example, Plotkin 1994). But it is also true that the ban imbued these symbols with a mystique beyond the realm of mere propaganda.

It was not until the new millennium, however, that Peronism became the political and ideological framework for an Argentine president turned superhero. In late August 2010 a meeting took place between the then former president Néstor Kirchner and the militant youth wing of the Kirchnerist movement under the slogan 'bancando a Cristina' ('standing by Cristina'). This rally was promoted by the group known as La Cámpora,[3] whose manifest aim was to show the widespread support of the militant youth for the president: Cristina Fernández de Kirchner. Néstor's wife and presidential successor, Cristina was embattled at the time as a result of a conflict with the country's major media conglomerates. In fact, Néstor Kirchner's election in 2003 had entailed a surprising shift to the centre-left of a Peronism whose recent presidents (Carlos Menem 1989–95, 1995–9; Eduardo Duhalde 2001–3) had positioned themselves clearly on the most neoliberal extreme of Argentine politics. Following the institutional crisis that included the resignation of several presidents during the final weeks of December 2001, Néstor Kirchner would be remembered as the political figure who took the country out of crisis, lowered poverty and unemployment rates, cancelled foreign debt, and reopened the Trials for Crimes Against Humanity, as well as a host of other policies that were diametrically opposed to the previous administrations.

The poster advertising the rally (Figure 9.1) revealed the former president wearing the Eternaut's characteristic diving suit in the midst of the deadly snowfall, walking with his archetypal smile. This poster was the birth of the 'Nestornaut'. Conceived as an advertising joke, the image would acquire huge popularity a few months later following the sudden demise of the former head of state. The Nestornaut would subsequently become a veritable emblem of the Kirchnerist movement, not only as one of the most representative images used by the vast crowds that attended the leader's funeral, but also as an icon of the political struggles that were to follow. The Nestornaut appeared on T-shirts, stencils, placards and banners as the symbol of resistance to powers which did not see eye to eye with the State, a power which the then head of state, Cristina Fernández de Kirchner, widow of the Nestornaut, was having to confront.

Figure 9.1 Political poster that first showed the Nestornaut, an image of former Argentine president Néstor Kirchner wearing the costume of Héctor G. Oesterheld's character the Eternaut.

There have been other studies – see Scolari (2014), Gago (2015), Francescutti (2015), Vacchieri and Castagnino (2015), as well as my own (Palacios 2012) – which either analyse the figure of the Nestornaut (Francescutti), read it as part of a global history of the character of the Eternaut (Scolari, Gago, Palacios), or see it as an example of transmediation within contemporary Argentine fiction (Vacchieri and Castagnino). Though I draw on these studies here, I focus more on determining what the necessary conditions for the emergence and success of an image like the Nestornaut were. As well as the political history of the Peronist movement and the social and political history of *El Eternauta* itself and its writer, Héctor Germán Oesterheld, I will argue that the role played by the national comic-strip industry as a catalyst for the political events of the 1960s and 1970s and during the return to democracy is also crucial. In the remainder of this chapter, I will unpack these various aspects, focusing in particular on the controversy that arose after the creation of the Nestornaut.

El Eternauta: A social and political history of a misunderstanding

The social and political history that would end up presenting *El Eternauta* as a symbol of successive acts of resistance against the invader embodied by multiple military regimes originates in Oesterheld's biography: he became a member of the Montoneros, a militant left-wing Peronist group, becoming its Press Secretary and writing the comic strip '450 Years of War Against Imperialism', which was published in the magazine *El Descamisado* (the group's official publication) from its tenth issue on 10 July 1973. Together with his four daughters (two of them pregnant at the time), Oesterheld was also one of the many 'disappeared' during the last military dictatorship (1976–83). In '450 Years . . .', analysed in Silvia Sigal and Eliseo Verón's now classic study of Peronist discourse (2003), a certain view of history was brought into play, by which the past as a symbol of the present was made up of a long succession of 17 Octobers (the date in 1945 when crowds demanded the release of the then imprisoned Perón) and Septembers 1955 (when he was deposed by a military coup) (Sigal and Verón 2003, 196). That is to say, this was an immobile history, anchored in a dialectic which entailed the legitimation of the movement itself, given that it had always been there, letting itself be killed and resisting. The Peronist Youth was just a new incarnation of those who had always, ever since the Conquest, defended the People-Homeland from an invading enemy identified with Imperialism.[4]

Surprisingly, a similar view of history had been forestalled in the second version of *El Eternauta*, which was published in *Gente* magazine in 1969 (Oesterheld and Breccia 1982). This second version takes up the storyline of the first and rewrites it but also adds some strange elements, even to the plot, in what might be interpreted as a blunder on Oesterheld's part, an attempt to insert a political reading that did not fit with the narrative. To begin with, the alien invaders in the new version have created a pact with the great global powers, the latter handing Latin America over to them. The intrigue that the 1957 version handled so well is replaced by a more naïve view of history that sets out a meaning which, as I have shown, the first *Eternauta* lacked: 'The invader used to be the exploitative countries, the large corporations. . . . Its deadly snowfalls were . . . poverty, backwardness, our own selfishness,' as the character

Favalli explains. Here, the interplanetary and impersonal horror of the first *Eternauta* has been disrupted by the presence of alien invaders who have been negotiating with the Pentagon and the Kremlin.

I would argue, then, that the allegorical reading of *El Eternauta*, particularly the way that it is subsequently connected to the figure of Néstor Kirchner, is based on a misunderstanding because the image itself alludes to the first version, which was devoid of the political slant that would be introduced by the second version. The latter, moreover, was drawn by Alberto Breccia in a style which contrasted not only with the earlier realism of Francisco Solano López but also with the propagandist tone that Oesterheld would come to acquire. That this second politicised version was published in *Gente* was an oddity, since the magazine was known as much for its frivolity as for its profoundly reactionary spirit. In fact, publication would later be suspended as readers started expressing their irritation not with the script but with Breccia's dark, avant-garde style.

Later studies would see this episode as the expression of a certain political unease on the part of a magazine whose views were diametrically opposed to the reading of history that the strip proposed: the deadly snowfalls and alien invaders, once the conquistadors, are now the great neocolonial superpowers. Such a reading was entirely in tune with that taken by the young editors of *El Descamisado*. *Gente* magazine presented an alternative view of history: that history moves forward in spite of those who should not, in any case, be classified as 'people' (since they are responsible for 'violence'). Progress is the inherent condition of history: 'I look at my country from a distance and it infuriates me that we are wasting so much time', wrote the editor Carlos Fontanarrosa from New York, later apologising to readers not for stopping the publication of *El Eternauta* but for having published it in the first place. In that issue, dated 18 September 1969, he writes:

> See you soon and let it be clear that my 'moment of truth' is near, that truth which cannot be replaced with strangers, buildings, different shows, the chance to get to know and experience a world like this one, nothing, nothing can replace the need to return to your own, to what belongs to you, to what you're about.
>
> (*Gente* 216, 18 September 1969)

For the editor, the enemies are those responsible for a violence that does not allow history to follow its inexorable course; for Oesterheld, on the other hand, the enemies are those who prevent change, allowing history to repeat itself. That these are diametrically opposed points of view passes unnoticed by both the editor and the readers in their letters to the editor. Instead, the complaints are directed at the 'graphic message' of Breccia's artwork: 'I will not deny the artistic quality of Breccia's drawings, but his value as comic strip illustrator is, however, debatable,' says a reader in issue number 209. Carlos Fontanarrosa for his part adds:

> [W]e had a great opportunity with 'El Eternauta' here in the magazine, a strip, as you all remember, which 'we could see' and that is why we published it. I hope Breccia will forgive me, he is a great illustrator, even, I would say, an artist, but in our mission to achieve communication we should have not surrendered to the aesthetic form of his drawing which at times became unintelligible.
>
> (*Gente* 216, 18 September 1969)

Trillo and Saccomano subsequently wrote a prologue for the comic edition in which they claimed that 'focusing on Breccia's formal ruptures allows [the editor] to avoid analysing the discourse of the story that Oesterheld tells, which would evidently force him to show himself as unfriendly to his readers. 'Form and content are always inextricably linked,' they argued:

> The drama of the story, that group fighting for their integrity, for a piece of life, betrayed by the great powers who have negotiated the invasion; that group, we mean, who in one of the thought bubbles remembers Tupac Amaru, needed to be drawn as Breccia drew them, with heartrending, sombre, harrowing expressionism.
>
> (Trillo and Saccomanno 1982, 11)

However, nowhere else in Oesterheld's work is there such a harsh contrast between what is being said and what can be seen. Not because what is said might be different from what is seen, but because the strategy the text uses to tell the story is radically different from the one used by the drawing. Trillo and Saccomanno, as well as Fontanarrosa, confuse the pairing of 'form/content' with the pairing of 'drawing/verbal text'. But if we recognise such a separation, then 'form' is also the way in which we choose to speak. That form, in this case, is at the service of 'communication', a 'literary message'. This idea, that the violence of the invasion does not differ in essence from the violence that the world's superpowers exercise on Latin America, does not appear, at least not in such explicit terms, in the first *Eternauta*.

This conception of the language of comics is similar to that put forward by Oscar Masotta in *La historieta en el mundo moderno* (Masotta 1970), one of the first theoretical studies of comics published in Argentina. Defining comics as 'drawn literature', Masotta was trying to legitimate an object of study which until then had never been addressed in theoretical terms. But in so doing he positioned drawing as being subordinate to other art forms, not least at a time when Argentine artists were producing the greatest innovations in terms of form. Breccia himself, not only in his *Eternauta* but also and perhaps even more so in his later adaptations of classics of world literature, distances himself from the illusion of transparency which the epigones of the language had so far demanded. In fact, this 1969 *Eternauta* marks Breccia's definitive leap into a type of illustration which does not subordinate itself at all to the word, which does not try to communicate anything so much as bring out the conventional nature of all representation. In that sense, this *Eternauta* marks the end of the adventure story in contemporary Argentine comics.

Robinsonian or not, the notion of adventure was subsequently replaced by Oesterheld's political experiment. But it was also part of a more general trend in Argentine and Latin American comics of the early 1970s, which believed that sacrificing adventure was the price to pay for admission into the world of art. Authors had begun to feel increasingly unhappy with the role of mass media art that had been ascribed to comics and they simultaneously felt compelled to address the violent events that were plaguing Argentine society at the time. Oesterheld's was just one strategy of many approaches to this problem.

There is, moreover, a substantial difference between the 1969 *Eternauta* and the final one, published in *Skorpio* magazine between 1976 and 1978 (Oesterheld was captured in 1977 and killed at some point later that year or in early 1978). This third version takes up the end of the first, continuing the plot and breaking the circularity of the original story. That is significant when considering the view of history that underpins Oesterheld's later work, which is very different to that found in *El Descamisado* and even more so to that in his famous publications of *Mort Cinder* (originally published between 1962 and 1964 in the magazine *Misterix*), *Ticonderoga* (originally published between 1957 and 1962 in the magazines *Hora Cero Extra* and *Hora Cero Semanal*), or *Sherlock Time* (originally published between 1958 and 1959 in *Hora Cero*

Extra and *Hora Cero Semanal*). Whereas the version published in *Gente* justified violence through the need for struggle, in this later case only completely unjustifiable violence remained. Turned superhero, Juan Salvo (and with him Oesterheld) espouses the pessimism of an unredeemable history. Many studies have claimed that the third version is the most political of the three. I would argue that this version, written clandestinely and after the abduction of two of his daughters, is only highly political insofar as it does not convey exasperation with politics but its total and utter negation.

Secret origins: From the *Eternaut* to the *Nestornaut,* and back again

The Nestornaut was just one of the three or four images used to advertise the rally of the Peronist Youth at Luna Park stadium on 14 August 2010 to celebrate 1,000 days of Cristina Fernández de Kirchner in office, a moment of crisis for the movement. Kirchnerism generally, and Néstor Kirchner in particular, had lost the 2009 legislative elections. The 2008 crisis in the agricultural sector (known as the 'crisis del campo' (crisis of the countryside)) had put the government in opposition to the more traditionally conservative sectors, fuelling its conflict with the mass media, particularly the monopoly represented by the newspaper *Clarín*, the TV channel *Canal 13*, and their subsidiaries. That conflict played out against the backdrop of the passing of the Ley de Medios (Media Bill), whose approval in 2009 would never be accepted by the mega corporations (and which would later be wiped out at a single stroke by Mauricio Macri, whose presidential campaign had been supported by that media monopoly, just a few days after coming to power).[5]

> Unlike the fictional character, which was promoted by subaltern intellectuals from the bottom up until it obtained the recognition of academics and political institutions, the trajectory of the Nestornaut goes in the opposite direction, as it is invented by a splinter group of the governing party, radiating out from there first to its followers and then to the wider public sphere.
>
> (Francescutti 2015, 34)

Nevertheless, the massive bicentenary celebrations, which those hostile to the government had tried to prevent, had proved effective. The festive climate of the day had brought back a historical memory, one that had been a political banner of Kirchnerism and which was in stark contrast to the non-existent politics of memory of Néstor's main opponent, Maurico Macri, the then mayor of the City of Buenos Aires.[6]

As I have demonstrated, that first poster, whose central image would go viral after the death of the former president,[7] incorporated a misguided metaphor in which the deadly snowfall and the alien invasion could be read as a figure, almost an allegory, of the political violence of the 1960s and 1970s. The main intention was to reactivate historical memory by associating Kirchnerism with the movements of that earlier period, presenting the enemies of the movement (particularly the president's enemies) as the 'aliens': the other, the threat, the 'Them' against whom the former president advanced, 'supporting Cristina', as the poster read.

However, when it comes to a deep understanding of the image, another detail is important: the erasure of the rifle that Favalli gave Juan Salvo to protect himself from potential threats during his first expedition outside the house. That detail gave new meaning to the story as, though the enemies are the same, the weapons are different. Once again, that view of history in which past and present merge into a single circular account whose episodes are mere repetitions of one same event, seemed to be re-updated, as both presidents were associated with the Peronist Youth which had at the time exploited the possibilities of a similar view as a way of legitimising the movement to which they belonged.

There was, however, a subtle difference, as Peronism had also changed. In fact, the way the poster with the image of the Nestornaut is framed is quite different from the solemnity typical of the strips of *El Descamisado* and from the usual way in which the archetypical figures of Perón and Eva had always been depicted. Instead, the background drawing, the choice of colours, the stereotypical, playful font of superhero comics, the rhetorical device of articulating the phrase as a palindrome – 'Néstor le habla a la Juventud le habla a Néstor [Néstor speaks to the Youth speak to Néstor]', with the frame of reference 'LA JUVENTUD' at the centre – the use of the imperative ('vienen todos, convocá [everyone's coming, invite]'), all speak of a cynical distancing which had not existed in the traditional imagery associated with the movement. The gesture which led the militant youth to liken the president to a comic-strip hero might seem similar to the glorification of the images of Perón and Eva in early Peronism. But it was substantially different because the use of a comic-strip character fell outside the conditions of possibility of first- and second-wave Peronism. Historically, either as cartoons or as more serious, educational tools, comic strips had incorporated political figures only in terms of satire and mockery, or by way of canonising historical figures from the past. They were never used to nod playfully to their followers.

The retrieval of the more mystical imagery of the Peronist movement was carried out, then, by means of a suggestive disbelief in the images it revered. Associated with the more popular sectors of Argentine society, traditionally hostile to the spheres of high culture whose most prominent members (writer Jorge Luis Borges, for instance) used to be decidedly anti-Peronist, new Peronism rescued from oblivion some of its most iconic symbols, which were now resignified as pop-art objects, as the use of the abbreviation 'Nac & Pop' (National and Popular) to refer to the cultural movement most clearly linked to Kirchnerism bears out. This cynical distancing enabled not only the emergence of figures like the Nestornaut, but also the success of TV character Bombita Rodríguez, referred to as 'el Palito Ortega montonero', by Argentine comedian Diego Capusotto.[8] Only through a similar strategy could Peronism reinstall an aesthetic that had been lost following the disastrous neoliberal policies of the Menem era.

Such cynical distancing entailed a double effect, characteristic of any humorous discourse. The comical draws on a common ideological field shared with its audience, 'a basic ideological pact' (Steimberg 1977). A 'recognition effect' occurs, which establishes complicity between author and reader. This recognition effect, which constitutes one of the essential aspects of any ideological effect (Verón 2004, 106), achieves a double result: the inclusion of the reader, who is now part of the producer's cultural universe and thus becomes 'complicit'; and the exclusion of those who do not have the necessary prior knowledge. That is to say, to those who knew and shared the doctrinal universe of Peronism, the joke underlying the image of the Nestornaut was clear. The superimposition of Néstor's smile and the archetypical smile of Perón is one such example of these gestures (another of the lines utilised by Diego Capusotto in Bombita Rodríguez's song is 'Mummy's smile is like Perón's').

Furthermore, and perhaps most interestingly, for any reader unfamiliar with the code, the recognition effect remains. The reader or viewer of a joke can reconstruct an ideological assumption unknown to him or her from the joke itself. Or, in the words of Umberto Eco: if the comical violates an implicit rule, even the spectator or reader who is unfamiliar with that rule can reassemble it based on the joke (Eco 1998). This means that the comical not only creates the object which it mocks, but also, by contrast, shows us what is serious, what is normal, what the rule is that we are escaping from. In this particular case, it involves the rediscovery of an unknown aesthetic based on the parody and transformation of that aesthetic. Such is the case, for example, of young people who had never read *El Eternauta*, who knew nothing about Oesterheld and, most importantly, who did not share in the repertoire of images typical of historical Peronism nor in the doctrine of heroism and the epic which it had traditionally supported.

This second effect, however, reached its limits in those who saw the image as incongruent or simply believed that *El Eternauta* (or even Peronism) meant something different. For instance, one of the main drivers behind the canonisation of the strip, Guillermo Saccomano, stated in an article published in the newspaper *Página/12* that 'if there was something that *El Eternauta* as a series embodied it was precisely the destruction of the individual and romantic view of the hero. Those of us who are in our sixties today, almost the age of Juan Salvo, know the risks of an elitist construction of the hero as a political adventurer' (2011). Another of the opposing voices was that of Alejandro Scutti, director of the publishing house *Récord*:

> They are misrepresenting the character, they are politicising him somehow, it is plagiarism [. . .]. They want to present Kirchner as a hero and to preserve him in time. As Perón was at the time [. . .]. We are the sole owners of the rights to *El Eternauta*; it is annoying that nobody looks for the relevant owner of the rights to do what they do.
>
> (*La Nación*, 10 October 2011)

The anger of sociologist Marcos Novaro, author of *Historia de la Argentina 1955–2010*, is perhaps more surprising, as he denies all similarities between the fictional character and the political leader, a gesture that entails taking the fictional character seriously, believing in him as a real person. He described Kirchner as 'A bloke who never ran any risks [. . .] who never distinguished himself for his fearlessness. And who therefore never paid personal costs [. . .] he was the prototype of the politician who takes no risks; he has nothing of the Eternaut about him' (cited in Francescutti 2015, 38).

José Pablo Feinmann published an article in *Página/12* in which he defended the figure of the Nestornaut against the onslaught of Mauricio Macri who, as a reaction to the debates around the Nestornaut, decided to ban the distribution of the comic strip *El Eternauta* in the schools of the City of Buenos Aires:

> *El Eternauta* was a symbol of my generation, of that 'decimated generation' which Kirchner mentioned in his inaugural speech, and the youth of today know it and they have decided that it should also be theirs; their symbol, no? The symbol of the struggle for a fairer, freer, more democratic country, one which respects, once and for all, all Indians, those with darker skin and all the good people. That is the message. That is what the much-feared (by you and by your advisers, because without your advisors, forgive me, you're nothing) Nestornaut symbolises. Nothing better than that message of life and respect for others. And of respect for politics as a means of transforming an evidently unjust world, the world that you represent.
>
> (*Página/12*, 27 August 2012)

Lautaro Ortiz, then editor-in-chief of *Fierro* magazine, also defended the use of the figure of the Nestornaut: 'Taking *El Eternauta*, Kirchnerism put forward a reading that, actually, is not far at all from the one Oesterheld himself had posed, and from that of scholars who studied that work: friendship, group struggle, the collective mission, the fate of societies, one's own strength when faced with the enemy' (cited in Francescutti 2015, 38).

Despite their differences, however, all these views amounted to taking the Nestornaut seriously. But such an attitude, I would suggest, was not congruent with the moment of its original creation. To the militant youths who came to Luna Park on 14 September 2010, the joke was clear. A few months later, however, Néstor Kirchner died suddenly at his home in El Calafate. The president's death provided the Nestornaut with a seriousness originally exempted from the character. Now a symbol of much more, it also implied the end of the cynical distancing which had characterised the retrieval of the Peronist imaginary for the new generations. That is why the controversies that followed were not able to recover for themselves the comical gesture that had been a feature of the image when it first appeared. The seriousness of the invectives was responding both positively and negatively to the way the figure of the president was being canonised. The sudden clash with the reality of death dissipated the risible effect and gave new life to the images of the movement. For many young university students like myself, it meant having to position ourselves in relation to the government at the time. Now it was acceptable to be a Kirchnerist. We could say it out loud. For better or for worse, the Nestornaut had become immortal.

Conclusion

The appropriation of the figure of the Eternaut by the Kirchnerist movement did not occur without certain resistance from those sectors which felt that a national symbol was being taken away from them and put at the service of a cause that they did not support. That was despite the fact that the legitimate heirs of its creators had previously agreed to such use.[9] If there were any objections to the political use of *El Eternauta* it was only from those who considered that it was a sacred object of Argentine culture which they were not prepared to give up. But the question remained over which Oesterheld and which *Eternauta* they had in mind. The enthroning of Oesterheld as the great Argentine comics writer had occurred prior to his abduction and murder and prior to his more distinctly propagandist work. Those who criticised the Nestornaut referred to the early Oesterheld, prior to his political conversion. Returning to the controversy surrounding the 1969 version, it is surprising how the complaints of the readers are all directed against Breccia's graphic work, with nothing being said about the ideological turn that the story takes or Oesterheld being left unscathed. By then the strip and its writer had already been canonised to the point that the declarations of the author himself were falling on deaf ears. On the other hand, those who defended its political use focused their gaze on the late Oesterheld, choosing to ignore his earlier work.

People entered a dispute over the figure of Juan Salvo similar in fashion to the controversies surrounding the deaths of Sherlock Holmes or Superman, a point that opens up questions about the status of characters in contemporary culture. Character theories present in narratology and in contemporary literary criticism focus on the classic Aristotelian discussion over whether the character precedes the plot or vice versa, taking for granted the reciprocal relationship between them. Writers such as William H. Gass maintain that both the stories and the characters that inhabit them are fundamentally made up of words (cited in Leitch 1986, 154). Algirdas Julien Greimas's (1990) actantial model, for example, deliberately omits any reference to psychological aspects or to identification with any human type. But, as the case of the Eternaut demonstrates, a character is much more than the agent of a certain succession of events. A character's life in society far exceeds the limits of a storyline in which they are born and develop. Superman, Sherlock Holmes, Ulysses, Dracula, Snoopy, Mafalda, Clemente or the Eternaut all have a life beyond the page, which cannot be explained by psychological identification or with reference to a scheme of events whose stability they would guarantee. The idea of narrative transmediatisation, which has garnered interest in recent years (Scolari 2014), is in fact implicit in the very concept of character itself.

Figure 9.2 Internet meme refashioning the Nestornaut but on this occasion with two money bags. The meme is entitled 'El Chorronauta', or 'The Robbernaut'.

To end I will mention one final example. In Figure 9.2 the Nestornaut has been transformed into 'El Chorronauta' (The Robbernaut), a clearly negative depiction of the figure of the former president consistent with the frequent accusations of illicit gain made by the opposition with the complaisance of the mass media, which was unsympathetic to him during his final years. In it, Kirchner can be seen surrounded by a shower of banknotes as he walks carrying bags of money. Next to him, the captions explain that 'Nestor Kirchner was president of Argentina, and he was the worst thief in the history of the country', before continuing 'Nestor Kirchner bears no relation to the strip "*El Eternauta*" [. . .] if anyone from *La Cámpora* lies to you or gives you the comic strip, tell your parents and call the police. These people are thieves'. There is also a visual comparison between the Eternaut and the Nestornaut (in fact, it is the 'Chorronauta' since he is surrounded by banknotes), respectively labelled as 'Real' and 'False'.

However, the virulence with which he is attacked, the insistence that you call the police, and the mention of a comic strip (*The Nestornaut*) that never existed, are all perhaps less interesting than the presence of Sponge Bob in the lower right-hand corner, who explains: 'a message from your friend Sponge Bob!'. Here the opposing political movement uses a well-known children's character in a denunciation that underpins the appropriation of Oesterheld's character. Characters have a social impact which goes far beyond the medium in which they are originally shaped. What is lacking even today is a discursive theory of the fictional character, a theory which accounts for the incorporation of characters into reality, their life in society, their ability to narrate us, and also to narrate themselves through us.

Notes

1 T.N.: Even though an English translation of *El Eternauta* exists (*The Eternaut*, tr. Erica Mena, Fantagraphics Books, 2012), the original Spanish title is preserved here due to its iconic status and to reflect the general trend in English-language scholarship. The English version of the character's proper name, 'the Eternaut', has been used to differentiate it from the strip.

2 In this short story an unknown something or someone gradually takes over the protagonists' house until they end up being expelled from their home. The story has traditionally been read as a metaphor for the irruption of the first wave of Peronism (1946–55) in the social life of the upper classes and their intellectual exponents.

3 The aforementioned group takes its name from José Cámpora, the first Peronist president elected following the end of the proscription law. He resigned from post after 49 days to allow Perón to return to power. His campaign slogan had been 'Cámpora to government, Perón to power'.

4 The political youth group known as Juventud Peronista, or 'JP', was a resistance movement of the most left-wing section of the party. From its ranks would emerge some of the clandestine armed organisations that would confront the successive military regimes of the 1960s and 1970s. It was historically refounded by Gustavo Rearte in 1957 after the dissolution of the original Movimiento de la Juventud Peronista following the overthrow of Perón in 1955. The youth movement was reactivated during Néstor Kirchner and Cristina Fernández de Kirchner's presidencies, taking shape as various different groups, including La Cámpora, JP Evita, JP Peronismo Militante or JP Descamisados. Néstor Kirchner and Cristina Fernández had themselves been militant members of the Federación Universitaria de la Revolución Nacional in their youth.

5   After Néstor Kirchner's death, one of the many offshoots of the Nestornaut – in this instance taking up Breccia's image – shows the leader removing his hood and exclaiming 'We can breathe now, kid!', an allusion to the declaration of constitutionality of the Ley de Medios by the Supreme Court of Justice on 29 October 2013.

6   In contrast with Kirchnerist memory politics, the politics of denial of historical memory has been characteristic of Macri's presidency. One of the first things his government did, for example, was to replace the images of the various historical figures who appeared on banknotes (the Kirchners had added Eva Perón to the 100-peso bill, for example) with animals. See, for example, https://www.politicargentina.com/notas/201612/18377-el-gobierno-reemplazara-a-los-proceres-de-los-billetes-por-animales.html

7   The image of the Nestornaut can be seen in many murals which adorn the city of Buenos Aires and its surroundings. Adorning school walls, soup kitchens, Justicialista Party grassroots centres, and often accompanied by allusive inscriptions ('love defeats hate', 'a thousand flowers will blossom', 'they can cut all the flowers but they cannot stop Spring'), the stencil can be found throughout the city of Buenos Aires and many other Argentine cities. Flags, banners, T-shirts, mugs, even shoes have been made with it. The image was used on the web throughout Cristina Fernández de Kirchner's second term, both as praise and criticism. On 19 February 2011, the website of the Argentine national press agency *TELAM* displayed the image of the Nestornaut on its homepage for a few hours, though it was later removed following a brief outcry.

8   The figure of Bombita Rodríguez combines the irreconcilable images of the Montoneros and Palito Ortega, a conservative and reactionary popular singer who would later become Governor of the Province of Tucumán during Carlos Menem's presidency. The contradictory combination of a type of 'cheap, popular, catchy song and lyrics which instigated revolution in Argentina' is comic because it not only contrasts two traditionally opposing worlds but also links the values, concepts, notions and names of a proverbially solemn Left. In this way, Bombita Rodríguez stars in soaps such as one which tells the story of a cab driver in Havana – 'Rolando Rivas Marxista', a pun on the title of the Argentine soap 'Rolando Rivas Taxista' – or takes part in hidden camera pranks on members of the bourgeoisie such as 'VideoMarx' (a pun on *Videomatch*, a TV programme famous for its candid camera sketches).

9   'Marina López, daughter of Solano López, the work's illustrator who died in 2011, said that her father agreed with the use of "the Nestornaut". Martín Mórtola Oesterheld, the writer's grandson, points out that "*El Eternauta* had already been used by other political groups" – the Darío Santillán Popular Front being one of them – and that its use by Kirchnerism had been authorised by Elsa Sánchez, the writer's widow' ('El héroe será llamado a la lucha', *Clarín*, 14 October 2014).

References

Eco, Umberto. 1998. *Faith in Fakes: Travels in Hyperreality*. London: Vintage.

Francescutti, Pablo. 2015. 'Del Eternauta al "Nestornauta": La transformación de un icono cultural en un símbolo político', *CIC Cuadernos de Información y Comunicación*, 20: 27–43.

Gago, Sebastián. 2015. 'La lectura de Oesterheld antes y después del retorno democrático', *La Trama de la Comunicación*, 19: 131–49.

Greimas, Algirdas Julien. 1990. *Narrative Semiotics and Cognitive Discourses*. London: Pinter.

Leitch, Thomas. 1986. *What Stories Are*. University Park: Pennsylvania State University Press.

Masotta, Oscar. 1970. *La historieta en el mundo moderno*. Buenos Aires: Paidós.

Oesterheld, Héctor G. and Alberto Breccia. 1982. *El Eternauta [1969]*. Buenos Aires: Ediciones de la Urraca.

Oesterheld, Héctor G. and Francisco Solano López. 2008. *El Eternauta [1957–1959]*. Buenos Aires: Doedytores.

Palacios, Cristian. 2012. 'Desfasajes: Entre la historieta y la política', *La Trama de la comunicación*, 16, no. 1: 105–17.

Plotkin, Mariano Ben. 1994. *Mañana es San Perón*. Buenos Aires: Ariel.

Sasturain, Juan. 1995. *El domicilio de la aventura*. Buenos Aires: Colihue.

Scolari, Carlos. 2014. 'El Eternauta: Transmedia Expansions, Political Resistance and Popular Appropriations of a Human Hero'. In *Transmedia Archaeology: Storytelling in the Borderlines of Science Fiction, Comics and Pulp Magazines*, edited by Carlos Scolari, Paolo Bertetti and Matthew Freeman, 55–71. Basingstoke: Palgrave Macmillan.

Sigal, Silvia and Eliseo Verón. 2003. *Perón o muerte: Los fundamentos discursivos del discurso peronista*. Buenos Aires: Eudeba.

Steimberg, Oscar. 1977. *Leyendo historietas*. Buenos Aires: Nueva Visión.

Trillo, Carlos and Guillermo Saccomanno. 1982. 'Una revista fresca y una historieta podrida'. In Héctor G. Oesterheld and Alberto Breccia, *El Eternauta*. Buenos Aires: Ediciones de la Urraca.

Vacchieri, Ariana and Luciana Castagnino. 2015. 'Narrativas transmedia: Cuando los relatos no se quedan quietos'. In *La cultura argentina hoy: Tendencias!* edited by Luis A. Quevedo. Buenos Aires: Siglo XXI.

Vazquez, Laura. 2005. '¿A quién salva Juan Salvo?: Otra lectura de El Eternauta'. *Tebeosfera*, 2 October. Last accessed 10 June 2019. https://www.tebeosfera.com/1/Seccion/AEC/03/Eternauta.htm.

Vazquez, Laura. 2010. *El oficio de las viñetas: La industria de la historieta Argentina*. Buenos Aires: Paidós.

Verón, Eliseo. 2004. *Fragmentos de un tejido*. Buenos Aires: Gedisa.

10
Comics and teaching architecture in Uruguay

Jorge Tuset
Translated by Mariana Casale

Introduction

The use of the graphic language of comics as a teaching resource goes back to the very origins of the medium. A friend of Goethe's, the Swiss teacher Rodolphe Töpffer (1799–1846) was not just one of the first comics artists but also one of the first educational practitioners of comics, as he started using drawn sequences with texts to keep the attention of his young students, a practice that led to the publication of a small album called *Les Amours de M. Vieux-Bois* (1839). At the same time, not least when designing and drawing backgrounds, whether historical, present or future, illustrators and comics creators have long turned to architectural forms as a key tool. In the early twentieth century, for example, Richard Fenton Outcault (1863–1928) set his famous Yellow Kid around Hogan's Alley, a typical street of New York's slums, and Winsor McCay (1869–1934) located Little Nemo not just in the imaginary universe of Slumberland but also in the colourful urban landscape of Chicago's skyscrapers. In this chapter I will look at both of these elements of the comics world: education and architecture, with a particular focus on a Uruguayan case study.

Comics are now widely recognised as an extremely effective vehicle for disseminating, conveying and debating ideas and concepts in education at all levels (primary, secondary and tertiary). To cite one contemporary example, the French company Cabrilog, which specialises in the development of teaching tools, has created interactive geometry software for the teaching of geometry and trigonometry based on the enigma and problems posed by the infinitely growing cube that is the central character of *La fièvre d'Urbicande* (The Fever of Urbicande) created by François Schuiten and Benoît Peeters (1985). In Uruguay, the work of architect and graphic designer Alejandro Rodríguez Juele, illustrator and comics scriptwriter Nicolás Peruzzo, and humanities scholar Victoria Saibene, are all significant in this field. These figures are key members of the Bandas Educativas (Educational Strips) collective, which brings together many authors (many of whom are comics professionals) who develop and disseminate a significant amount of digital teaching material to support the teaching of national history at primary school level. Rodríguez Juele himself developed and published a series of stories based on little-known incidents in Uruguayan history past and present (*La isla elefante* in 2011 and a series of stories based on the experiences of the Uruguayan Army as part of the Peace Corps in the Congo, published in *Lento* magazine).

Comics and architecture are, in any case, closely linked. In his paper at the XV COMICON, which took place in Naples in April 2013, Italian architect and comics scholar Andrea Alberghini (2013) said:

> If we define architecture as the device which allows individuals and communities to represent themselves in a particular social context, the connections between this art and the language of images seem obvious. Specifically, comics and architecture share a basic generative tool: drawing. While it is true that the aim of architecture is to build and transform the world, the function of drawing is a propaedeutic one, as it prefigures the result of such transformations, translating ideal aspirations into images, and constituting a powerful critical and reflective tool.

Nowadays many architects and architects' groups see comics as an important vehicle for disseminating and debating their projects and proposals, as well as for expressing their different ideological stances. Some examples of such approaches can be found in the work of the Spanish firm bRijUNi architects, notably 'Vivir y dejar Rotterdam [Living and Leaving in Rotterdam]' (2006), or the well-known monograph by the Danish architect Bjarke Ingels about the work of his firm, BIG, entitled *Yes is More: An Archicomic in Architectural Evolution* (the title making direct reference to the graphic medium; Bjarke Ingels Group 2009). The list of architects who have utilised comics has grown over the past 20 years or so. Prominent figures who have availed themselves of comics include: the

Dutch architect Rem Koolhaas, who, together with Tomas Koolhaas and Louis Price, used comics in *Byzantium*, part of the voluminous *S, M, L, XL* (1995, 354–61); François Henninen, Tony Neyeux and Florian Tayssié, who created a mural in the shape of a gigantic comic strip to present the plan for the city of Valencia in 2005; the French architect Jean Nouvel in the work *Littoral*; the Swiss architects Jacques Herzog and Pierre De Meuron, with the support of Eth Zurich, as part of their proposal for *Metrobasel: A Model for the European Region* (2009); or the award-winning *00110 Arquitectura*, a collective of young Spanish architects whose 'Efecto Arenal' and their 'Cómic Urbano' won a special mention in the 2017 edition of the European 14 competition. There are also a growing number of studies that analyse the various perspectives taken by comics that address architecture and architectural forms, including works such as *Sequenze Urbane: La Metropoli nel Fumetto* (2006), a book by Italian architect and comics scholar Andrea Alberghini; *Comics and the City* (2010), a compilation by Jörn Ahrens and Arno Meteling; and Laura Cassará and Sebastiano D'Urso's essay *Goodbye Topolina*: *Su architettura e fumetto* (2013).[1]

Despite these practices and studies, and the close affinity between comics and architecture, there are relatively few examples of comics being used to teach architecture, either at degree or postgraduate level. Experiences are limited and partial even at first-rate academic institutions. Some isolated examples include Paloma Úbeda Mansilla's study for the Universidad Politécnica de Madrid, 'El cómic contextualizado en la clase de ESP para arquitectos: El diseño de una unidad' (2000), where she points out that 'teaching methods in some particular fields in the world of teaching fail to meet the needs for designing activities which fit with the most immediate and real interests of students in an enjoyable way'. Spanish architect and teacher Koldo Lus Arana has also published papers in the context of the Harvard Graduate School of Design as well as MAS Context no.20 *Narrative* (2013). Finally, Jimenez Lai from China has published *Citizens of No Place: An Architectural Graphic Novel*, an essay on contemporary urban planning (2012).

The current position of this line of research and work within the School of Architecture, Design and Urban Planning of the University of the Republic of Uruguay, a state higher education institution, differs little from this general reluctance to embrace comics. In the last 20 years, this institution has displayed rather endogamous behaviour in terms of its vision of architecture as a cultural product, and it has focused particularly on architecture's social and technological aspects, obviously fundamental facets for all study of architecture, not least in the diverse contexts of Latin

America. The new curriculum introduced in 2015 gave no indication that this endogamous attitude would be modified, which means that the programme has gradually been distancing itself from contemporary discourses and debates within the discipline, specifically in terms of a vision of architecture as a wider, complex and open cultural product and as a field for innovative exploration and new initiatives. Such shifts have, at the same time, been evident in other cultural disciplines (most notably, for example, in the symbiosis carried out in the field of music, where typically popular musical genres such as *candombé* or rock are being mixed with music commonly labelled 'cultured' or highbrow). Architecture is a discipline that requires constant connections with other areas of national culture, something that provides the architect with the necessary analytical tools with which to approach their work, art and trade. But such needs have not been addressed with the necessary intensity or direction that contemporary society demands of the world of academia.

Bit by bit and not without difficulty, comics are trying to enter the School of Architecture. Unfortunately many colleagues see comics as a minor figure in the pantheon of the University, a popular cultural pastime rather than the domain of 'high culture'. One might wonder what Rodolphe Töppfer, Le Corbusier, Yona Friedman, Peter Cook or even Benoît Peeters might have to say about this belief, but it will no doubt not be the last example of the cultural myopia of academics, determined to defend their own cultural perceptions rather than challenge clichés and expand intellectual frontiers and boundaries. As a response to this context of superiority, then, in this chapter I undertake a critical evaluation of a teaching experiment that took place between 2014 and 2017 within the School of Architecture, Design and Urban Planning at the University of the Republic of Uruguay, one which complements another, more recent, experience in the Teacher Training Institute, the latter aimed at training secondary school teachers. In essence, I want to demonstrate why comics are a powerful medium for teaching and analysing architectural ideas.

The course(s)

The original aim of the course was not only to study architecture and its visual representation in comics but also to delve into comics' potential for communicating critical reflection about architecture itself and the city and, therefore, for being an effective way of learning about the built environment. As a precursor, I should mention the activities led by Benoît Peeters during two fleeting visits to the university, during which he gave talks and facilitated a workshop with students. During his visits to the School of Architecture, Design and Urban Planning in 1988 and in 2016, I had the opportunity to discuss comics and architecture with Peeters. In his talks, he examined the genesis of his work and its direct and explicit links with architecture, noting that his colleague and partner in his comics works, the Belgian François Schuiten, is the son of architects and that one of his brothers is a renowned theorist of contemporary Belgian architecture. The workshop that I ran was named after Peeters' well-known comics series *The Obscure Cities* (originally *Les Cités obscure*; also published as *Cities of the Fantastic* in English).

In my case, I wanted to work with the city of Montevideo and wanted findings to be presented in the form of a short comic strip. In fact, the first use I made of comics as a teaching strategy was designed not so much to teach architecture as landscape, part of a Landscape Project course that was included in the degree of the same name. This course took place at the East Regional University Centre located in the east of Uruguay, in the city of Maldonado, not far from the seaside resort of Punta del Este. This partial exercise included the participation of a very diverse group of students in terms of age and background, with some graduates from secondary school or from courses in technical gardening, as well as technicians who qualified for the degree because of their previous experience in related areas. As a result it was necessary to offer a series of brief lectures about the origins of comics and their relevance within contemporary society, as this form was not familiar to most of the students. The methodology was a workshop in which students were put into groups of two or more to optimise knowledge exchange, time and resources.

The first presentations addressed the impact of rampant processes of urbanisation typical of large tourist developments. Students were required to set out potential political and design strategies to avoid the deterioration caused by such processes and to restore environmental quality. Supporting bibliography included the graphic novel *Brüsel* (Schuiten and Peeters 1993), part of the aforementioned cycle *The Obscure Cities*, which narrates events in the imaginary city of Brüsel (a distorted reflection of the real Brussels), which is subject to rampant growth and consequent destruction of the old urban fabric with new, high, svelte and aseptic tower blocks; and the theoretical essay *Vers une cité végétale: Projets urbains et ruraux de demain* (Towards a Vegetal City: Urban and Rural Projects for Tomorrow), written by Luc Schuiten and Pierre Loze (2010), a piece that offers a series of strategies for the recovery of our urban landscapes and the integration of green spaces as the fundamental and predominant elements of urban life.

One study submitted by the students depicted a verdant landscape with a stark blue river and trees. Each panel of their comic, however, depicted that landscape rife with tower blocks, highlighting the consequences of uncontrolled urbanisation (the tower blocks here are a kind of alien force that gradually occupy the virgin territory in rampant fashion). A huge fist in the final frame depicts the response of a despoiled nature that finally rebels in an attempt to re-establish some kind of original balance. The work demonstrates how the narrative form of comics can be used to highlight the shifting nature of the architectural landscape.

In the wake of this early foray into using comics, I subsequently ran the first version of the full course, submitted via the standard university curricular review procedures. This course was aimed at advanced students of the degree of Architecture and the degree of Design and Visual Communication, as well as some foreign students (particularly French and Mexican) who were taking the course as part of the university's exchange programme (most of them with some pre-existing knowledge of the field of architecture). The teaching team consisted of myself and my colleague, the architect and comics scholar Carolina Tobler. The development of the course was complemented by the one-off participation of comic-strip authors, including the aforementioned Rodríguez Juele and the architect, urban planning scholar, doctoral candidate and lecturer in the History of Contemporary Architecture, Diego Capandeguy.

As part of the planning process we developed an in-depth preparatory study, setting out a series of stages aimed at minimising the difficulties and uncertainties that the course posed for both students and faculty. These arose, primarily, from the novelty of the course, at least as far as the institution was concerned, as there were no precedents for developing a teaching strategy in this area. The only somewhat direct referent was the aforementioned experience of the group Bandas Educativas, though that had been aimed exclusively at primary and secondary school students and more as a way of illustrating stories. There were, moreover, some difficulties with the fact that the student cohort was diverse in its make-up and not everyone was familiar with the strategies and potential of contemporary comics. In this particular case, the presence of foreign students, especially those from France, enriched the course, no doubt due to the more pervasive presence of comics in French culture. On the course, we tried to put together teams of students from different backgrounds so that they would be confronted with a wide range of views and approaches.

To address lack of knowledge about comics we included a series of talks and presentations about different aspects of the history of comics, their evolution and basic structural concepts (codes, composition, means of communication, etc). Thematically, we used the city of Montevideo as our urban focus, asking students to consider the city itself, its evolution and its likely future. Many lines of argument touched upon dystopian visions of that future. Some looked at population growth related to immigration, particularly from Asia, which at one point had been modelled as a political strategy by government advisers to solve Uruguay's extremely low population growth rate.

A broader cultural context was established by including references to cinema, including films such as Richard Fleischer's *Soylent Green* (1973) or Marco Brambilla's *Demolition Man* (1993), and literature, including texts such as *Paris in the Twentieth Century* by Jules Verne, a little known novel by the French author, written in the late nineteenth century but only published in 1994, and *Brave New World* by Aldous Huxley, written in the 1930s. As well as the treatise written by English architect and critic Charles Jencks in 1971, *Architecture 2000*, we also required students to read material related to the creation of comics, including Scott McCloud's *Making Comics* (2007), *Comics and the City* (2010) edited by Jörn Ahrens and Arno Meteling, and the graphic novels *Dropsie Avenue* (1995) by Will Eisner and *Transmetropolitan* (1999) by Warren Ellis and Darrick Robertson. The latter were chosen as they fit with the ideas about the future evolution of the city of Montevideo outlined above. Eisner's story clearly and accurately illustrates the inception and development of urban life from the point of view of those who inhabit, build, enjoy and endure it. And, with a high degree of cynicism, Ellis's work describes life in a dystopian city of the future, in which the abundance of heterogeneous social groups, famous and small-time criminals, and corrupt politicians constitute a simultaneously peculiar and recognisable urban society that is being permanently bombarded by digital images that create an almost schizophrenic urban space.

The most difficult element of the course was defining a script around which to structure a narrative. Being a comics scriptwriter is a complex task and, in addition to knowledge of the topic or topics being addressed, it also demands an ability for concision so that underlying concepts and ideas can be explained within the context of the page. At the same time, we had to address preconceptions that stemmed from the different university degrees that were being taken by the students on the course. Such differences are evident in some of the students' proposals. Architectural students tended to emphasise spaces, buildings and other urban elements, such as the street, the square or the city block as a way of thinking through the way setting is constructed. Graphic design students took a different approach, however. In one example, some design students used graphic resources in the style of Richard Hamilton's early works of the mid-1960s, specifically his collage *Just What is it Makes Today's Homes so Different, so Appealing?* (1956), and the canvas painting by the US pop artist Roy Lichtenstein, *Whaam!* (1963), both works referred to openly during the course.

The second version of the course, aimed at a group of students with a similar level of training, set out to address some of the shortcomings of the first, mainly those related to lack of knowledge about comics. A series of short exercises in the form of workshops were put in place, supported by presentations by staff about the development and making of comics. Much as in the previous version, these were intended to help students learn about the guiding principles of the genre and about different comic strategies developed by various relevant authors, from Winsor McCay to Chris Ware, through classic authors like Moebius, Hergé or Hugo Pratt.

An initial exercise looked at the graphic and expressive strategies of comics based around a series of categories which were applied to a particular story and author. We chose the US graphic novel *Asterios Polyp* (2009) by David Mazzucchelli because we saw it as encapsulating a number of graphic characteristics that, apart from being evidently explicit, were relevant to the objectives of the planned analysis. On this basis, among others, the following aspects were addressed: the formal aspects of the panel (types, layout, gutters, framing, shots, etc), transitions or passages from panel to panel (action to action, scene to scene, etc), the page (ways of reading, treatment of time, etc), and specific iconography (conventions, visualisation of metaphor and onomatopoeia). The story developed by Mazzucchelli seemed particularly relevant as it addressed the existential and professional crisis of a renowned architect and academic teacher.

We highlighted the connections between the communicational structure of a comic strip and architectural design by drawing on *Comics and Sequential Art* (1988) by Will Eisner and *Making Comics* (2007) by Scott McCloud, which take an analytical approach based on semiotics and on architecture as a language. In class we discussed and debated the logic implicit in the notion that architecture has always been an appropriate and pertinent medium for the transmission of certain values. This approach was developed in the 1990s by writers, philosophers and semioticians like Paul Virilio (*Esthétique de la disparition* (1980)), Jean Baudrillard (*Los objetos singulares* (2002), with the collaboration of the French architect Jean Nouvel) and Umberto Eco (*Apocalípticos e integrados* (1968, although first published in 1964) and *Tratado de semiótica general* (1975)).

In a second exercise we set out to explore strategies for the graphic interpretation of a given text. Here we selected extracts from Georges Perec's novel *La Vie mode d'emploi* (Life: A User's Manual) (1988), in which Perec offers a comprehensive and obsessive description of the spaces and situations that arise among the residents of a typical Parisian building, each chapter in the novel describing the particular characteristics of the occupants. The scenes in the novel were taken as a kind of plot-script that could serve as the basis for the development of a formalised graphic interpretation. Working individually or in pairs, students had to tackle one of the chapters. We provided students with some examples to inspire them, including the well-known 1875 etchings by Bertall (Charles Constant Albert Nicolas d'Arnoux de Limoges Saint-Saëns) which depict life in a mid-nineteenth-century Parisian building via a classic architectural style, a graphic strategy used more recently by the group of Japanese architects Bow-Wow to present many of their projects. We also referred to the work of the Spaniard Francisco Ibáñez, *13 rue de la Percebe* (1961), which takes a similar approach to Bertall.

We gave students total expressive freedom to develop their story, whether in terms of number, size, form, expression or layout of the panels. The aim was to ensure harmony between expressive resources and narrative, so that readers could grasp a full understanding of the episode being narrated.

The third and final exercise of the course, longer and more demanding than the previous tasks, centred on the critical development of a model of a city chosen in advance. Apart from a critical commentary on the model, the aim was to conjugate and make explicit the links between comics, architecture and the city. In view of the difficulties that arose in the previous version when trying to determine an anecdote around which to construct a plot, we presented the situation posed in King Vidor's film *The Fountainhead* (1949) as the key reference point. Setting aside the romantic situation between architect Howard Roark (Gary Cooper) and Dominique Francon (Patricia Neal), the daughter of a wealthy property developer, the film presents the conflict between the young and idealistic professional facing the harsh demands of reality imposed by the client's aesthetic perceptions and economic concerns. Students were asked to address that clash between idealism and pragmatism, a classic trope in the history of architecture.

These models covered a wide range of projects drawn from different moments in the history of architecture. Some examples included the Ideal City of 'Baltimore' (attributed to the school of Fra Carnevale, 1470), a collage city that existed many centuries before the architectural theorist Colin Rowe coined the term; the Royal Saltworks in Chaux (Claude Ledoux, 1775), an example of high abstraction by eighteenth-century French rationalists; the Garden City (Ebenezer Howard, 1903), an idyllic organisation of territory that aimed to improve the extremely poor living conditions of the working classes following the Industrial Revolution; the Gross Berlin (Albert Speer, 1937), the new capital of the Third Reich which attempted to immortalise its ideology; The Seaside Urbanization, Seaside, Florida (Andres Duany and Elizabeth Plater-Zyberk, 1984), where most of the location shots of *The Truman Show* (Peter Weir, 1998) were filmed; Kowloon (1993), considered, until it was demolished, as the densest and most chaotic concentration of humans in the world; and Waterfront Dubai (OMA, 2008), which sought to recreate the grandeur and the charm of the great Arabian palaces with gardens and fountains. Each team of students had to research their allocated model, learning about its history, genesis and the ideas and architectural and city planning concepts underlying their case study. Students were also asked to express their findings in the form of a comic strip.

At the next stage students were expected to develop a script that would set out a series of critical comments about the city model, focusing on its positive as well as its negative aspects in what we called a 'graphic essay', a play on the contemporary term 'graphic novel'. This work was presented in the form of a small fanzine using a variety of expressive techniques in line with the story being narrated and the meaning that was being constructed (digital, hand-drawn, photomontage, etc).

This course aimed to address two fundamental aspects: first, to introduce students to topics related to the city and urban design in an attempt, by means of the analysis of the various proposals and examples put forward, to tackle these topics from the point of view of project strategies. And second, to encourage students to experiment with methods and means of the presentation, representation and critical dissemination of ideas by using resources which are unusual in architectural design courses. We concluded that high levels of student participation and commitment on the course were in part due to the fact that using comics stimulated the imagination and helped students create and visualise scenarios and places which were often only expressed as conceptual statements or, at best, simple schemes accompanying written text.

With the modifications and reorganisation brought about by the application of a new syllabus, to attain the marks required to move forward in their studies students subsequently had to choose from a range of courses that included a great variety of themes, perspectives and approaches. Our course was one of the options offered by the Architectural Composition Workshop. This time around the course was no longer aimed at advanced students but at first-year students. This shift posed a challenge to staff, as we had to adapt the topics, materials and exercises to the new student body.

The first part of the year drew on previous versions of the course by focusing on the study of comics, their history, evolution and current tendencies within the form. Will Eisner's *New York: The Big City* (1986), Schuiten and Peeters's *Brüsel* (1993) and David Mazzucchelli's *Asterios Polyp* (2009) were again used for the analysis of the different aspects which shape the structure of comics. All three were chosen for their clear links to architecture and its problems. But on this occasion we also included work by other comics authors who have a more experimental approach, such as Marc-Antoine Mathieu's *Le dessin* (2001), Chris Ware's *Building Stories* (2012) and Robert McGuire's *Here* (2014). We chose these works for their innovative approach to presenting narrative in graphic terms.

For the main exercise on this version of the course we took advantage of the fact that the Architectural Composition Workshop was looking specifically at the topic of individual urban dwellings designed for a particular user. As a result, the exercise we designed meant that for many students the course offered them an opportunity to continue their work on a pre-existing part of the curriculum but to approach it in more depth. On this occasion, once again to avoid difficulties in terms of developing a narrative script, we set the students the same departure point: the Argentine film *El hombre de al lado* (The Man Next Door) (2009), directed by Mariano Cohn and Gastón Duprat. The story set out in the film deals with a topic of architectural interest: a man wishes to add a window to his house which would look out onto the exterior patio of his neighbour's house, where the film's protagonist lives. The main character is a famous furniture designer and well-known university lecturer but even more significantly he lives in La Casa Curutchet (The Curutchet House), a residence designed for an Argentine doctor in 1949 by Le Corbusier in the city of La Plata (Argentina) and one of only two buildings ever completed in the Americas that was designed by the French architect. The conflict in the film revolves around the clash between Víctor (the working-class neighbour artisan) and Leonardo (the middle-class, sophisticated designer-intellectual); Víctor wants a new window to let in some sunshine and Leonardo wants to protect his privacy. The students were asked to analyse the issues arising from the film and to learn about Le Corbusier's project, which was also developed by Argentine architect

Amancio Williams. Based on their research, they were required to draw a relevant moment in the film on one page, which allowed us to evaluate the resources they used to convey a particular message at the same time as making the drafting of a storyline quite straightforward. Even though the plot provided the basis for the script, in-depth knowledge of the case study allowed students to establish relationships between abstract architectural spaces and the complex situations that can arise around them when they become sites of social conflict.

Each individual student or pair of students was expected to set their story in a paradigmatic house taken from the history of architecture. The house was to constitute the central element around which the text would revolve. The repertoire of selected houses was very wide ranging, spanning different historical periods, styles, dwellers and architects. International examples included Villa Rotonda (A. Palladio, 1566), the Farnsworth House (Mies van der Rohe, 1946), and Villa Dall'Ava (R. Koolhaas, 1985); Uruguayan examples included Casa Paysée (M. Paysée Reyes, 1954) and Casa Buceo (Martín and Marcelo Gualano, 2007). Other architects that were referred to included the US architect Robert Venturi, the Swiss Mario Botta, the Luxembourg Leo Krier and the Chilean Smiljan Radic, among others.

The exercise was divided into four stages:

(1) a prologue, which had to present the dwelling in question, be drawn in comic-strip format, and be designed to introduce the lay reader to the chosen architectural example
(2) a script outline presented on a storyboard which would later define the central body of the story
(3) a sketch of the history that had been set out which indicated how to bring text and image together
(4) the final presentation using different expressive media to develop the story.

The final presentation was displayed on the predetermined A5 page format, which lent uniformity to work across the class, avoiding previous problems with huge variances in terms of format, quality and type of presentation. This universal approach also meant the stories could be collected in a standardised colour publication of approximately 150 pages (in the event, the expense of such a publication meant that only one copy was printed). The format that we chose was based on the idea that the final work should be envisaged as a small graphic novel or, as in this case, 'graphic essay'.

The most important references were, in this case, the short critical essay by the Spanish architectural collective bRijUNi architects about the city of Rotterdam, *Living and Leaving in Rotterdam* (2009); the graphic novel created by the US architect Wes Jones, 'Re:Doing Dubai' (included in *Beyond No.1: Scenarios and Speculations* (Gadanho 2009)); and *L'Enfant Penchée* by Schuiten and Peeters (1996; part of the *The Obscure Cities* cycle) and *The Building* by Will Eisner (1987).

The storylines that were developed ranged from costume dramas with elements of soap operas, fairly conventional science fiction, to stories with a markedly *noir* tone, as is the case with a story set in the house built by Le Corbusier for the painter Amadée Ozenfant in Paris in 1922. A remote artist's refuge was transformed into the setting for a frivolous and mundane life but one in which a crime of passion is subsequently committed.

On the other hand, the idyllic residence built by Frank Lloyd Wright, a luxury refuge of sorts built amid the solitude and charm of a virgin forest (Falling Water or Kaufmann House, built between 1936 and 1939 in Pennsylvania), became a dwelling for ghosts and paranormal activity (a storyline that draws on Stanley Kubrick's *The Shining* (1980)).

The final outcomes of the course, both the preliminary and final exercises, were compiled in the printed publication referred to above. The document pays testament to a number of issues that, I would argue, highlight the value of comics as a vehicle for learning about and debating issues within the field of architecture.

As mentioned above, our final experience of using comics was aimed at students on the teacher-training course in the area of visual communication and was, therefore, not centred on the links between comics and architecture. These students had little or no training in or knowledge of architecture and, at best, their only experience of architecture had been on courses in History of Art. As a result, we had to rethink the general approach that we had used up to this point, focusing this time on the graphic structures and communication value of comics, as well as on comics' ability to develop and convey ideas beyond the narrative storyline. For these reasons, the preliminary exercises that we used centred more on these more general topics than on approaches related to a survey of architecture and architectural thought.

We set out to highlight the structural elements constitutive of comics, from the handling of visual planes, panel sequences and composition, through to coherent graphics (drawing style) and the handling of chromatic palettes in relation to the situations and environments in which stories are set. For this course, comics experts took part and contributed by sharing their perspectives on the genre as makers rather than as academic scholars. Architect Andrés Milano gave a paper on the similarities between comics and film, especially in relation to the handling of shots and framing (close-up shots, *plan américain* shots, high-angle shots, low-angle shots, etc); another talk, by Uruguayan comics specialist and historian Gabriel Mainero, focused on the ability of the form to relate transcendental stories that go beyond adventure or humour. To discuss these issues we focused on Art Spiegelman's award-winning *Maus*, first published in 1973 and recipient of the Pulitzer Prize in 1992. Focusing on these issues meant having to redefine the final exercise of the course. This time we focused more specifically on developing a story based on other famous graphic novels, chosen to represent the diversity of the field, including historical, testimonial, and utopian and dystopian science fiction. The graphic novels selected were: the aforementioned *Maus* (1973) by Art Spiegelman; *Brüsel* (1993) by Benoît Peeters and Francois Schuiten; *It Was the War of the Trenches* (1993) by Jacques Tardi; *El gaucho* (1995) by Hugo Pratt and Milo Manara; Will Eisner's adaptation of Herman Melville's *Moby Dick* (2001); and *La mudanza* (*The Move*) (2013) by Uruguayan Nicolás Peruzzo. In their final presentation students were required to include a version of the text as well as a brief analysis of the selected stories by way of a prologue.

In certain aspects, the work carried out by the students aligned itself with the categories of analysis described by Peeters in *Lire la bande dessinée* (1998), which can be summarised as follows: firstly, there were those who, following the analysis of one of the works cited, proceeded to compose a storyboard of sorts, focusing more on the storyline than the graphics; a second line of work sought to rely on graphic skill, which led to extremely elaborate drawings of high technical execution but clearly very different to their chosen story; and a third approach saw students create their own original story, one not necessarily conceived as a sequel to the original text but presented in a style that was almost an imitation of the original.

Conclusion

I start my conclusion by quoting Caín Somé Laserna from the Department of Contemporary History of the University of Seville:

> Conventional University teaching methods based primarily on masterclasses are a thing of the past. Nowadays the introduction of

new technologies and various tools into the University classroom are commonplace . . . looking for new tools must be an essential task for the lecturer and on occasion, those tools, far from being new, are simply tools that were already in existence but whose use is dismissed. Such is the case with comics. . . .

('El cómic como herramienta de trabajo en el ámbito universitario', 2012)

Similarly, Jimenez Lai writes in the Preface of *Citizens of No-Place*:

Dancing between the line of narrative and representation, cartooning is a medium that facilitates experimentation in proportion, composition, scale, sensibility, character plasticity, and the part-to-whole relationship as the page becomes an object. More importantly, this drawing medium affords the possibility of conflating representation, theory, criticism, storytelling, and design.

(Lai 2012, 7)

Teaching architecture through comics has not been without its frustrations. Despite our best efforts, staff who taught on these courses have still not managed to carve out a significant space for comics within the School of Architecture, Design and Urban Planning. Nevertheless, in general terms, I regard the courses that we taught as a success in terms of achieving the aims and expectations that we set out. Apart from working with a cultural field often only reserved for experts and connoisseurs, students were able to draw a series of possible links between comics and architecture. As a result students developed a way of approaching and learning about architecture that is not common in our teaching institutions, which are more concerned with preserving their own status than with trying new and provocative teaching experiences and didactic practices. Comics allow for a more direct approach to architectural work, one that has greater visual appeal than that usually found in academic texts and publications. Comics allow us to familiarise ourselves with and learn from significant architectural works and the ideas and concepts handled by their authors. I am convinced that knowledge cannot move forward unless it pushes its own disciplinary boundaries, which makes it all the more a shame that, two centuries after Töpffer's first experiments, the pedagogical potential of comics has still not been fully exploited.

Notes

1. It is important to mention two other texts that I do not refer to in the body of this essay as they were published after the courses discussed in this chapter concluded. They will form part of core reading for future iterations of these courses. The first is the work by Enrique Bordes, a Spanish 'comicarchitect' as he calls himself, entitled *Cómic, arquitectura narrativa*, which analyses the relationship between drawing comics and architecture. In his introduction to this book he writes: 'la relación entre tebeos y espacios construidos [. . .] va mucho más allá de la metáfora que implica que el autor de cómic construye sus páginas igual que el arquitecto sus edificios [the relationship between comics and built spaces [. . .] goes beyond the metaphor that implies that a comics author builds his pages in the same way that an architect builds his buildings]'. The other is the recent conceptual work by Spanish artist Daniel Torres, *La casa: Crónica de una conquista* (2017).

References

Please note that the list of references includes publications that were taught on the units referred to in this chapter, even if they are not cited in the chapter.

Ahrens, Jörn and Arno Meteling. 2010. *Comics and the City: Urban Space in Print, Picture And Sequence*. New York: Continuum.

Alberghini, Andrea. 2006. *Sequenze Urbane: La Metropoli nel Fumetto*. Rovigo: Edizioni Delta Comics.

Alberghini, Andrea. 2013. 'Architettura e Fumetto'. Paper presented at XV Comicon, Naples (25–28 April). Last accessed 2 December 2019. https://whereiscomics.wordpress.com/2015/09/03/parallelismi-xv-napoli-comicon.

Baudrillard, Jean and Jean Nouvel. 2002. *Los objetos singulares*. Buenos Aires: Fondo de Cultura Económica.

Bjarke Ingels Group (BIG). 2009. *Yes is More: An Archicomic in Architectural Evolution*. Copenhagen: Big Ap 5.

Bordes, Enrique. 2017. *Cómic, arquitectura narrativa*. Madrid: Ediciones Cátedra.

bRijUNi architects. 2009. 'Vivir y dejar Rotterdam [Living and Leaving in Rotterdam]', *Future Arquitecturas*, 15: 235–9.

Cassará, Laura and Sebastiano D'Urso. 2013. *Goodbye Topolina: Su architettura e fumetto*. Catania: Maldor D'Edizione.

Christin, Pierre and Olivier Balez. 2014. *Robert Moses: The Master Builder of New York City*. Grenoble and London: Editions Glénat and Nobrow.

Eco, Umberto. 1968. *Apocalípticos e integrados*. Buenos Aires: Editorial Lumen.

Eco, Umberto. 1975. *Tratado de semiótica general*. Buenos Aires: Editorial Lumen.

Eisner, Will. 1987. *The Building*. Northampton, MA: Kitchen Sink Press.

Eisner, Will. 1988. *El cómic y el arte secuencial*. Barcelona: Norma Editorial.

Eisner, Will. 2000. *Dropsie Avenue*. Barcelona: Norma Editorial.

Eisner, Will. 2001. *Moby Dick*. New York: NBM Publishing.

Eisner, Will. 2008. *Nueva York: La vida en la gran ciudad*. Barcelona: Norma Editorial.

Ellis, Warren and Darrick Robertson. 1999. *Transmetropolitan*. Barcelona: Norma Editorial.

Groensteen, Thierry. 2007. *The System of Comics*. Jackson: University Press of Mississippi.

Hernandez, Gilbert. 2011. *Luba*. Barcelona: Ediciones La Cúpula.

Herzog, Jacques and Pierre De Meuron. 2009. *Metrobasel: A Model for the European Region*. Zurich: ETH-Bibliothek.

Huxley, Aldous. 1932. *Brave New World*. London: Chatto & Windus.

Jencks, Charles. 1975. *Arquitectura 2000: Predicciones y métodos*. Barcelona: Editorial Blume.

Jones, Wes. 2009. 'Re:Doing Dubai'. In *Beyond No.1: Scenarios and Speculations*, edited by Pedro Gadanho, 89–102. Amsterdam: Sun Publishers.

Kidd, Chip and Dave Taylor. 2012. *Batman: Death By Design*. New York, NY: DC Comics.

Koolhaas, Tomas and Louis Price. 1995. 'Byzantium'. In *S, M, L, XL*, edited by Rem Koolhaas and Bruce Mau. Rotterdam: 010 Publisher.

Lai, Jimenez. 2012. *Citizens of No Place: An Architectural Graphic Novel*. New York: Princeton Architectural Press.

Lus Arana, Luis Miguel (Koldo). 2013. 'Comics and Architecture, Comics in Architecture'. *MAS Context*, 20: 16–31.

Lutes, Jason. 2010. *Berlin: Ciudad de piedras*. Bilbao: Astiberri Ediciones.

Mathieu, Marc-Antoine. 2001. *Le dessin*. Paris: Delcourt.

Mazzucchelli, David. 2009. *Asterios Polyp*. Toronto: Pantheon Books.

McCloud, Scott. 2007. *Como hacer un cómic*. Bilbao: Astiberri Ediciones.

McGuire, Robert. 2014. *Here*. London: Hamish Hamilton.

Moix, Terence. 2007. *Historia Social Del Cómic*. Barcelona: Editorial Bruguera.

Nebiolo, Guiseppe, Jean Chesnaux and Umberto Eco. 1976. *Los cómics de Mao*. Barcelona: Editorial G. Gili.

Nouvel, Jean. 2012. 'Valencia Litoral'. In *Bricks & Balloons: Architecture in Comic Strip Form*, edited by Mélanie van der Hoorn, 169–70. Rotterdam: 010 Publishers.

Ortega, Álvaro. 2010. *Los arquitectos*. Vitoria-Gasteiz: Ikusager Ediciones.

Peeters, Benoît. 1998. *Lire la bande dessinée*. Manchecourt: Flammarion.

Perec, Georges. 1988. *La Vie mode d'emploi* [Life: A User's Manual]. Paris: Hachette.

Peruzzo, Nicolás. 2013. *La mudanza*. Montevideo: Ninfa Comics.

Pratt, Hugo and Milo Manara. 1995. *El gaucho*. Barcelona: Norma Editorial.

Rébéna, Fréderic, Jean-Marc Thévenet and Baudoui. 2010. *Le Corbusier: Architecte parmi des hommes*. Brussels: Editions Dupuis S.A. Marcinelle.

Rodriguez Juele, Alejandro. 2011. *La isla elefante*. Montevideo: Malaquita Ediciones.

Santullo, Rodolfo and Matias Bergara. 2012. *Dengue*. Montevideo: Editorial Belerofonte and Editorial Estuario.

Schuiten, François and Benoît Peeters. 1985. *La fièvre d'Urbicande*. Tournai: Casterman.

Schuiten, François and Benoît Peeters. 1993. *Brüsel*. Barcelona: Norma Editorial.

Schuiten, François and Benoît Peeters. 1996. *L'Enfant Penchée*. Tournai: Casterman.

Schuiten, Luc and Pierre Loze. 2010. *Vers une cité végétale: Projets urbains et ruraux de demain*. Brussels: Mardaga Editeur.

Sousanis, Nick. 2015. *Unflattening*. Cambridge, MA: Harvard University Press.

Spiegelman, Art. 1989. *Maus I*. Barcelona: España Para Muchnik Editores S.A.

Spiegelman, Art. 2012. *MetaMaus*. New York And Toronto: Pantheon Books.

Tardi, Jaques. 1993. *1914–1918: La guerra de las trincheras*. Barcelona: Norma Editorial.

Töpffer, Rodolphe. 1839. *Les Amours de M. Vieux-Bois*. Paris: Aubert. Last accessed 2 December 2019. http://www.gutenberg.ca/ebooks/toepfferr-amoursdemrvieuxbois/toepfferr-amoursdemrvieuxbois-00-h-dir/toepfferr-amoursdemrvieuxbois-00-h.html.

Torres, Daniel. 2017. *La casa: Crónica de una conquista*. Barcelona: Norma Editorial.

Tuset, Jorge. 2011. 'El otro lado del espejo: La arquitectura en el cómic y en la obra de Schuiten y Peeters'. Doctoral Thesis. Universidad Politécnica De Madrid. Last accessed 30 June 2019. http://oa.upm.es/10597.

Úbeda Mansilla, Paloma. 2000. 'El cómic contextualizado en la clase de ESP para arquitectos: El diseño de una unidad'. *Didáctica: Lengua y literatura*, 12: 265–78.

Van der Hoorn, Mélanie. 2012. *Bricks & Balloons: Architecture in Comic Strip Form*. Rotterdam: 010 Publishers.

Various. 2010. *Archi et BD: La ville dessinée*. Paris: Monografik éditions.

Various. 2013. 'Narrative', *Mas Context* 20.

Verne, Jules. 1994. *Paris au XXe siècle* [Paris in the Twentieth Century]. Paris: Hachette.

Virilio, Paul. 1980. *Esthétique de la disparition*. Paris: Éditions Balland.

Ware, Chris. 2012. *Building Stories*. New York: Pantheon Books.

Appendix

Preguntas sin respuestas:* Notes on teaching the armed conflict in Perú

Text and drawings by Jesús Cossio
Translated by James Scorer

Reference

Aguirre, Carlos. 2011. 'Terruco de m… Insulto y estigma en la guerra sucia peruana', *Histórica*, 35(1): 103–39.

* Questions and Answers.

Text and drawings: Jesús Cossio / Translation: James Scorer
* Questions without Answers

In Peru teaching about the years of violence that lasted between 1990 and 2000 is still inadequate. Though the events affected many people and their impact is still being felt today, it remains difficult to talk about them openly. The main problem is the oversimplification of the conflict as an example of "terrorism". Many divide the internal war between...

...and leave to one side the social, cultural, economic and historical threads that inform it.

If someone criticises the military they are often accused of being "pro-Sendero". And if they are left wing they are often accused of siding with Sendero Luminoso. Such people are known as "terrorist sympathisers".[1]...

1. Translator's note: the author uses the terms 'terruqueo' and 'terruco' here. These are colloquial Peruvian expressions for 'terrorist sympathiser' and 'terrorist' that were coined during the period of armed internal conflict. Carlos Aguirre has pointed out that the term is also now used to refer to anyone with left-wing views, to members of human rights organisations, or even to indigenous populations more broadly (see Aguirre, 2011).

Certain sectors of society vehemently deny that the military committed crimes, either claiming that there were only isolated "excesses" or that such actions were appropriate in a counter-subversive war.

In Peru it has been estimated that there are around 15,731 missing people and 6,462 mass graves throughout the country. Between 80% and 90% of these graves are located in Ayacucho.

After Ayacucho, the other most affected regions are: Huancavelica, Apurímac, Junín and Huánuco.

Peru also has a Terrorism Law,[2] which is used by conservative political groups to threaten...

TERRORISM LAW

...those who flag up the role of the State, the Armed Forces and the Police in human rights violations.

JUSTICE FOR THE
STERI

WATE
YES
MININ
NO!

NO TO PARDON FOR FUJIMORI

2. Translator's note: the Peruvian Terrorism Law [Ley de Apología al Terrorismo] criminalises the act of praising or justifying terrorist activities.

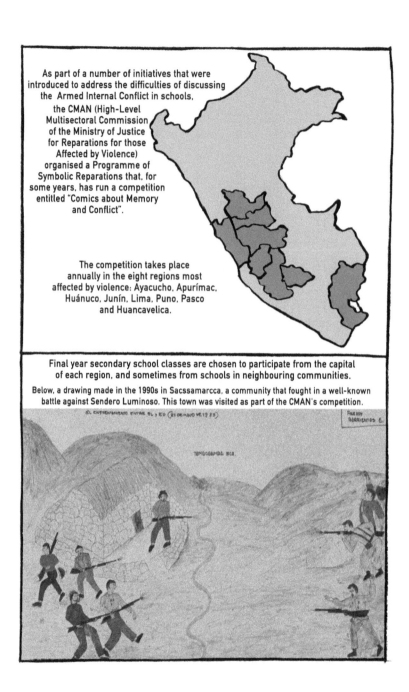

As part of a number of initiatives that were introduced to address the difficulties of discussing the Armed Internal Conflict in schools, the CMAN (High-Level Multisectoral Commission of the Ministry of Justice for Reparations for those Affected by Violence) organised a Programme of Symbolic Reparations that, for some years, has run a competition entitled "Comics about Memory and Conflict".

The competition takes place annually in the eight regions most affected by violence: Ayacucho, Apurímac, Huánuco, Junín, Lima, Puno, Pasco and Huancavelica.

Final year secondary school classes are chosen to participate from the capital of each region, and sometimes from schools in neighbouring communities.

Below, a drawing made in the 1990s in Sacssamarcca, a community that fought in a well-known battle against Sendero Luminoso. This town was visited as part of the CMAN's competition.

Many of the workshops take place in cities that now house enforced migrants from rural communities that were threatened by State or Sendero violence. Nevertheless, widespread racism in Peru means that younger generations are often reluctant to admit openly that they are the descendants of enforced migrants.

It takes some time before they are willing to acknowledge their background.

THIS CITY HAS NEIGHBOURHOODS WITH MIGRANTS WHO CAME FROM THE COUNTRYSIDE BECAUSE OF SENDERO THREATS.

YOU ARE THE DESCENDANTS OF THESE MIGRANTS, THEY CAME WITH ALMOST NOTHING AND AND MADE GREAT EFFORTS TO STAY HERE.

HIGHLANDERS!

NEWCOMERS!

PEASANTS!

WHEN MY GRANDFATHER WAS MAYOR HE HAD TO FLEE FROM HIS VILLAGE BECAUSE THE TERRORISTS WERE GOING TO KILL HIM.

MY AUNT AND UNCLE HAD TO COME BECAUSE THEIR NEIGHBOURS TURNED UP DEAD.

MY MOM AND HER FAMILY ESCAPED WHEN SHE WAS A GIRL.

Some less frequent cases depicted in the comics relate to sexual violence. Indeed, discussion about the extensive number of sexual crimes during the Armed Conflict has been very limited. Only in the last few years, as a result of recent condemnation of sexual assaults and femicides, have accusations related to such crimes gained prominence.

THE SOLDIERS CAME AND TOOK ME TO ANOTHER HOUSE. I BEGGED SO MUCH FOR MY LIFE... THEY TIED UP MY HUSBAND AND RAPED ME. I WAS PREGNANT AND AFTER THAT THE BABY GROWING INSIDE ME DIED. MY HUSBAND SAW EVERYTHING THEY DID TO ME WHILE HE WAS TIED UP. THAT WAS THE GREATEST EVIL THAT THEY DID TO ME.

WE WERE WALKING NEAR THE POLICE STATION, CROSSING THE SQUARE. THEY WERE IN THE DOORWAY, DRUNK. FOUR POLICEMEN APPROACHED US AND TOOK ME AND ANOTHER WOMAN INTO THE STATION BY FORCE. I DID NOT SEE WHAT HAPPENED TO THE OTHER LADY BUT THEY PUT ME IN A SMALL ROOM AND ABUSED ME.

Two victims of sexual violence relate a little of their cases (testimony from the book Lo inescuchable [The Unhearable], by Ana María Guerrero).

Finally, it is worth noting that some teachers and headteachers are wary of addressing in any meaningful way the Armed Internal Conflict for fear of being accused of "meddling in politics" and "talking about Sendero Luminoso", even though the Peruvian State has included the Armed Internal Conflict in the national curriculum and the Truth Commission Report recognises the responsibility of both Sendero Luminoso and the Armed Forces and the Police in human rights violations carried out between 1980 and 2000.

Unfortunately, this fear is part of the accusatory and negationist climate fomented by, on the one hand, the press and right-wing politicians and, on the other, the MOVADEF (the Movement for Amnesty for Sendero Prisoners). Those who are coming off worst are the vast numbers of Peruvian children and young people who lack reliable forms of education about the Armed Internal Conflict.

WHY IS THE LUGAR DE LA MEMORIA CALLED LUM, WHICH IS THE START OF "LUMINOSO"? IS IT A COINCIDENCE THAT THE ARCHITECTURE OF THE LUM IS A DARK PATHWAY, IN OTHER WORDS, A "SHINING PATH"?

Congressman Donayre

A GENERAL AMNESTY FOR CIVILIANS, THE MILITARY AND THE POLICE WOULD BRING ABOUT NATIONAL RECONCILIATION.

CORTE DE JUICIOS
LIBERTAD PARA ABIMAEL

NO MAS ODIO NI VENGANZAS AMNISTIA

MOVADEF activists

Index

Lightning Source UK Ltd.
Milton Keynes UK
UKHW020410140320
360310UK00002B/9